TSV

BROTHER SHALL NOT LIFT HIS SWORD AGAINST BROTHER

The Roots and Solution
To the Problem in the Holy Land

Liad Publishing

www.the-engagement.org

Third Edition

March 2008

ISBN: 1-4196-8900-2
9781419689000

Translation: Daniella Ashkenazy

Linguistic Editing: Joan Hooper, P

Cover design: Yael Saranga

Printed by: BookSurge

TABLE OF CONTENTS

iii

Introduction

"We cannot solve our problems with the same thinking we used when we created them."

Albert Einstein

The Israeli-Palestinian Conflict stems from two conflicting positions in the historical dispute regarding rights to the Land of Israel (henceforth, Eretz-Israel). Each side in the conflict bases its position on ancient roots and believes fervently in the justness of its own narrative. The endless struggle between the two sides is detrimental to all the country's inhabitants, while the conflict has only escalated since the 1920s.

The situation as it stands at the beginning of 2008 will ultimately lead to the signing of a long-term *hudna* (cease-fire) between Israel and the veteran Palestinian political leadership, who will continue to lead the Palestinian Authority from the position of its chairman. According to the agreement, a Palestinian state will be established in Judea, Samaria (the West Bank) and the Gaza Strip. Not the veteran Palestinian leadership, but rather the Palestinian terrorist leadership will be the ones who determine the success of the plan. This leadership will determine when the Palestinian state will be transformed into a far more dangerous form of southern Lebanon, a version in which only **Eilat** will remain immune to improved Katyusha and Kassam rockets.

The Palestinian terrorist leadership is comprised of the heads of an assortment of organizations and gangs and part of the Palestinian political leadership. The rest of the veteran political leadership is unable to control the terror leadership, even if it desires to do so. The victory of Hamas in Palestinian Authority elections in January 2006 and the battles between Fatah and Hamas factions in 2007 have unequivocally underscored this fact. The loyalty of most personnel serving in the Palestinian Authority's security forces lay

1

first and foremost with the terrorist leadership. The concept of 'two states for the two peoples in Eretz-Israel' does not go to the roots of the problem. Yet, due to American and European pressure, this 'solution' will be carried out despite the victory of Hamas in the elections, and without it being possible to uproot terror. Under such conditions, acting on the 'two state' concept will prompt the terror leadership to launch a third *Intifada*, when it becomes expedient.

All those who are in a quandary as to the future of the region, need only answer one question: 'What has changed?' The only legitimate reply one can give is "primarily rockets, missiles and weapons of mass destruction have become more prevalent, and Hamas, Iran and Hizbollah have replaced Yasser Arafat as the party pulling the strings of terror leadership from above."

With the end of the American presence in Iraq, sure to happen in the near future without defeating terrorism in Iraq, the United States will emerge as the leading force in the diplomatic process in the Middle East, and as a broken reed in the military sphere. Israel has also demonstrated its inability to effectively fight terrorism in the Gaza Strip and against the Hizbollah guerrillas in the Second Lebanon War. Under such circumstances, Iran with its arsenal of non-conventional weapons – including a nuclear capability, will, with the assistance of Palestinian and Hizbollah leadership, become the most influential party of all in the region. An air strike on Iran's nuclear facilities will only postpone the peril, and serve as an excuse for taking the tremendous risk inherent in establishment of a Palestinian state.

This reality – the inevitability of a Palestinian state and the risks it poses to Israel – obligates the Israeli leadership to provide much better answers to the Palestinian issue, including the issue of sovereignty over Eretz-Israel. It is imperative to find a solution that will provide a natural solution to the yearnings of both sides.

2

Israel must move beyond the assumptions that have shaped conventional thinking on this issue and **bring into play an old-new finding regarding Palestinian identity – a finding that offers a just and lasting solution to the conflict**.

The above-mentioned finding is based on a series of studies on various topics, the most extensive among them being genetic research and historio-demographic research of Eretz-Israel over the past two thousand years. Examination of these studies leads one to an amazing conclusion:

Not only are contemporary assumptions regarding the Arab identity of the Palestinians unfounded, but there is a solid foundation for another Palestinian identity – one that will come as a surprise to many. This thought was raised in the past during the period of WWI and following it by **David Ben-Gurion** (who declared the establishment of the State of Israel and became Israel's first prime minister), and by **Yitzhak Ben-Zvi** (who became the second president of the State of Israel). These two key leaders were already cognizant then of the need to address the complex issue of Eretz-Israel's non-Jewish population.

The Holocaust of European Jewry led to widespread support through most of the world in favor of the Zionist solution. Consequently, the Zionist leadership at the time was liberated from the necessity of grappling in any deep manner with this problem. As the years passed, and the impact of the memory of the Holocaust began to wane and the problem of terrorism began to rise, the Zionist leadership was forced to deal with the problem, which had been neglected and became all the more serious. Because Ben-Gurion's and Yitzhak Ben-Zvi's approach has so many serious ramifications vis-à-vis the conflict and the way it can be solved, it deserves to be raised and re-examined.

3

Conventional historical thinking holds that those Jews in Eretz-Israel who remained in the country after the destruction of the Second Jewish Commonwealth were obliterated in various and sundry ways, opening the way for foreigners to become the majority in Eretz-Israel until the establishment of the State of Israel. This thought, however, is not based on any historical fact. How exactly Jews 'disappeared' from Eretz-Israel has been left an enigma.

Ben-Gurion's and Ben-Zvi's postulations regarding the Palestinian identity issue received serious corroboration and became significantly more validated as a result of a series of genetic studies published of late. Such research shows that from a genetic standpoint, the Palestinians are closely related to Jews, more than to Arabs or to any other People. In the wake of publication of this research, additional studies have been conducted and published that further substantiate such a revolutionary assertion as to the Palestinians' identity. Such specific evidence regarding Palestinian identity can have far-reaching implications on the future of the region. First and foremost, it should be disseminated and made part of public discourse by Israeli public relations in order to curtail the scope of animosity between the sides.

Most important – even if this requires a complete turnabout in conventional thinking, it would be a terrible mistake to ignore such evidence in any attempt to settle such a complex and complicated conflict. This issue is particularly critical since after so many years, no one has succeeded in finding a solution based on negotiations that is acceptable to both parties. Any agreement between the sides that is based on conventional thought emerges from lack of any other alternative. Consequently all agreement of this kind has been transitory, or a ruse. Therefore, everything agreed to in the past after considerable effort, has only exacerbated the conflict, with serious consequences in both the local and international arena.

4

Partition of Eretz-Israel does not address the roots of hatred between the sides, and it is far from providing a solution for their respective aspirations and wishes. Prospects are very good that partition ('the two state solution') will become but another stage in the history of growing violence in the Middle East. The long-term *hudna* that will ultimately be agreed upon will only be a temporary affair. In order that such a *hudna* will not culminate in resumption of violent conflict, one needs a solution that will allow comprehensive peace and justice. **In order to bring about a just and lasting solution to the conflict, there is no alternative except to establish a format based on recognition of the genuine in-depth roots of the conflict and to suggest a fitting solution!**

This book constitutes an abridged and simplified presentation of a broader and more detailed work published in Hebrew in March 2006. The English volume at hand is designed for a popular audience. Readers and scholars who seek more demographic detail are referred to the author's Hebrew original, *Ye'uman ki Yesupar.*[1]

---

[1] See Bibliography Source 6.

Chapter One

Genetic Findings and Analysis of the Problem

Genetic Research

In the years 2000-2001 a number of genetic studies were published that indicate a linkage between Jews and Palestinians. Professor **Ariella Oppenheimer** from the Hebrew University in Jerusalem conducted a series of genetic studies, together with other research institutions.[2] The crux of the research was first reported in the spring of 2000, and subsequent findings in November 2001 in *Haaretz* newspaper. In studies of the male Y chromosome, it was found that **there is a tremendous relatedness from a genetic standpoint between Palestinians and Jews, similar to the linkage between various Jewish ethnic subgroups, which were found to be closer to one another than their distance from other Peoples.**

The study also found that *Ashkenazi* **Jews have a closer linkage to Palestinians than to other Arabs**, and are also very close to *Mizrachi* Jews (from Arab countries) and Muslim Kurds. These findings not only strengthen the historical finding presented here; they also refute claims, such as those held by former president of Syria, Hafez Assad, that the roots of Ashkenazi Jews are Khazar[3] and therefore the Jews have no historical rights to Eretz-Israel.

Another genetic study was published in 2001 in *Human Immunology*. The study received wide exposure and reverberated

---

[2] See Bibliography, Sources 12-14.
[3] A Caucasian-Turkish people located northeast of the Black Sea, that adopted Judaism in the 8th century A.D. and later most of them deserted it.

throughout the academic community and the media due to the scholarly journal's call upon subscribers to either ignore or "physically remove the relevant pages" from their copies due to the author's alleged mixing of political opinions and scientific research. The study in question was immune system research carried out by **Antonio Arnaiz-Villena** from **Complutense** University in Madrid and co-authors, which found that the immune system of Jews and Palestinians are very close to one another in a manner that indicates an almost identical genetic match.

Research during the same period at Tel Aviv University[4] concerning a particular hereditary form of deafness, common among a certain portion of the Palestinian population, also showed a clear and exclusive linkage (!) with Ashkenazi Jews who suffer from the same disability. This genetic mutation exists only among these two population groups out of the entire world population. The findings indicate, among other things, that there is a genetic link between Jews and Palestinians that is entirely not coincidental.

The scope of genetic studies conducted represents only a very small portion, relatively speaking, of the sum total of gene types that have yet to be compared. Even though only partial in scope, these findings are sufficient to point out the strong genetic relatedness between Palestinians and Jews.

Because the conflict between Jews and Palestinians is generally on an escalation course, and because the number of failed attempts over the years to solve this conflict has continuously increased, one has no choice but to examine the implications of the genetic findings. Yet, in order for such a study to be serious, one needs to carry out a historio-demographic analysis of how such a huge linkage between the two sides of the conflict came about.

---

[4] See Bibliography, Source 15.

8

Furthermore, for such an exercise to be a serious endeavor, one must translate the findings into a solution to the conflict between the parties – a solution that itself stems from the relatedness of the contenders. The ramifications of such a solution must be examined and an implementation strategy has to be formulated. This book is devoted to these issues – a historio-demographic analysis and a solution that arises from the linkage between the two parties.

In order to propose a <u>successful</u> solution to such a complex problem, and in order that one be able to grasp why superficial solutions are not forceful enough to solve the problem and why a revolutionary solution is needed, one must first understand the problem in depth.

Three Fundamental Problems in the Israeli-Palestinian Conflict

The fundamental problems preventing the achievement of peace, security and economic prosperity in Eretz-Israel are:

A.   A situation where two people (different according to conventional perceptions) believe that the same land is the homeland to each one of them – separately.

B.   The feelings of wretchedness, deprivation and hatred among the Palestinians.

C.   The endemic rifts that divide the Jewish people.

The first fundamental problem: <u>Two rival claims of 'ownership' of Eretz-Israel</u>.

This problem is well known and needs no expansion. The genuine question is – how did this problem arise? Most of what we know has little anchor in reality. The historical narrative presented in this volume will reveal in detail how this problem evolved.

The second fundamental problem: The feelings of <u>deprivation</u> <u>and hatred</u>.

These feelings are so extreme among some Palestinian rank-and-file and some of their leaders, that they seriously exacerbate the situation and the conflict that stem from the existence of the first problem. Such elevated animosity cannot be addressed with superficial 'band-aid' solutions that don't go to the root of the first problem. Under such conditions, bringing calm to the Middle East, and, to a great extent, to the world as a whole, is unattainable.

Intensification of the conflict and the behavior of Palestinian leadership in the Second *Intifada* have led to increased animosity towards Palestinians among some Jews. This state of affairs has made it all the more difficult to solve the conflict. If we understand how Palestinian hatred was sparked, if we can pinpoint its roots and deal with them, we can curtail its scope. This can help achieve the calm milieu that is so essential to solving the first problem – the most complex of all.

Many believe that the genuine crux of the problem regarding Palestinian behavior is terrorism. Yet, despite the gravity of terrorism and the need to uproot it, one must understand that to do so it is imperative to first pinpoint the roots of terrorism. Terrorism would not be sustainable for so many years without the sense of disinheritance Palestinians feel and the hatred it fuels. On one hand, terrorism might have died out without the support of external forces (extreme Arab and Moslem regimes). On the other hand, outside support would not have succeeded in pushing the Palestinians to sacrifice so much in their war with Israel, without the endemic sense of disinheritance and injustice they harbor.

Despite the tremendous importance and validity of the war on terrorism, in order to uproot terrorism, it would be judicious to address the underlying problem that created it. This is the first pre-

10

condition to a solution, any solution. Only such an approach can ensure that even after terrorism is defeated it will not reappear with force from an unexpected direction. All attempts to date to treat the roots of terrorism have failed because the genuine roots have not been identified at all, because how the first fundamental problem came about has never been elucidated.

The third fundamental problem: The endemic rifts that divide the Jewish people.

Parallel to events among the Palestinians, belief in the indispensability of continuing on a Zionist track at this 'advanced' stage of Israel's development has weakened among many Israelis. This trend had its advent in the tremendous increase in the standard of living in Israel; many Israelis have become addicted to 'a comfortable life' and have gradually lost their willingness to continue the Zionist struggle in the face of an indefatigable enemy.

Palestinian wretchedness and the 'bitter lives' that a significant portion of Palestinians lead in contrast to what has been happening among Israelis has undermined to a large extent faith in the justness of the Zionist way, both in Israel and among some of its friends. Many around the world and among the Israeli Left have found it difficult to support traditional Zionist worldviews if their own wellbeing comes at the expense of Palestinians, if many Palestinians appear to be the victims of Zionism.

Loss of Zionism's way due to the Palestinian problem has created two alarming problems among Zionist leadership. The first, the breakdown of Zionist ideology that had been the driving force for Zionist leadership in the past has been replaced by an economic and personal hedonism. This is to a large extent due to the lack of a national-Zionist challenge, because of frustration in the face of their inability to reach a settlement of the Palestinian problem. The pursuit of pleasures and personal gain has led to a rise in corruption among the leadership and in society as a whole. The

11

high echelons in Israel, including no small number of senior public servants with tremendous clout, have invested most of their time and energy, while fulfilling senior government posts, in promoting themselves and their own vested interests: enhancing their standing and increasing their own personal assets.

Widespread corruption has led many in Israel to give up on their leadership and in their despair join the ranks of those who have lost faith in the Zionist ethos, atrophying the wherewithal of part of the Jewish public in the struggles they continue to face.

Loss of faith in Zionism has also led to an additional problem: a severe schism within the Jewish people and its leadership. The Israeli Left, out of sensitivity to the Palestinian problem and the desire to solve it, has abandoned traditional Zionist dedication to the settlement of Eretz-Israel and the determined battle against terrorism which they themselves led for so many years.

The Israeli Right, the majority of whom have continued to embrace traditional beliefs and outlooks, have become the standard-bearers of traditional Zionist values and visions that were once led by the Left. The split in diplomatic paths has created a huge rift between Right and Left in Israel that is unprecedented in magnitude.

The division within the Israeli camp has worsened greatly since the outset of the Oslo Process. And worsening of the Israeli-Palestinian conflict in the wake of the failure of the Oslo Process has already led the Left – in a last-ditch attempt to bring about an end to the conflict – to adopt positions that constitute a jeopardy to the security of Israel. The weakness that a lack of unanimity projects threatens the very existence of the Jewish people.

One of the most serious ramifications of the Right-Left chasm is that the majority of Israelis are unable to unite (except in times of war or major crises) in order to act together over time to meet the internal economic-social perils that put the country in jeopardy. Most of the public is cognizant of the dangers, but do not always fathom the genuine scope and seriousness they present. Neglecting

12

these dangers allows them to grow; such circumstances could ultimately lead to a breakdown of the country's security. The destructive consequences of internal disunity among Israelis multiply when Israel's enemies are aware of its weakened condition. They wait for Israel to be weakened from within to the point when the time will be ripe to attack it with weapons of mass destruction, to bring about the total annihilation of the State of Israel without sustaining any great damage to themselves. This state of affairs, together with the hatred of Israel harbored by some of the Muslim inhabitants of the Middle East and first and foremost among the Iranians and their allies in Lebanon and in the Palestinian Authority, encourages such elements to invest extraordinary resources in armament and preparations for the 'next round' of violence.

The clash between some Israeli secularists and religious Zionists, which reached its peak in the Israeli disengagement from Gaza in August 2005, has further weakened Israel internally. Islamist extremists merely rub their hands with glee in anticipation of Israel's downfall from within, quoting apt passages from the Koran as a prophecy about to be fulfilled:

Chapter 2 Verse 253:

"And if Allah had pleased, those after them would not have **fought one with another after clear arguments had come to them, but they disagreed; so there were some of them who believed and others who denied**; and if Allah had pleased they would not have fought one with another, but Allah brings about what He intends."

And in Chapter 2 Verse 84-85:

"And when we made a covenant with you: **You shall not shed your blood and you shall not turn your people out of your cities**; then you gave a promise while you witnessed. Yet you it is who slay your people **and turn a party from among you out of their homes, backing each other up against them unlawfully and exceeding the limits...**What then is the reward of such among you as do this but disgrace in the life of this world, and on the day of resurrection they shall be sent back to the most grievous chastisement, and Allah is not at all heedless of what you do."

In light of the above, it is imperative that every possible vehicle be used that can minimize the terrible rift among the People of Israel in order to stabilize Israel's policies, its economy and security. Doing so will ease a solution to the problem of Palestinian suffering (the second fundamental problem), because reduction in internal division in Israel will convince those devoted to terrorism that they had better not fall for the illusion that all they have to do is be willing to sacrifice, suffer and inflict enough suffering on the enemy in order for the Palestinians and radical Islam to win in the end.

A Dead End Situation

Curtailing the third fundamental problem – the division among Israelis, will enhance the prospects for calm in the region. As in the case of mitigating hatred, such calm is necessary to solve the first, core problem of two different claimants to Eretz-Israel. Of course, the first problem is the source of the others.

One faces a **Circular Cascade Effect**: Each problem must be solved as a preliminary to solving the others. In order to end the cycle of bloodshed, one must find a comprehensive solution to all three problems together in order to bring about a solution to each problem itself. This complexity is the reason the ongoing crisis in the Middle East not only has failed to be solved to date; it is also the reason attempts to reach an diplomatic agreement of one sort or another, that ignore the complexity of the problem, have only exacerbated the situation.

14

Any attempt to solve the Middle Eastern morass without going down to its roots demands use of force or coercion which only deepen the existing muddle. Contrary to all other approaches, this volume, by going to the roots of the conflict, is designed to present one solution that will address simultaneously all three fundamental problems. This volume does not claim that the road to a solution is short. The author does not claim that efforts to follow the path suggested will be simple or that the objective will be easy to realize. After all, if the situation was indeed simple, the path to a solution would have been found and applied successfully a long time ago. The importance of this book is the very presentation of a different *modus operandi*, a path that will lead to peace and security in Eretz-Israel, while at the present time there is not one party that has yet to suggest that they have an alternative path for solving the crises.

Chapter Two

A Path that Doesn't Lead to a Solution - Past Failures

The ramifications of unsolved problems between Israelis and Palestinians don't just boil down to unending wars and terrorism and the suffering they cause Israel's inhabitants.

The cycle of bloodshed from terrorist attacks and Israeli counter-responses, side-by-side with recognition of Palestinian suffering and the necessity of its removal, have prompted the Israeli government, with the support of and pressure from most of the world community, to 'reward' Palestinian terrorism with the Oslo Accords, the Disengagement Plan and the Road Map.

Once the world acquiesced to terrorism and made it worthwhile, it spawned a new generation of terrorism that reached its present peak in the events of September 11, 2001 in the United States – the terrorist attack that led to the collapse of the World Trade Center.

Extremist Islamic terrorism has enjoyed a tail wind as the result of the success of a chain of terrorist attacks in the United States, Bali, Russia, Iraq, Morocco, Saudi Arabia, Turkey, Egypt, London, India, Jordan, Spain and France (the last, riots by Muslims in Paris) that expressed the determination of extremist Islamists to step up their global terrorist offensive. Iranian and North Korean leaders were drawn into thinking that a policy of force and deception, combined with development of weapons of mass destruction and their proliferation, is a recipe for success.

A burning hatred towards Americans and towards Israel spread by extremist Islamist elements 'stir the pot,' as well. The propaganda, incitement and 'education' fanned by extremist Islam increases hatred round-the-clock. Parallel to this, Israel does nothing to speak of in order to turn this trend around – and its weakness in this regard is not the absence of gestures (that are then viewed as a

16

sign of weakness and mobilized by terrorist leaders to further intensify their attacks).

The first and most immediate quandary is **how to get out of the present predicament?** Solutions have already been offered and attempted, that have turned out to be merely partial and temporary, and ultimately ended in failure. One must conclude that bigger and more genuine questions must be asked, the answers to which are indispensable if we are to extricate the conflict from its present entanglement: How can one settle the complex problems in Eretz-Israel?

If one examines the history of Israeli relations with the Palestinians since 1967, one encounters after the Six Day War the **first Israeli approach** to such a relationship. It was Moshe Dayan who strived to establish a rational and worthy Palestinian leadership. This effort did not succeed due to threats against the budding local Palestinian leadership by PLO terrorist leadership abroad. Thus, this first solution to the problem failed.

At the outset of the 1970s, Israel changed its approach, with a lengthy offensive on PLO terrorism, inflicting serious damage to the PLO. This **second Israeli approach**, while it struck back at terrorism, failed to bring an end to terrorism. Israel's focus on the 'war against terrorism,' however, was detrimental: First and foremost, such focus was a contributing factor to Israel's lack of preparedness for the 1973 War and the surprise when it broke out (a phenomenon that repeated itself in the Second Lebanon War in July 2006, when fighting the *Intifada* disrupted training exercises and preparedness for an entirely different kind of warfare).

Despite achievement of peace between Israel and Egypt – diplomacy in which **Menachem Begin** raised the concept of **autonomy**, nothing has been done to realize this idea since then, and the war against terrorism intensified, reaching its peak in 1982 in the first Lebanon War (the 'Peace for the Galilee' Campaign). As a result of this war, PLO headquarters was evacuated to Tunis.

This move not only left the PLO intact and 'on the map' in the struggle against Israel; the power vacuum it created in Southern Lebanon with the PLO's departure as a result of the war, produced a new adversary for Israel – Hizbollah.

Parallel to Israel's focus on the war against terrorism, the Palestinian masses were totally neglected throughout this entire period in every domain beyond economics and education. Even in these two areas treatment was faulty: In the economic sphere, over-dependence on the Israeli economy was created, while in the educational field there was not enough direction of education towards reconciliation.

Furthermore, the investment in the well-being of Palestinians and even in Israeli Arabs was insufficient. Both faced relative discrimination compared to Jewish Israeli citizens. While Israel made efforts to move some of the Palestinians out of refugee camps to permanent housing, the Palestinians refused to do so under pressure of terrorist leadership. Thus, Israel became an unwilling accomplice to the perpetuation of the refugee problem alongside the Arab countries and the PLO.

For the State of Israel, dealing with terrorism became akin to 'occupational therapy.' This skewed attention away from the need to find a solution to the Palestinian problem. In the first decade after the 1967 War, the solution to the conflict offered by Israel was the Alon Plan which envisioned the return of most of Judea and Samaria (the West Bank) to Jordan, except the Jordan Valley and some areas adjacent to the Green Line. In 1977 another plan was offered to the Palestinians: Begin's autonomy plan ('autonomy for people, not autonomy of territory'). This plan as well failed to give sufficient expression to Palestinians' national longings, and therefore nothing came of it.

Along the road, the idea of a 'transfer' was raised – that Palestinians should be transferred to Jordan where, it was argued, there was already a Palestinian majority. Although transfer did not garner much support in Israel, it frightened Palestinians in Eretz-Israel who found themselves under the threat of becoming refugees again, but this time outside Eretz-Israel.

Parallel to its unrelenting battle with the PLO, the State of Israel encouraged the growth of alternative political organization in Palestinian territories. But as a result of the above-mentioned neglect, coupled by financial support from Saudi Arabia, the alternative that sprouted as a substitute for the PLO was extremist Islam in the framework of Hamas.

This process took place primarily in the Gaza Strip where the impact of neglect was the worse due to a high birth rate in a confined area that led to severe crowding and poverty. Against the backdrop of such conditions, it is not hard to fathom why the first *Intifada* broke out at the end of 1987.

The first *Intifada* overshadowed Israel's achievements in the war against terrorism, and added the threat of a Hamas takeover on the street. This situation underscored the failure of the second Israeli approach to the problem. The result was the **third Israeli approach**: Bringing the PLO, the enemy whose headquarters were in Tunis, to the Territories and signing the Oslo Accords with them, in the hope that the PLO would serve as a force capable of stopping the growth of Hamas. As became apparent with the outbreak of the second *Intifada* in 2000, and Palestinian parliamentary elections early in 2006 that culminated in a Hamas landslide victory, this third approach also failed.

Parallel to efforts to curtail the damage inflicted by terrorism, a **fourth Israeli approach** was adopted: Neutralizing Arafat as a partner to negotiations and to the bilateral relationship. This approach was at best only marginally effective in Arafat's lifetime and – some would argue – backfired, nor was his power over Palestinians politics 'neutralized' by his death. Arafat's spirit as a terrorist leader and as an entrenched symbol of Palestinianism continues to reign over most Palestinians, without anyone seriously trying to change this.

Israel, which did not know how to respond to the situation that developed with the death of Arafat – arrived at a **fifth Israeli approach**: Unilateral disengagement from the Palestinians as unworthy as negotiation partners. The election of Abu Mazen as Chairman of the Palestinian Authority was met by a half-hearted, qualified dialogue with Arafat's successor that led to **a sixth Israeli approach** – a partial bilateral disengagement. A **seventh Israeli approach** was almost a foregone conclusion: an imposed settlement to negotiate establishment of a Palestinian state with one out of two Palestinian governments, that at the most will result in a *hudna* with both of these goverments, without peace.

Since a *hudna* is not a permanent solution, it is hard to know how many other new approaches will be required, between timeouts, to keep up the bloodbath.

In one of the fables written by the renowned Russian writer Ivan Krylov, a father and son owned a donkey and needed to get to a faraway city. They tried every possible solution to the absurd predicament they found themselves in; unable to find a resolution, they were driven to one experiment after another, each more absurd than the previous one.[5] The predicament of two Peoples

---

[5] The fable tells of a son who had a donkey. The two needed to get to a faraway city. Naturally, the father rode the ass and the son walked beside him. They met a wayfarer who asked the father: "Don't you have mercy on the young man?!" So the father let his son ride the donkey. Not very long after, they encountered another wayfarer who asked the young man: "Don't you have mercy on your father?!" The two had no choice but to ride the animal together. A third wayfarer asked: "Don't you have any mercy on the donkey?!" So all three – the father, the son and the donkey – were left to hoof it on their own steam. When a fourth wayfarer encountered the threesome, he commented sarcastically: "I don't understand why three asses are walking together. The father and the son had no choice but to put the donkey on their shoulders and continue on their way.

20

claiming title to the same land is no less complicated than the fable. It would be wiser to learn from it: In other words, rather than creating growing suffering and death for one another in attempting to solve an illogical situation to no avail, it would be wiser to try and turn the situation into a logical one.

A new approach to solving the problem is needed!

In order to break the chain of failures, one needs to take a timeout to discuss the roots of the problem and the direction a solution must therefore take. The only prospect for embarking on a new path is to lower the level of hatred in an effective manner – and not through gestures that are liable to worsen the situation. Such an approach requires one **'go to the roots' in order to bring about a just solution to the conflict!**

One must provide a decisive answer to the first problem presented at the outset: **How did two Peoples come to see the same country as their homeland?** One cannot continue to ignore the question of how this came about – and how to solve this problem.

The new element that is required to solve the problem is a change and an improvement in Israel's public relations apparatus, and the position Israel takes vis-à-vis the conflict. Israel must change its argumentation so that its position will be acceptable to the majority of world opinion. Once the Israeli public is surer of the justice of its case, it will be more unified, enhancing the changes of winning the battle for peace and security. The more the world will become convinced of the justness of Israel's case, the more latitude Israel will have to operate decisively in uprooting terrorism. The less convinced Palestinians will be that terrorism is the right way to go, the sooner terrorism will fade away.

When one is caught in a deadlock, as the situation in Eretz-Israel seems to be, one must break conventions! Doing so is no small matter. It demands freeing oneself from years of brainwashing, and

21

the way unconsciously such brainwashing has shaped ways of thinking and led to fixated thinking!

The reader will need a lot of openness and forbearance to comprehend the revolutionary **finding** presented in Chapter Three and Four. In Chapter Five substantiation of this finding is presented from various perspectives, validation that will assist readers accept this finding. The importance of the finding is magnified by the absence of any other serious solution, thus prospects that it will be accepted are greater now than in the past.

Chapter Six of the book details a new approach to solving the conflict based on the finding. Its innovative nature makes this approach difficult to assimilate. Various parties that are captives to present conventions will have difficulty accepting it at first, but fundamentally the approach is very simple and harbors the facility to finally bring a just and lasting peace to Eretz-Israel.

The Foundation of the Finding

The finding presented in this book is founded upon examination of historical facts regarding Eretz-Israel in the course of the past two thousand years that are commonly ignored. These historic facts put things in a different light and have significant implications for the present and the future as to the identity of most Palestinians and the solution of the conflict in Eretz-Israel.

This finding will at first glance seem new. In essence, it expands on a relatively old approach that was already hinted at by two key fathers of the Zionist movement – David Ben-Gurion and Yitzhak Ben-Zvi – in a book the two coauthored, entitled *Eretz-Israel ba-Avar ooba-Hoveh* ('Eretz-Israel in the Past and the Present').[6] The raising of this issue by two core leaders of the Zionist Movement in Eretz-Israel was prompted by the desire to justify Zionism, since the two men were aware of the problem Arab inhabitants of Eretz-

---

[6] For the Yiddish version from 1918, see Source 1 in the Bibliography.

Israel presented. Yitzhak Ben-Zvi went even farther, devoting much time to researching this issue.

For various reasons, including the hostility between Jews and Palestinians with the intensification of Palestinian terrorist activity in the years 1936-1939, Yitzhak Ben-Zvi dropped the subject. Then, in the wake of the Holocaust of European Jewry, there was no longer a need to justify the Zionism case, and the issue was abandoned almost entirely.

But today, there is a new constellation of forces at play: On one hand, the situation in the region has reached a deadlock. In an era of proliferation of terrorism and weapons of mass destruction one simply cannot afford to continue to neglect the problem. In fact, the necessity of solving it has become critical. Under such circumstances, together with fading memories of the Holocaust as the years go by, not only has it become imperative to justify the Zionist case; time has also taken its toll among Jewry as well, along with non-Jews who have withdrawn their support of Israel, no small number of Jews have also lost their belief in the Zionist way.

On the other hand, in the closing decade of the 20th Century, the 'old approach' first raised by Ben-Zvi and Ben-Gurion has been seriously bolstered by genetic research of Jewish ethnic groupings, the Palestinians and other Peoples.[7] In addition, information and communications technologies and their widespread access have made it far easier to reach a host of new and old information sources and examine their validity. All this has contributed greatly to bring to the forefront new supportive evidence of the finding detailed in Chapters Three to Five.

Demographic patterns during the past two thousand years that serve as a foundation for the finding may appear to be very far

---

[7] See discussion at the beginning of Chapter One, and Sources 12-15 in the Bibliography.

removed from present problems. The need to re-examine history emanates first and foremost from the complexity and difficulty of the problem itself, but also from Palestinian longings to roll back history, to raise the issue of the Right of Return and transform it into stumbling block on the road to peace in Eretz-Israel.

Beyond this, the two sides of the conflict tie themselves and their respective collective memories and right to Eretz-Israel thousands of years back in time. As is the case in psychoanalysis, sometimes one must go back into the distant past in order to understand the roots of current problems. In the case before us, the quandary is: How did two Peoples come to view the same country as their homeland, and how can one untangle this muddle?

Chapter Three

Eretz-Israel from a Demographic Standpoint between the Second Commonwealth Period and Modern Times

The Profile of Inhabitants of Eretz-Israel from the Second Commonwealth Period

Edomites and Moabites – Brother Nations of the Israelites

There are two parties from the past who seem, at first glance, insignificant vis-à-vis the present: the Edomites and the Moabites. Yet, on closer examination it becomes evident that these two groupings are a central component in the present conflict over Eretz-Israel, and therefore knowledge of their history needs to be elucidated.

The preferential treatment that the Israelites gave the Edomites and Moabites was evidenced at the time of the conquest of eastern Eretz-Israel (Canaan) in the last days of Moses, prior to the Israelite tribes crossing the Jordan River westward under the leadership of Joshua. The Israelites were commanded to treat the Edomites, the Moabites and the Ammonites differently than the other peoples occupying the Promised Land.

As they prepared to enter Eretz-Israel, the Israelites were commanded to cleanse the Land of its inhabitants – the **Canaanites** and the **Amorites** and members of other Small Nations. The primary reason for doing so was the need to remove any negative influence by idol worshippers on the Israelite Nation. Another motive was not to leave in place in Eretz-Israel parties with prior rights, who ultimately would most likely try to uproot

25

the Israelites from their lands. This act of ethnic cleansing was carried out, except for vestiges of the original populations that remained along the coastal plain of western Eretz-Israel that was not conquered by Joshua and remained in the hands of the Philistines and the Canaanites.

As for the Edomites, the Moabites and the Ammonites – as the Israelites moved northward up the eastern side of the Jordan River, on their way passing through Edomite, Moabite and Ammonite territories the Israelites were commanded to buy and pay for the food and water they needed, and not to harm the locals.

Such preferential treatment towards the Moabites and Ammonites stemmed from the fact that they were the offspring of Lot, the son of the Patriarch Abraham's brother. As for the special treatment the Edomites enjoyed, this was because they were the offspring of Esau – the Patriarch Jacob's twin brother. Edom was Esau's nickname, and the Edomites had sprung from Esau's loins. Despite the tensions between Jacob and Esau in their youth when the two competed for their father Isaac's birthright, their relationship had improved in adulthood.

The good relations between Jacob and his twin brother grew the more their sheep and cattle business prospered. Due to the shortage of grazing land they faced in western Eretz-Israel, Esau – on his own initiative and of his own volition – took his family and herds and migrated east of the Jordan River to the vicinity of the Seir Mountain.

The circumstances surrounding the conquest of Eretz-Israel and its cleansing of foreign elements during the period of Moses' and Joshua's leadership played a significant role in the close relationship of these nations to the Israelite Nation – and their common origins: Terah, the father of Abraham. These nations inhabited the south-eastern sector of Eretz-Israel on the frontier of the territory designated for Israelite settlement. In this manner, the sons of **Brethren Nations of Israel** – as we have labeled the offspring of these ancient nations in this volume – were not supposed to intermingle with the Israelites. Consequently, the risk of them infecting the Israelites with pagan practices was marginal.

The preferential treatment of Brethren Nations also stemmed from the fact that they did not present a demographic threat to the Israelite Nation, while other nations were not allowed to remain in territories overtaken from previous inhabitants (except for the Gibeonites, who were small in number) in order not to jeopardize the Israelites' exclusive title to the Land. Thus, to make their presence acceptable, the areas where they resided were viewed at the time as beyond the borders of Eretz-Israel.

The Israelite Nation's close relationship with the Edomites and the Moabites prevailed and even deepened over time, despite the fact that the relationship was the product of acts of conquest. In the course of King David's conquests, the Moabites, the Ammonites and the Edomites were converted and made an extension of the Israelite Nation, although their kings were allowed to continue to directly hold the reins of power. In the case of the Edomites, their fierce opposition to Israelite occupation led King David to take the extraordinary step of killing all male Edomites. Thus the women in Edom had no alternative but to marry members of the Israelite garrison and other Israelites. Consequently, at the time and at later stages of history, those who were designated Edomites, in fact, had bloodlines that were half-Israelite.

Despite the close relationship that developed, the Edomites continued to bear their original names and were not incorporated into any of the Israelite tribes. They remained only part-Israelite, and they continued to reside in Edom as the subjects of an Edomite king.

To understand King David's conduct one should keep in mind that he himself was the great grandson of a convert – Ruth the Moabite. This family link surely was in his mind when he chose – first of all, to embrace and view as close brethren those who were blood relatives of his own great grandmother, while acting towards them in a humane manner compared to his treatment of the Edomites. His attitude towards the Ammonites – who were related to the Moabites – was much the same.

Nebuchadnezzar, the King of Babylon, permanently exiled a considerable part of the Edomite and Moabite Nations following the destruction of the First Jewish Commonwealth. But a significant number remained in Eretz-Israel and continue to be considered part of the Israelite Nation parallel to their original identity. The fate of the Ammonites was far harsher: Nebuchadnezzar exiled the majority without leaving them significant numbers in Eretz-Israel. Those who remained lived near Moabite communities and underwent a gradual process of assimilation, and the differences between them faded away.

The kinship between the Edomites and the Moabites, and the Israelites continued throughout the period of the Second Commonwealth and henceforth. After the destruction of the First Commonwealth, in the absence of the hegemony of an Israelite regime, the Moabites' and Edomites' devotion to their brethren the Israelite Nation and their religious beliefs waned. To bring them back into the fold, the Hasmonean leaders decided to re-convert them a second time. Jokhanan (John) Hyrcanus began this process by converting the Moabite minority that resided on grazing lands that Hyrcanus had conquered and added to his Kingdom.

Alexander Yanai (Alexander Jannaeus) completed the conversion of the Moabites and converted the Edomites after he added their territory to his Kingdom – which included the Gulf of Eilat in the South. The proximity of the Edomites and Moabites to the **Nabataeans**, their neighbors to the East, led to a small number – several hundred – to join the Nabataeans. But other than this small marginal group, following their conversion by the Hasmoneans, all the Edomites and Moabites continued for the next 1,600 years to be an inseparable part of the People of Israel.

28

The most famous among this population was Herod the Edomite king of Judea. Herod's paternal grandfather had been converted in the time of Alexander Jannaeus, when Herod's father, Antipater, was just a boy. In order to gain the consent of the Jewish People to reign over Judea, Herod married Mariamne, of the Hasmonean royal house. To further endear himself to the Jewish masses, King Herod invested greatly in renovating the Temple.

The Edomites and Moabites participated in the Great Revolt against the Romans (i.e., the First Jewish-Roman War) and inflicted more damage on their enemies, relative to their small numbers, than the Jews. This population will be referred to primarily as "**Brethren Nations [of Israel].**" (The Moabites were the dominant group within this population, which also included no small number of Ammonites – but being relatively small in numbers and assimilated among the Moabites, the Ammonites will not be cited as a separate entity in this work.)

The Samaritans – Remnants of the Kingdom of Israel

Another grouping that appears to be irrelevant in regard to the present is the Samaritans. In fact, the Samaritans are important to solving the problem of Eretz-Israel.

One of the results of the factionalism that has been an enduring feature of so much of the history of the People of Israel has been the mistaken way Jewish leadership has related to the Samaritans as a foreign element. Numerically small today, the Samaritans would seem to be unimportant, but this is erroneous. An historical survey of events reveals that the Samaritans are a very important component in resolving the Conflict in Eretz Israel, and, therefore, it is important to set the historical record straight.

In *An Abridged History of the Samaritans*[8] (*Kitzur Toldot HaShomronim,* in Hebrew), **Benyamin Tzadka** cites sources that claim most Samaritans were the offspring of tillers of the soil

---

[8] See the Bibliography, Source 11.

among the Israelite Tribes, part of whom were never exiled by the Assyrians or the Babylonians during the period of the destruction of the First Jewish Commonwealth.

Historical research of other conquests reveal a common pattern: the strong tie mountain peoples have to their lands, and the relative stability of such populations compared to inhabitants of the plains and valleys. It is natural that many of these tillers of the soil that resided in the mountains of Samaria at the time were not exiled by the Assyrians. Assyrian documents discovered in modern times cite only a modest number of exiles from Samaria, relative to the overall population of the Kingdom. This is also evidenced in references after the destruction of the Kingdom of Israel, citing that the King of Judea invited those who remained there to celebrate Passover in Jerusalem.

In practice, the Assyrians only exiled the leadership and strong elements of the population, consciously intermixing them in their places of exile with local lower class inhabitants, to manage their economy and civil order. The Babylonians behaved in the same manner. For example, in the Bible in Second Kings it is said that with the conquest of Jerusalem by the Babylonians, the conquerors exiled approximately 10,000 persons, while the poor classes, the vine growers and farmers from the city and its environs, remained.

Only a small minority of the population of Samaria was the offspring of established classes of the **Small Nations** (those who came from Cuthah and others) who were exiled to Eretz-Israel by the Assyrians. Moreover, the majority of the exiles returned to their homeland following the fall of the Assyrian Empire. In addition the population of Samaria included inhabitants of mixed parentage – Israelites and aliens. The alien minority who remained in the country, adopted the Israeli (Samaritan) religion in the course of time, after the destruction of the First Temple.

Despite this, the Babylonians, who followed the Assyrians as the dominant entity in the Fertile Crescent, were more thorough than their predecessors in the manner in which they exiled inhabitants of conquered lands. Samaritan sources cite that many Samaritans were exiled by the Babylonians. The Babylonians, however, skipped over a significant portion of the Samaritan population: By the time they arrived in Samaria, the Babylonians found many alien elements that were not native to Eretz-Israel and had not yet left. Consequently, the Babylonians did not undertake a thorough expulsion from Samaria (since the Assyrians had led many areas to being viewed as places whose indigenous population had already been replaced by aliens and needed no further expulsion).

Parallel to the Small Nations who left Samaria for their homelands after the fall of Assyria, a portion of the Samaritans who had been exiled by the Assyrians took advantage of the Babylonians' ignorance as to their identity and the opportunity (i.e., the geographic-demographic 'vacuum') that presented itself, to attempt to return to their homes after they were abandoned by the Small Nations. According to the Talmud, in the days of King of Judea Josiah (639-609 BCE) Jeremiah the Prophet repatriated a portion of the Israelite exiles.

The name Samaritan, given to the community during the Second Commonwealth Period, is based on the geographic designation Samaria, which in turn received its name as the capitol of the Northern Kingdom of Israel (Samaria) built by the 6th and 7th Kings of Israel Omri and Ahab.

Unfortunately, a constellation of circumstances led the Jews returning from the Babylonian Exile during the Return to Zion under Ezra and Nehemiah to mistakenly identify the Samaritans and relate to them as strangers. Among the circumstances: The designation 'Samaritan' as an separate entity from the time of the First Temple which Returnees were familiar with; the differences in religious practices between Returnees coming from the Diaspora and those who remained in Eretz-Israel – tension and 'rivalry' exacerbated by the religious zealousness of both sides; the breakdown into two separate communities of Israelites exiled to a strange land and Samaritans who remained in the homeland who developed under different circumstances; and the long-harbored animosity that had been an undercurrent between the Samaritans and the Jews from the time of the First Commonwealth. A more detailed discussion of the background to this schism is set forth in Appendix A.

The upshot of this mistake in viewing Samaritans as Others rather than brethren **led to a schism within the People of Israel, that began at the height of the First Commonwealth Period and was not healed during the Second Commonwealth Period or henceforth**. If there was a period of deepening ties between Israel and Judea during the First Temple period, it shriveled in the period of the Second Temple.

Already at the time of the building of the Second Temple, the Jews rejected Samaritans who requested to partake in the building process. Subsequently, relations went from bad to worse – from estrangement to hatred – which reached one of its peaks in the destruction of the city Samaria by the Hasmonean leader Jokhanan Hyrcanus.

The fact that the Samaritans were even more meticulous in fulfilling the commandments of the Torah than the Jews did not prevent the Jews and their sages through the Second Commonwealth Period and afterward from viewing the Samaritans as strangers and gentiles who followed the Religion of Israel only because their forefathers had converted. In other words, their conversion did not necessarily carry recognition at this point that they belonged to the People of Israel. The Samaritans were required by their tradition to dwell in the Land of Israel; Samaritans who left Eretz-Israel ceased to be Samaritans in the eyes of the Samaritan community, unless their departure was temporary in nature.

Inhabitants of Eretz-Israel who did not belong to the People of Israel

The fate of the Small Nations dwelling in Eretz-Israel in the time of Nebuchadnezzar was similar to those described above when most of the population was exiled by the Babylonians. These Small Nations include the Philistines who threatened the People of Israel until they were finally subdued by King David. Thus, in the Second Commonwealth Period and henceforth, only remnants remained in Eretz-Israel of the Small Nations.

At the close of the Second Commonwealth Period, remnants of these small groupings that did not belong to the People of Israel resided along the coastal plain of the Mediterranean. They were comprised of no more than several tens of thousands of inhabitants, at the most. The largest minority in Eretz-Israel were the Phoenicians, most of whom resided in Lebanon.

In addition, in Eretz-Israel there were remnants of the Philistines, Canaanites, and a small number of Greeks who had remained from the Hellenistic period and Persians who remained from the period of Persian rule, as Babylonians and Assyrians who had remained in Eretz-Israel due to similar circumstances. In addition, there remained in Eretz-Israel thousands of offspring of other ancient peoples. All of these remnants were Hellenized populations who had adopted Greek culture and worshiped Greek deities during Greek rule.

Under the reign of the Hasmoneans – Jokhanan Hyrcanus and his heirs, members of these small minorities were converted. All those who were not Jewish, Samaritan or Hellenist were converted to Judaism. Thus, no foreign elements nor members of Small Nations remained who had not been Hellenized. In the course of history which is traced in this book, over time, the distinctions in origin that separated all these small minority populations, foreign and local, faded away. All have therefore been bundled together as one category: the **Small Nations of Eretz-Israel, or Small Nations.**

Almost all the Greeks who came to Eretz-Israel during the Greek conquest were expelled by the Hasmoneans in the course of liberating the country from Greek rule. Only a few thousand remained. In addition to the above mixture of ethnicities, there were approximately 40,000 Arabs who engaged in idol worship under Hellenist influence.

Definitions and Basic Data

The composition of the People of Israel in Eretz-Israel from an ethnic and religious standpoint during the period under study was rather complex – and grew in complexity as the years passed. In order to clarify for the reader, this needs to be defined at the start:

The concept **Ethnic Jews** does not include the Edomites and the Moabites. Their number prior to the destruction of the Second Temple was in the vicinity of 4.8 million. This designation includes Jews who converted to Christianity, and later even Jews who accepted Islam in one form or another – provided that they resided in Eretz-Israel.

The concept **Jews** is more inclusive – encompassing the Edomites and the Moabites in addition to Ethnic Jews. Prior to the destruction of the Second Temple the total Jewish population in Eretz-Israel was some 5.5 million souls. At the close of the Second Commonwealth Period there were some 700,000 Edomites and Moabites in Eretz-Israel.

The concept **People of Israel,** as distinguished from the **Jewish People**, includes Jews and Samaritans together. The People of Israel numbered 6.4 million souls, including 900,000 Samaritans.

The concept **People of Israel from an ethnic standpoint** does not include the Edomites and the Moabites.

The concept **Religion of Israel** includes the Jewish and Samaritan religion together.

In the course of the book, other additional definitions follow where relevant. The reader who wants an explanation of a particular concept without having to search through the body of the text can find a complete list in Appendix 6, at the very back of the book.

The Historical Survey:

From the Outset of Roman Rule in Eretz-Israel to the Great Revolt

The bitterest period for the People of Israel in Eretz-Israel began with the conquest of Eretz-Israel by the Romans in 63 BCE, and reached its peak in the Great Revolt, whose repression was completed in 70 CE after the Romans destroyed the Second Temple. The Jews' decision to rise up against Rome – the superpower of the times – stemmed first and foremost from the discrimination they faced and the religious decrees imposed on them. The Jews, who had given up hope of national independence, merely sought to maintain freedom of religious expression; however, they were forced to endure unbearable forms of religious coercion including idol worship, which reached its height when the Romans introduced statues of their deities into the Temple itself.

Yet, the grounds for the Great Revolt ripened over a period of time. The Romans gave the Small Nations of Eretz-Israel – a tiny minority numerically – preferential treatment over the huge majority of inhabitants who belonging to the People of Israel. These gentiles were allowed to enlist in the Roman army and gained positions of power and enhanced their economic status. Among the Jews there was high unemployment that led many to conclude that they had nothing to lose by rising up against Rome. Disputes between gentiles and Jews in mixed areas multiplied. The gentiles plotted against the Jews and the Roman consuls systematically handed down judgments in clashes between the two in favor of the gentile side.

In the year 66 CE, **Nero** ruled that the gentiles would control Caesarea, a town populated by a large Jewish community. This event was the 'point of no return' for the Jews. The Great Revolt broke out in earnest in the year 68 CE, following introduction of idols into the holiest sanctuary of Judaism – the Temple.

68 A. D. – Prior to the Great Revolt		
Ethnic Group	No. of Inhabitants	Percentage of Population
Jews	4,800,000	72%
Samaritans	900,000	14%
Edomites & Moabites	730,000	11%
Total People of Israel	6,430,000	97%
Arabs	40,000	1%
Phoenicians	30,000	0%
Philistines	28,000	0%
Canaanites	24,000	0%
Other Small Nations	67,000	1%
Romans	10,000	0%
Total	**6,629,000**	**100%**

Table 1: The Population of Eretz-Israel Prior to the Great Revolt.

The decision to embark on an uprising suggested that the insurgents in Eretz-Israel would soon be joined by large forces among the Jewish communities in Babylon. The Jewish community of Babylon, particularly those who resided northwest of the Euphrates River, was renowned for its military force. But expectations of assistance failed to materialize. To this one must add the military prowess of the Romans – their superior battle experience and advanced war technologies.

Another factor that had far-reaching ramifications on the chances of the Great Revolt's success was internal disarray – divisions within to the Jewish People, in-fighting among the Jews that often was extremely brutal and entailed the spilling of blood. The results were catastrophic. Internal fighting culminated, among other things, in the burning of most of the food that had been stockpiled in Jerusalem in the event of a siege on the city. All the above factors played a decisive role in the outcome of the Revolt, despite the heroism and willingness to sacrifice exhibited by many Jews.

In the course of the Revolt, 2.5 million out of 6 million inhabitants of Eretz-Israel were murdered or killed throughout the country, or died of hunger during the siege of Jerusalem. Close to **two million others were exiled and sold into slavery.**

Out of 5.5 million Jews (including Edomites and Moabites) and 900,000 Samaritans dwelling in Eretz-Israel before the Revolt, only 2 million Jews and some 280,000 Samaritans remained. The number of Edomites and Moabites dropped from 730,000 to 150,000. Table 2 in Appendix 5 contains the data on the breakdown of the surviving population after the Revolt. The data show that the Samaritans, the Edomites and the Moabites took a more active part in the Revolt and were extraordinarily devoted to the People of Israel. Relatively speaking, these minorities paid a much higher price than did the Ethnic Jews.

The destruction of the Second Jewish Commonwealth was **the first among many great calamities** in the history of Israel. The destruction of the First Commonwealth was a great calamity from a national-political standpoint. But in magnitude it hardly held a candle to the sheer genocidal scope of what transpired in the course of the destruction of the Second Commonwealth and later periods to People of Israel.

The destruction of the Second Commonwealth was also the **first significant depopulation point** in the number of inhabitants in Eretz-Israel since the destruction of the First Commonwealth. Further down the course of history there were additional events that led to other significant losses in population.

Subjection of the Great Revolt peaked in horrific events. In the course of a mere two weeks, 600,000 corpses were removed from the walled city of Jerusalem – Jews who had died of starvation after having been trapped in the siege of Jerusalem after participating in the annual Passover pilgrimage.

In terms of single catastrophic events, even the worst single atrocity committed by the Nazis in the course of the Holocaust against European Jewry pales in comparison with the terrible sight of the bodies of hundreds of thousands of Jewish inhabitants being carried out the gates of Jerusalem.

The Romans allowed the removal of the dead from Jerusalem due to the stench which plagued both sides. Even the Roman soldiers laying siege to the city couldn't keep back their tears at the terrible sight.

The Diaspora Revolt

The Jews who had been expelled from Eretz-Israel by the Romans following the Great Revolt refused to accept their fate passively. The Jews had been exiled to parts of the Roman Empire to the West that were relatively close to Eretz-Israel – Asia Minor, southeastern European, Cyprus and northeast Africa. These Diaspora Jews, like their brethren in Eretz-Israel, suffered discrimination and heavy taxes imposed by the Roman Empire.

In addition Jews in the Diaspora hated the Romans for the calamity they had visited on the Jewish People during the Great Revolt. At the same time, there was tremendous unrest among the Greeks against the Romans, for overrunning and destroying the Greek Empire, as well as discrimination against Greeks by Rome. All took advantage of the opportunity that arose when the Roman Emperor **Marcus Traianus** or Trajan (98-177 CE) was occupied for an extended period in wars with the Parthians, wars that cut deep into the ranks of the Roman Army and keep it pinned down on the eastern front.

In the year 114 CE, another Jewish revolt against the Romans broke out. The Jews were joined by many Greeks. The revolt was called the **Revolt of the Diasporas** or the **Revolt of the Exiles**. The Jewish side was led by zealots; exiles from Eretz-Israel among them constituted a good proportion of the Jews in the Empire. The revolt continued until the year 118 CE. In the course of the uprising, Jews and their allies killed many Romans and those who sided with the Empire.

Relatively few people are aware of the far-reaching impact the Roman Emperor **Hadrian** had on history. Prior to his ascendancy to the throne, Hadrian was Traianus' military commander. When he became Emperor upon the death of Traianus in the year 117 CE, Hadrian came to the conclusion that conduct of a two-front war was impossible. He therefore forged a peace treaty with the Parthians and directed most of his military force towards brutally putting down the revolts within the Empire. In the course of stamping out the revolt, the Romans killed 1.2 million Jews, approximately a third of all the Jews in Asia Minor, Europe and North Africa.

In the wake of the revolt, the Roman Emperor forbade the Jews, mostly in areas where the uprising had taken place, from continuing to fulfill the commandments of Judaism. The primary commandment they outlawed and imposed strictly was prohibition of circumcision – a commandment, unlike others that could be conducted in hiding without being caught, that it was hard to hide.

The Bar Kokhba Revolt and Its Results

Another horrific event took place at the close of the Bar Kokhba Revolt in 135 CE. This revolt broke out towards the end of Hadrian's rule. The reason for unrest among the Jews that laid the ground for the uprising was a new tax that the Romans imposed that again discriminated against the Jews.

The new tax was part of a tax reform carried out by Hadrian which abolished certain taxes and set new ones in place. The taxes that were abolished had little significance for the Jews of Eretz-Israel whose livelihoods were not tied to international commerce. On the other hand, the new taxes were relevant for Jews. The new taxes were imposed, however, during a period of economic prosperity in Eretz-Israel, and at a time when there had been a significant improvement in relations between Jews and gentiles. Consequently, the reforms were not significant enough to spark an uprising, but the taxes were a source of ferment among the Jews.

At the outset the Jews in Eretz-Israel and Babylon were under the impression that Hadrian was pro-Jewish. He was a military man, who with his appointment as Emperor became a man of peace, renowned for his construction projects, his spiritual nature and his care for the poor. In the wake of the peace treaty he forged with the Parthians, some of the Roman army commanders mutinied and the Senate ordered them executed.

40

One of the Roman army commanders who had been responsible for a brutal massacre of Babylonian Jews was also executed. The Jews in Eretz-Israel interpreted his execution as a pro-Jewish act on the part of the Emperor. Another reason for the Jews' sympathetic attitude towards Hadrian, even more so the Samaritans, was the fact that Hadrian had a Samaritan wife whom he had brought from the village of Yashuf (today, Yasuf) in Samaria.

The initial impression among the Jews of Eretz-Israel in regard to Hadrian for the most part preceded the Emperor's actions in putting down the Revolts of the Diasporas. Another factor in this good impression was the close ties the Jews of Eretz-Israel had with the Jewish center in Babylon, Jews who resided in a rather narrow area and who were well organized, in contrast with Jews scattered through the west with whom contact was poor. Moreover, the revolt took place over a very wide geographic area and only several years after the revolt was put down did the Jews fully comprehend the scope of the calamity the Jewish People had suffered at Hadrian's hands.

Hadrian revitalized the glory of Hellenism and merged it with the Roman idol worship. In fact, his command of Greek was better than his command of Latin. The Emperor frequently traveled throughout his far-flung Empire, rebuilt and constructed new Hellenist temples – including ones in Athens and Rome. In addition, in order to thwart wars with possible invaders, he fortified the boundaries of the Roman Empire, including the famous Hadrian Wall in the British Iles.

In Judea he entered into a dialogue with Jewish sages on religious philosophy seeking the common denominator among various religions, and was looked on favorably by the scribes. In the framework of his works rebuilding temples, he promised the Jews that the Temple in Jerusalem would be rebuilt. This 'sign' and a host of other circumstances combined to kindle false messianic hopes among the People of Israel.

Given the positive reception Hadrian received in his contact with Jewish religious leaders, the Emperor did not encounter the abhorrence Jews harbored towards idol worship or its intensity and remained oblivious that this was a very sensitive issue. With the best intensions, in the course of his efforts to advance Hellenism, Hadrian had a temple built to **Jupiter** (the Roman god parallel to the Greek deity **Zeus**) on the ruins of the Second Temple, and settled gentiles in Jerusalem to serve the gods in the newly-established shrine. The Jews' great expectations of Redemption were dashed, replaced by bitter disappointment. This was exacerbated by news arriving in Eretz-Israel of the horrific casualties inflicted on the Jews in the Revolt of the Exiles. The attitude of the Jews toward Hadrian underwent a total reversal.

Shimon Bar-Kokhba, an extremely able Jewish military commander, began to organize the Jews to rise up in revolt, with the blessing of the venerated spiritual leader **Rabbi Akiva**. Unlike the Great Revolt, this time the Jews prepared themselves well and made impressive gains, exhibiting extraordinary fighting courage. The revolt which broke out in the year 131 CE totally surprised the Romans and particularly the Emperor, who honestly thought his actions in Jerusalem were beneficial to his Jewish subjects. In putting down the revolt, as well as revenge for the casualties the rebels inflicted on the Romans, the Romans murdered many among the 2 million Jews who remained in Eretz-Israel at the end of the Great Revolt. In addition Hadrian had many others exiled and sold into slavery.

The Romans chose to inflate reports of the number of Jews killed – 580,000 – in order to explain their own great losses to the Jewish insurgents. Actually the number of Jews who fell in battle or were murdered in retribution was about 250,000. Another 450,000 members of the People of Israel were exiled or sold into slavery.[9]

---

[9] In order to balance the number of Jews who disappeared from Eretz-Israel, the Romans deflated the number of exiles in their reports, claimed to be 200,000.

Roman losses in military personnel and auxiliary forces reached 120,000. The scope of causalities was way beyond what the Roman army was used to. In an unprecedented step, the Emperor Hadrian did not mark the end of the revolt by announcing the victory before a cheering Senate: "If you and your sons are healthy it is better, I and the army are well." The heroism of Bar Kokhba's followers and their capabilities were so great that the Roman Army was afraid to engage them in face-to-face combat and adopted a tactic of encirclement and severing supply lines.

The great calamity that befell the portion of the People of Israel residing in Eretz-Israel with the suppression of the Bar Kokhba Revolt, following on the heels of the calamity of the Great Revolt, sparked widespread despair. In the wake of the tribulations, the killing and the cruelty of the Romans towards the rebellious population, and primarily due to the period of oppressive and punitive actions that the Revolt spurred, 300,000 more Jews left the country and migrated to the great Jewish center of Diaspora in Babylon. To sum up the negative demographics: By the period following the Bar Kokhba Revolt the number of inhabitants belonging to the People of Israel in Eretz-Israel had dropped by a million inhabitants.

All told, the series of Jewish revolts against Rome led to very significant demographic change in Eretz-Israel. From a point where Jews constituted a large and decisive majority of the inhabitants, their numbers dropped to approximately one million, including the Moabites. The Samaritans, who had not participated in the Bar Kokhba Revolt, remained unaffected. Their numbers rose due to natural population growth and the period of peace and economic prosperity they enjoyed after the Great Revolt.

The majority of the population of Eretz-Israel was by now comprised of elements that did not belong to the People of Israel. This only came about as a result of the influx of foreign elements to Eretz-Israel, primarily Arabs who filled the vacuum left by those who perished or were exiled in the Great Revolt.

135 A. D. – Following the Bar Kokhba Revolt		
Ethnic Group	No. of Inhabitants	Percentage of Population
Jews	900,000	32%
Samaritans	300,000	11%
Edomites & Moabites	100,000	4%
Total People of Israel	1,300,000	46%
Arabs	1,300,000	46%
Phoenicians	74,000	3%
Philistines	40,000	1%
Canaanites	39,000	1%
Other Small Nations	60,000	2%
Romans	18,000	1%
Total	2,831,000	100%

Table 3: Demographic Composition after the Suppression of the Bar Kokhba Revolt.

The Arabs at this time were the largest population group among the inhabitants of Eretz-Israel. The Arab Province of the Roman Empire extended eastward and southward of Eretz-Israel, from the eastern portion of what is today Jordan that was never considered part of Eretz-Israel. The drop in Moabite and Edomite populations in the course of the Great Revolt allowed **Nabataeans** and Arabs to take possession of fertile holdings east of the Jordan. They established the Nabataean Kingdom and built the city of **Petra** as their capital, the remains of which are considered one of the great architectural wonders of the ancient world.

44

In the year 106, the Romans conquered the Nabataean Kingdom and annexed it to the Arab Province. This move led to an additional influx of Arab immigrants from their Province into the relatively superior and more fertile sectors of eastern Eretz-Israel, migration that reached its peak in the year 127. After the Bar Kokhba Revolt which had further decimated the Jewish population, more Arabs entered Eretz-Israel, and the Nabataeans took possession of the Negev regions. All the Arabs at this time (this was some 500 years prior to the advent of Islam) were pagan.

Among the gentiles belonging to the Small Nations in the western part of Eretz-Israel, the Phoenicians grew in numbers. Following the Great Revolt, many migrated from Lebanon to Eretz-Israel which had been depopulated to a certain degree and contained unclaimed agricultural lands. The population of other Small Nations also grew as a result of natural demographic growth.

Although prior to the Bar Kokhba Revolt and even in its aftermath, as a result of the arrival of the Arabs, the overall population of Eretz-Israel grew compared to the number of inhabitants left after the Great Revolt, yet the Bar Kokhba Revolt itself became **the second significant depopulation point** of the overall population of Eretz-Israel in the period covered by this study.

At the close of the Bar Kokhba Revolt the Jews (including the Edomites and the Moabites) constituted only 36 percent of the inhabitants of Eretz-Israel. The Arabs were concentrated east of the Jordan, where they held a majority. As a result, the Jews constituted the majority (about 50 percent) of the population west of the Jordan. The vast majority of the Jewish population was concentrated in the North – The Galilee, The Golan and the Beit She'an Valley. The remaining Jews of Eretz-Israel resided in the Jordan Valley and to the east – as well as Judea, but these areas also had a large majority of gentiles of all kinds. The Samaritans lived primarily in Samaria, where they constituted a decisive majority.

The Romans, in a symbolic act that has great importance in our times, changed the name of the country from Judea to **Palestina**, after the Philistines. The name was chosen by the Romans despite the Philistines being a tiny minority of the population of Eretz-Israel – only a bit more than one percent even after the Jewish population was largely depleted.

The Romans embarked on this step in order to detach the linkage between Eretz-Israel and the People of Israel. The Emperor was very angry at the rebellious Jews and couldn't fathom how deeply he had offended them and why they had risen up against him. Moreover, as a military leader, the Jews military achievements in the revolt were an unprecedented blemish to his legacy in the annals of Roman history.

The revolt had not been the first revolt by the Jews against Rome, and had been the second that the Emperor had been forced to put down, and since the Emperor was familiar with the expulsion of the Greeks and the uprooting by the Hasmoneans of the same Hellenism he championed, he decided to bring an end to Jewish insurgency once and for all, by breaking the linkage between the Jews and their land, and leave them 'without a homeland to their name.' In any case, the Jewish community in Eretz-Israel had not only become a minority among the inhabitants of Eretz-Israel; its position in the Jewish world had been broken and pushed into periphery status from the demographical point of view by the hegemony of the large Jewish center in Babylon. The change of name was a *coup de grace* designed to put an end to the tie between the People of Israel and its Land.

The Emperor hoped that once Eretz-Israel lost its Jewish identity and centrality in the lives of the Jews, who in any case by then resided for the most part in the Diaspora, the Jews would assimilate and cease to be a obdurate and divisive element for the Empire.

46

Prior to the Bar Kokhba Revolt, the Small Nations of Eretz-Israel who were idol worshippers became close allies of the Roman regime. They even occupied senior positions in Roman governance of Eretz-Israel.

When they changed the name of Judea to Palestina, the Romans purposely chose the name of the Jews' most tenacious and vexing enemies (until they were finally subjugated by King David): The Philistines. Another reason for the choice – the Philistines' loyalty to the Roman Empire and their high personal qualities which enabled the Philistines, more than members of other Small Nations, to attain senior positions in the governing institutions of the Roman regime. By contrast, the Jews did not succeed at all in fulfilling positions in the Roman 'colonial government.' The status thus achieved by the Philistines and their amiable working relationship with their Roman masters played a decisive role in the decision to rename the country Palestina. The new name gained acceptance in place of Eretz-Israel, and is used in contemporary discourse by no small number of discussants. Despite this, the deep connection between the People of Israel with the Land of Israel remained strong through thick and thin, but the name change resulted in a disconnection of another type – highly damaging to contemporary times: The population that remained in Eretz-Israel began to be called by this designation – Palestinian.

Even before the Bar Kokhba Revolt, the Romans changed the name of Jerusalem to **Aelius Capitolina** ('the new city of Aelius'), and in the wake of the Revolt, Jews were forbidden to reside in Jerusalem. The city was named in honor of the Emperor, whose family name was Aelius. However, due to the holiness of the city to Christianity and Islam, the Roman name was forgotten over generations.

Byzantine Rule

Eretz-Israel's importance rose with adoption of Christianity as the official religion of the Empire – marked by the construction on many Christian holy sites in Eretz-Israel. Monasteries were built throughout the country to serve as centers for dissemination of Christian doctrine. Jerusalem was transformed into a Christian city. In 335 after **Constantine I** embraced Christianity and became Emperor, he built the **Church of the Holy Sepulcher** on the site where Jesus was crucified and buried. For many years the Church served as the most important holy site in the Holy Land for Christians and symbolized the supremacy of monotheistic religions over the city.

During the same century, the Roman Empire split into two political entities – the western Latin-speaking empire whose capital remained Rome, and the eastern Greek-speaking empire whose capital was **Constantinople.**[10] Eretz-Israel, due to its geographic position, fell within what came to be known as the Eastern Roman Empire or **Byzantine** Empire or **Byzantium** (Latinization of the original name of the mythical Greek city Byzantium).

After the collapse of the western empire a short time after the split, the Byzantine Empire was considered the successor of the Roman Empire, although Rome was not part of it. The Empire's military, which prior to the schism was called the Roman Army, continued to bear that name even after the split since those forces quartered in the Eastern Empire did not undergo any significant change following the schism.

The new edicts that the adoption of Christianity by the Empire brought upon the Jews in Eretz-Israel, together with a high head tax, rekindled bitterness. In 351 the Jews of the Galilee, whose center was in Tzipori, rose up in protest against the Romans and

---

[10] Today Istanbul, the largest city in Turkey.

48

Gallus, the Governor of the Syrian Province. The uprising – called the **Tzipori Revolt** or the **Gallus Revolt** – only galvanized a portion of the Jewish population and was easily put down without any major ramification on the fate of the country or its demographics. Throughout Byzantine rule, the People of Israel (Jews and Samaritans) continued to be a target for discrimination and oppression, as part of pressures to accept Christianity. The primary targets of killings were Jewish and Samaritan leaders. Many Jews were unable to withstand such pressures and persecution and, indeed, became Christians. The loyalty of the Small Nations to the Empire led many members of such minority groups to embrace the official state religion – Christianity – as a matter of course. Such a step was also a 'conversion of convenience' that allowed the converts to maintain their senior positions in the Empire's 'colonial machinery' and their superior status among the subjugated populations of Eretz-Israel, superior to that of the Jews and Samaritans.

Alongside such local 'new Christians,' there were foreign Christians who came to settle in the Holy Land out of religious motivations, and personnel in the Roman Army whose soldiers and families had to accept Christianity once it became the established religion of the Empire. Thus Christians became the majority in Eretz-Israel by the close of the 4th Century CE. In contrast with these converts, the majority of Arabs did not want to convert to Christianity and left due to persecution. On the other hand, many Nabataean Arabs agreed to convert to Christianity and remained in Eretz-Israel.

The edicts against the Samaritans, including intense pressures to abandon their religion were worse than the steps taken against the Jews, who enjoyed a certain degree of respect and consideration in the eyes of the Byzantine regime. For instance, in contrast with the Jews, the Samaritans were forbidden to circumcise their sons. Less hostile attitudes towards the Jews were the product of two factors: Jesus 'and the Apostles' Jewish origins, on one hand, and cognizance of Jewish zealotry and willingness to sacrifice demonstrated during the Bar Kokhba Revolt that made Byzantine rulers reluctant to increase their wrath on religious matters, while the Samaritans – who had not participated in the Bar Kokhba Revolt – were viewed as less problematic and a lot less intimidating.

Another factor in the greater level of pressure brought to bear on the Samaritans was the fact that they were far more zealous in the practice of the Religion of Israel than some of the Jews, and didn't surrender to conversion. One reason for this was a practice among the Samaritans that any Samaritan who left the Religion of Israel was no longer considered a Samaritan and would be spurned and repudiated by family and friends.

Among the Jews, attitudes were different: Jews who converted to Christianity continued to be considered part of the People of Israel as long as they continued to live in Eretz-Israel. If there were a small number of Samaritans who succumbed to pressures and converted to Christianity, they did so for appearance sake, and in essence remained crypto-Samaritans.

Those Samaritans and Jews who converted were entitled to positions in the machinery of government. Yet there was one area where Samaritans who remained faithful to their religion received preferential treatment compared to Jews who remained Jews: The Byzantines allowed the Samaritans to join the Roman Army – a mercenary army that was a source of livelihood for its personnel. Not having taken part in the Bar Kokhba Revolt, they were considered a community loyal to the regime. The Samaritans took advantage of this opportunity and consequently the Samaritan community included a large reservoir of able warriors.

The two factors – pressures imposed by the Byzantines on one hand and military expertise on the other – combined to spark a series of Samaritan revolts in the Empire between the years 484 and 572, which peaked in the Great Samaritan Revolt that took place in 529.

50

The Samaritan Revolt was brutally snuffed out by the Byzantines whose numerical superiority was significant. As a result of the war – the casualties and those exiled – the number of Samaritans in the population of Eretz-Israel diminished. One of the byproducts of the subjugation of the Samaritans was the genuine conversion of some of the Samaritans.

Towards the close of the 6th Century the population of Eretz-Israel was similar to that at the end of the Bar Kokhba Revolt. Demographically, the primary changes were the conversion to Christianity of the overwhelming majority of those who had not previously belonged to the Religion of Israel, and the departure of most of the Arabs. The Jewish People (including the Christians among them) numbered in the vicinity of one million souls.

The number of Edomites and Moabites was relatively smaller than in earlier periods as a result of pogroms at the hands of their Arab neighbors. A significant portion left the country. The number of Christians among the Jewish People in Eretz-Israel peaked at 270,000. Among the Samaritans, due to their deep devotion to the Religion of Israel, only a handful – several thousand – converted to Christianity and were no longer considered Samaritans.

Thus, in the 6th Century, most of the inhabitants of Eretz-Israel were Christians. This included a number of groupings beyond the converts among the People of Israel. The primary group was 600,000 members of the Roman-Byzantine Army – a garrison that included the soldiers' families. Another large group was Christian Arabs. Most were Nabataeans who resided east of the Jordan River and in the Negev. The others were nomads who lived in western Eretz-Israel.

The other Christians included members of the Small Nations who for the most part adopted Christianity and consequently enjoyed improved conditions that enhanced natural population growth relative to their numbers during the period of the Bar Kokhba Revolt.

In fact, most population groups enjoyed population growth after the Bar Kokhba Revolt, propelled by economic prosperity and a progressive regime that strived to develop the country. Transformation of Eretz-Israel to an important province in the Empire attracted both attention and investments by the Byzantine leadership. Most of the Arabs, who had preferred to remain pagan, left the country due to persecution by the Christians and only a small minority of those that continued pagan practices remained in the country. In addition, a small number of Canaanites and Philistines remained who continued idol worship, out of sight of officialdom.

On one hand there was a decline in the Samaritan population and thinning out of Arabs after the inauguration of the Byzantine rule. On the other hand stood a high natural population growth and the magnitude of military personnel in the country increased significantly. Thus, the overall population in Eretz-Israel remained relatively static, relative to the pre-Byzantine period.

As a result, the People of Israel again became the largest *ethnic* group in Eretz-Israel – half the overall population. From an ethnic standpoint the three largest groups in Eretz-Israel were the People of Israel (48 percent), various Romans (24 percent) and the Arabs (18 percent). From a *religious* standpoint, Christians (62 percent) were the largest grouping. The ethnic and religious compositions of the overall population during this period appear in Tables 4 and 5 in Appendix 5.

The Wars between the Parthians and the Byzantines

From the close of the 6th Century until 628 CE, Eretz-Israel became a battlefield crossed by armies in a series of wars between the Byzantines and the Parthians (the Sasanian Dynasty then ruled the Parthian Empire, which was also called the **Sasanian** Empire). As the armies passed through Eretz-Israel, local inhabitants were viewed by each side as collaborators with the other.

Each army in turn 'lived off the land,' plundering the local population for food, capital and other supplies necessary to sustain themselves. Each conquest brought new taxes. All these placed a heavy burden on the inhabitants. As a result of this phenomenon, the population of Eretz-Israel during this period was depleted, although there was no specific event or policy decision designed to do so.

In 614 CE, the Parthians conquered Eretz-Israel. Tens of thousands of Jews from the Galilee assisted the Parthians in expelling the Jews' much hated enemy, the Byzantines. The Jewish-Parthian alliance was facilitated by the lobbyism of Babylonian Jewry. Indeed, the Parthians had been easy on the Jews and allowed them to resettle Jerusalem, and even expelled the Christians from the city. In the course of capturing Jerusalem, Parthians had killed thousands of Christian Jerusalemites.

By the year 617 CE, however, Parthian power had waned and the Parthians began to cooperate with the Byzantines leading to a change for the worse in the Parthians' attitude towards the Jews. In 628 CE, the Byzantines succeeded in regaining control of the Holy Land.

During this lengthy period of wars in Eretz-Israel and surrounding territory a significant portion of the inhabitants left. Among them were nearly half the members of the Jewish People. These included the majority of the Christians that belonged to the Jewish People. Over the years, their affinity to their people and their homeland weakened, and most left Eretz-Israel in the face of growing hardships.

The number of Christians among the People of Israel in Eretz-Israel dropped to 27,000 as a result of the massacre and emigration. Among the Edomites and the Moabites, approximately a third left. The other émigrés among the People of Israel included the majority of Samaritans.

Among the Christians, the scope was only slightly lower. Like the Christians among the Jewish People, during this period the majority of Christian Roman civilians and a significant part of the Small Nations (who for the most part were by then Christians) departed. The number of pagans among the Small Nations remaining in Eretz-Israel was reduced to approximately 1,000 souls.

The other Christians who left were for the most part Nabataeans, whose overall numbers in the overall population had become marginal. Among all the Arabs who remained in the country, only a small portion was Christian. Despite this, in order to conquer the country and prevent the Parthians from retaking Eretz-Israel, the scale of Roman Army forces in the Land was increased to an unprecedented 700,000 persons.

The Jews and the Samaritans who were tillers of the soil in the mountain country were the least affected. The reason: Most of the military traffic and the battles took place in the plains and the valleys. In the Arab Conquest that came later, warfare was also confined primarily to these areas, except for the conquest of Jerusalem.

After the expulsion of the Parthians from Eretz-Israel, the Christian-Byzantine regime decided that the conversion of the Jews to Christianity should be brought about in a more amicable fashion, and even had some success in this endeavor. There were attempts to get masses to abandon the Jewish faith, and the number of Christians among the People of Israel almost doubled. The primary logic in the Christian argument was as follows: Your hopes for redemption have failed and there is no logic in your continued devotion to your faith. The Christian conversion phenomenon did not overlook the minority of Arabs who had been pagans previously.

In contrast with the trend to leave the country in wartime, one group was an exception: The Arab Judham tribe, that numbered several thousand souls, immigrated to Eretz-Israel. Almost all settled in Jerusalem in the year 630 CE, and a small minority subsequently settled in Hebron. Members of the tribe were pagans, and constituted the majority of idol worshippers that remained in Eretz-Israel.

The period of wartime that began in the 7th Century was **the third significant depopulation point** in the overall population of Eretz-Israel in the past two thousand years. Due to the actions of the Christian regime, almost no longstanding pagan or Hellenized inhabitants remained in Eretz-Israel, except marginal groupings of Canaanites and Philistines. Within a short period, Byzantine control of Eretz-Israel came to a close with the completion of the Arab Conquest in the year 640 CE.

The Arab Conquest

During the Arab Conquest the number of inhabitants belonging to the People of Israel still residing in Eretz-Israel was nonetheless rather significant. They included 500,000 members of the Jewish People, including some 30,000 Edomites and Moabites. In addition to these, there were some 70,000 Samaritans. Among the Jewish People there were 72,000 members of the Christian faith who were still considered members of the Jewish People. Those members of the Jewish People who remained in Eretz-Israel at the time were for the most part inhabitants of the mountain regions of the country, primarily villagers who were tillers of the soil. The armies passing through Eretz-Israel and the battles they fought between themselves rarely came near their villages (except in the area of Jerusalem, where those members of the Jewish People who were Jews by religion had not resided for quite a time), and thus these inhabitants of the mountain regions continued to live their lives largely unaffected by the clash of civilizations in their backyard.

These mountain people constituted the hardcore 570,000 members of the People of Israel, who for the most part clung to Eretz-Israel throughout the next 800 years. Throughout most of this period, this nucleus increased in size through natural population growth. But as the situation deteriorated and the plight of the country grew, their numbers gradually declined by the beginning of the 15th Century to their original scope. Only in the worst years of the 15th Century was there a significant drop in the overall population of Eretz-Israel, including members of the People of Israel.

Most of the inhabitants of Eretz-Israel at the time of the Arab Conquest in the 7th Century were Christians. The largest Christian group was the Roman garrison and their families who remained despite the Arab Conquest! At the time, they constituted the largest population grouping, but their importance and scale declined over time. They will be labeled henceforth **The Roman Army** or **Descendants of the Roman Army**.

The other Christians were primarily more than 100,000 Arabs and twice as many members of the Small Nations. The Judham were forced by the Arab occupiers to convert to Islam immediately following the Arab Conquest. In addition, Arab soldiers were garrisoned in Eretz-Israel to protect the regime.

The conquest of Eretz-Israel by the Arabs did not entail significant losses among the People of Israel. The Jews and the Samaritans hated the Byzantines and did not take part in the defense of the Empire against the invading Arabs. Nor did the Roman Army suffer great losses, and there were no serious inroads in their numbers since the majority surrendered at Caesarea.

The ethnic and religious compositions of the population of Eretz-Israel and their numbers at the time of the Arab Conquest are detailed in Tables 6 and 7 in Appendix 5. The decline in the overall population of Eretz-Israel and the proportion belonging to the People of Israel since the beginning of the Great Revolt are presented in Graph 1:

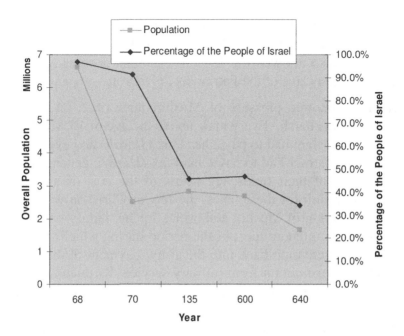

Graph 1: Changes in Population Size and the Proportion of People of Israel between the Years 68 – 640 A.D.

Arab-Muslim Rule

Arab-Muslim rule in its various forms used economic (discriminative policies), physical (pogroms) and psychological (threats) pressures to Islamize the local population. This took place despite hopes that the Jews had nurtured that the end of Byzantine rule would bring relief, not more oppressive decrees. These expectations were based on the **Caliph Omar I (a-Khittab)** who had called upon the Jews to return to Eretz-Israel declaring that their exile had come to an end.

Towards the close of the 7th Century the Arabs allowed the Jews to return and settle in Jerusalem. The first to do so were Jews from Tiberias who built the Jewish quarter south of the Temple Mount.

57

They were allowed to settle at this site after promising to take upon themselves to care for the cleanliness of the sites holy to Islam. The Arabs also allowed the Jews to establish a synagogue at the entrance to the Cave of the Patriarchs in Hebron.

Yet, the economic pressure of Muslim authorities on Jews and Christians was harsh. Every male above the age of 15 who had not submitted to Islam had to pay a head tax (*Jizyah*) and every Jewish or Christian farmer had to pay a land tax (*Haraj*), generally a fifth of the yield of their fields, regardless of the cost of agricultural imputs. In return for these taxes, the Jew or Christian was entitled to the protection of Muslim authorities for his family's safety and his assets. Throughout most of the period during which subjects of the Empire were mobilized into the army, payment of the head tax provided an exemption from military service. Parthians who were members of the Zoroastrian faith received similar treatment. Those who converted to Islam were exempt from the tax. While the fate of pagans is almost irrelevant to the situation in Eretz-Israel, the Arabs for the most part dealt severely with such idol worshippers, who were made to accept Islam through measures to be detailed.

Beyond the head tax and land tax, Muslims received preferential treatment in the payment of other taxes. In addition Muslims enjoyed certain privileges reserved for Muslims only, such as licenses to provide the regime with goods and services. In addition to such regular ongoing discrimination, there were periodic physical attacks on Jews, Samaritans and Christians, and specials edicts issued from time-to-time – particularly during the reign of the second dynasty – **The Abassid Caliphate**.

At the outset, the attitude of the Arabs towards the Samaritans in Eretz-Israel who followed all the commandments in the Five Books of Moses was akin to their attitude towards Jews and Christians. All were considered People of the Book, *Ahal l-*

58

Kitab.[11] Like the others, the Samaritans were discriminated against economically and required to pay head and land taxes in exchange for the protection of the Arabs.

Today, in order to win the hearts of the faithful, Islamic education hides from Muslims the coercive acts and discrimination Islam imposed in its past. The educators are cognizant of criticism of Islam on this issue, and they teach the faithful that those who claim that Islam was forced on those who joined the faith are in error. They rest their case on the Koran saying (Sura 2:256) "There is no compulsion in religion."

Unfortunately, a number of Muslim leaders during the Arab Conquest did not uphold the Koran as written, and many more Muslim leaders have failed to uphold its spirit – submission meaning accepting Islam as an act of free will. Unfortunately intolerance is not a thing of the past: In contrast with enlightened Islam, dark forces within Islam continue to this day in their call for Jihad against those whom they perceive as heretics, along the lines of the same violations of the Koran committed in the past. The mechanisms behind mass conversion following the Arab Conquest and how it worked need to be elucidated.

The objective of the Arabs was to bring Islam to conquered, subjugated peoples, particularly the pagans among them. Often they could achieve this while fulfilling the spirit of the Koran fully: The Arabs succeeded in convincing many pagans to accept Islam since in many cases idol worship was anchored more in folklore than religious belief. Few remained entrenched in their ways. Encouragement, side-by-side with the material advantages that being a Muslim carried – exemption from taxes and later participation in further conquest and the booty this brought, and even empowerment through access to positions in government – led many to 'join the winning side.'

---

[11] Literally, 'sons of the family of the Book.'

Nevertheless, in many instances, the burning desire to convince subjugated peoples to accept Islam encountered two phenomena that undermined Arab proselytizing efforts – refusals that forced the Muslim to be more sophisticated in order to realize their mission without breaking with the Koran, as written:

The primary stumbling block to accepting Islam stemmed from the success of local leaders in convincing their communities to remain faithful to idol worshiping. Here no one was accused of refusing to accept Islam, because the Koran forbade this, but the leaders themselves were accused of interfering with the spread of Islam, which the Koran did not forbid. The leaders were given the choice of accepting Islam immediately and calling on their people to follow suit …or to be put to death. Those who broke down and converted to Islam led to the conversion of their entire communities. The execution of those who refused, conducted in a brutal and public manner, removed any barriers to the conversion of the entire community, who needed no additional 'elucidation' of what was in store for them should they continue to refuse to accept Islam willingly.

The secondary phenomenon that impeded the spread of Islam was apathy toward Islam, its commandments and benefits – without being devoted to any particular pagan beliefs or practices or faith in a leader. In such cases, the first method served as inspiration for another tactic of 'convincing' pagans to convert: A local leader was forced to convert to Islam and expected to then willingly 'assist' in disseminating its doctrine – amplified, if necessary, by threats that failure in this mission could lead to trumped up accusations of interfering in the dissemination of Islam whose punishment was well known… There was no need to carry out any executions. One could always choose another dignitary to take on the task, if the first leader's missionary work failed to produce results.

As the Muslims conquered more and more territory in the name of Islam their 'reputation' for cruelty when faced by refusals to

60

accept their religion spread – snuffing out almost all resistance and making it unnecessary to apply these tactics at all. In many places there was no talk of coercion and few cases of coercion in practice, and if there were, they were not documented, thus preserving the good name of the Muslim and the purity of their religion in the eyes of many subjugated peoples.

The Arabs were successful using the first tactic in most quarters, but from the outset failed in their efforts to convert the Jews of the Arabian Peninsula, whose devotion to their faith remained strong despite their suffering and attempts to intimidate them into submission on pain of torture and death. The Jews' tenacity led Islam to see Jews as a special case, to endow Judaism with special status as a monotheistic faith and to focus their duties as Muslims on spreading belief in One God. Similar status was then given to Christianity, and a number of other faiths.

Another consideration that strengthened this attitude towards Jews, Christians and others as 'exceptions' was the rulers' desire to continue to receive lucrative taxes from non-Muslims in various areas. This source of revenue was important in the period following completion of the Arab Conquest as the Arabs consolidated their hold. (Initially, taking of war booty that accompanied the Conquest filled the coffers of the rulers.) Since those who converted to Islam were generally exempt from most if not all the taxes, taxes could be exacted only from non-Muslim parties, a ransom forfeited on an ongoing basis for refusing to accept Islam. Such an arrangement allowed the rulers to get rich while giving those who did convert preferential treatment, without undermining the spread of the belief in One God.

This trend reached its height in the 7th Century when four different Caliphs from the Omayyad Dynasty sent rabbis from Babylon to newly-conquered areas of North Africa (Tunis, today) in order to convert prosperous Phoenicians to Judaism rather than Islam, thus enjoying the best of both worlds: converting non-believers to monotheism without losing their most lucrative tax base. They

61

preferred Judaism over Christianity, since Christianity by its sheer size and power challenged Islam's hegemony, and the Muslims had no interest in adding to the ranks of the faithful of a rival faith.

Those who were most effected by Muslim religious coercion in Eretz-Israel during this period were the Arabs in particular. Members of the Judham Tribe who resided in Jerusalem immediately converted to Islam in the wake of the Arab Conquest. Yet there were only a handful of Canaanites and Philistines who were idol worshippers, and they did not attract the attention of the authorities, being scattered throughout the coastal plain.

The **Omayyad Dynasty** had a positive attitude towards Eretz-Israel and its inhabitants and was characterized by its building enterprises. At the beginning, the Omayyads built the mosques on the Temple Mount: The Dome of the Rock (Mosque of Omar) in 691, constructed by the Caliph **Abd al-Malik**, and the El-Aqsa Mosque, built in 710 by the Caliph **Al-Walid**. The two mosques were constructed on the ruins of the temple to Jupiter built by Hadrian, after the Omayyads raised the level of the foundation and the surrounding supportive walls.

In 715, the Caliph **Sulayman** built the city of **Ramle**. The city became the southern capitol of Eretz-Israel, a government center and a place of residence of the Caliph himself. Prior to that, nearby **Lod** (Lydda) was the capital of the south. The founding of Ramle was, however, the exception that proves the rule: Other than Ramle, during its entire reign up until the 19th Century, Muslim rulers did not build any other new settlements in Eretz-Israel.

Arab Settlement in Conquered Lands

In contrast to the Arab Conquest's pattern in other lands, in Eretz-Israel Arab settlers were not brought in. The primary objective of Arab settlers was first and foremost to ensure loyalty to Islam and the belief in One God of longstanding inhabitants who had been idol worshippers before accepting Islam under duress. Since the

62

majority of the inhabitants of Eretz-Israel were Christians, Jews or Samaritans, there was no need to keep a watchful eye regarding their devotion to One God.

To this day, dissemination of Islam is the most important objective of the Arabs – even more than dissemination of Arabism. Success in the spread of Islam is considered an Arab achievement. The individual's collective identity (and which group the individual belongs to vis-à-vis other groups) has long been the primary point of reference and self-ascription for Arabs, and this overriding 'collective self' within the individual operates as a driving force even today. First and foremost, one belongs to the **Islamic Nation**. Only after that comes membership in the Arab Nation, and farther down the scale belonging to this or that national polity. Beyond the uppermost importance Arabs ascribe to the dissemination of Islam, it was clear to them at the offset, because of their relatively small numbers, that disseminating Arabism as part of the dissemination of Islam would impede the spread of Islam.

Another objective of Arab settlement beyond the Arabian Peninsula was the desire to ensure the continuity of Arab rule, to ensure that loyalty of subjects to Islam would continue. To do so, Arab settlers intermarried with local populations in order to erase over the generations any distinctive local nationhood and to transform the inhabitants into loyal subjects of the Arab-Muslim regime.

Because Eretz-Israel is geographically closer to the crucible of Arab culture in the Arabian Peninsula, and its territory is small, the continuity of Arab control did not appear problematic, as other countries' control did. Its importance resided in its geopolitical position as a narrow, fertile, strategic land bridge between the desert and the sea that afforded passage between Arabia and the vast territories to the north and the west conquered by the Arabs, and Eretz-Israel's essentialness for territorial continuity of their holdings.

Because the number of Arabs who were available to settle elsewhere was limited, Arab leaders preferred to focus their settlement endeavors in areas where idol worship was rampant prior to the Arab Conquest. Many Arab settlers arrived in Eretz-Israel, but this was done in passage to other lands, on the way to Syria, Lebanon and North Africa.

Muslim Extremism during the Reign of the Abbasid Dynasty

In 750 CE the ruling dynasty of the Muslim world changed hands when the Caliphate that had been headed by the Omayyad Dynasty and whose center was in Damascus was followed by the Caliphs of Beit Abbas whose center was in Baghdad.

The Abbasids exerted far more pressure than their Omayyad predecessors to bring the Jews and the Samaritans to convert to Islam. The regime intensified destruction of synagogues throughout the country in order to persecute and suppress the Jews. Already in the course of the 7th Century, and even more so during the 8th, Muslims destroyed countless synagogues. As if oppression by the authorities was not enough, the Jews found themselves in the clutches of another calamity when a major earthquake in the year 748 destroyed 30 synagogues in Tiberias.

Despite all the special edicts, the discrimination, persecution and destruction, the scope of conversion to Islam was small. By the end of the 8th Century only 6 percent of the Jews and 4 percent of the Christians had embraced Islam. The rate of conversion rose significantly under the Abbasids, compared to the moderate Omayyads under whom only a few thousand Christians and Jews converted to Islam – less than 1 percent.

Towards the end of the 8th Century and during the 9th and 10th Centuries the pressure of the regime on the Jews in Eretz-Israel abated. This period was ushered in by the rule of the enlightened

Caliph **Harun al-Rashid**[12] who invited tillers of the soil among the People of Israel to return to Eretz-Israel. This followed the exodus of a portion of the Jewish peasant class to neighboring countries following the weakening of established government in Eretz-Israel that left inhabitants at the mercy of bandits and nomads.

Almokdasi, a 10th Century Muslim geographer from Jerusalem, stated in his writings that in Jerusalem at the time there were almost no Muslims: **"The mosques are empty and the Muslim holy books are not taught. Most of the population of Jerusalem are Jews and Christians who feel like the lords [of the land] and behave with insolence."**[13]

In contrast with the moderate stance the Abbasids adopted in the period of relaxed relations with the Jews, their attitude towards the Samaritans was more aggressive. At the beginning, mainly due to the relatively small number of Jews and Christians, they did not attract the attention of the Abbasid regime, but after Abbasid authorities gave up forcing the Jews and the Christians to accept Islam, they focused their energies on the Samaritans.

Since the Samaritan religion was considered inferior to Judaism in the eyes of the Muslims, the Abbasids viewed the Samaritans 'easy marks' for a more forceful approach to conversion. They decided that the Samaritans did not enjoy the status of *Ahal l-Ketab*, and greater pressures could legitimately be applied to make them change their faith.

Already at the outset of the 9th Century, after the death of Harun al-Rashid, the Abbasids began a concentrated persecution campaign against the Samaritans. As a result of the pressure, a tenth of the

---

[12] The first in the Dynasty, that ruled between 809-786 CE.
[13] See Source 10. This was the degree of importance that Arabs and Muslims assigned to Jerusalem throughout most of the period that the city was under their control. This attitude was the opposite of the importance that Muslims assigned once Jerusalem was no longer in their hands.

Samaritans converted to Islam. This transpired only after several thousand of the Samaritan community were exiled from Eretz-Israel. Since the Samaritan community in Nablus was well organized, it stood firm against Islamic pressures. The Samaritan villagers, however, were the target of most of the pressure, and it was from there that the Muslims chose the exiles and 'won' most of their new converts.

Another wave of persecutions by the Abbasid regime against the Samaritans took place in the years 905-935. This oppression led some two thousand Samaritans to convert to Islam. This time the pressure was directed towards the city of Nablus and its 'stubborn' and recalcitrant population. Even after the Abbasids murdered thousands of Samaritans, their coercive tactics only yielded skimpy results in terms of new converts.

The Abbasid Caliphate gradually degenerated and disintegrated. Control in practice of what remained of its territories passed into the hands of other parties. In the course of this decline, the Abbasid Caliphs continued to formally hold the reins of government, but in terms of real power, this degraded into little more than a symbolic role. The period between 868 and 1517 was rife with chaotic changes in governance in the Middle East, turnovers that were also registered in Eretz-Israel.

From the year 878, Eretz-Israel changed hands repeatedly, subject first to the control the central Abbasid government, then the rule of Turkish emirs whose seat of government was in Egypt. Compared to the Abbasid regime, the emirs were enlightened rulers who invested in the development of the territories they controlled. The development of Eretz-Israel reached a peak in the expansion of the Akko (Acre) port and fortification of the city initiated by the governor of Jerusalem.

In the year 961-962 Jerusalemites, most of them Jews and a minority Arabs, rebuilt the walls of the city. In the year 963 works continued and focused on fortification of the Temple Mount – the site of two of Islam's important holy shrines. The supporting understructure of the Temple Mount was built by Herod. This was then elevated by Hadrian who added to its height, including the only remaining section of the western wall of the Temple Mount. Since the Temple Mount itself was occupied for the most part by the mosques, without the Muslims intending to do so, in the course of time this small section – the Western Wall – became the holiest spot in Judaism.

The Key-Period – The Fatimid Regime and the al-Hakem Edict

In the year 969, the Muslim regime again changed hands in Eretz-Israel. The new rulers were the **Fatimid Caliphs**. These heads of the **Fatimide** tribe – a branch of the Ismailian sect of the Shi'ite faction of Islam – established itself as a ruling dynasty in northeastern Algeria in 909 and reigned parallel to the Abbasids, who continued to control the lion's share of Islamic territory. At the outset, the Fatimid Dynasty was a principality under the Abbasids, but further on the principality declared its independence as an autonomous caliphate.

In the course of a territorial campaign, members of the tribe – who were named after **Fatma**, the daughter of Mohammed and the wife of **Ali** (the father of Shi'a) – succeeded in taking control of Eretz-Israel and southern Syria. The Fatimids, aided by a Berber Army (North African natives), conquered Egypt in 969. The Fatimid Caliph **al-Muezz Badeen Illah** transferred the seat of the Caliphate to Cairo, built the **al-Azhar** Mosque on the site, transforming Cairo from a village to a center of the Muslim world.

The majority of Fatimid Caliphs focused on constructive works in a milieu of religious tolerance and economic development. But at the outset of the 11th Century, the Fatimid reign took a very extremist turn. The height of Islamist decrees came in the year 1012. The Caliph at the time was **Abu Ali al-Mansûr**, but he was

67

better known as **Al-Hakim bi-Amr Illah** (**'Reigning by Allah's Word'**). Foreigners shortened his name which varied from Hakem to Hakam, Hakim, al-Hakem and al-Hakim (henceforth, in short – **al-Hakem**).

Al-Hakem – who held the exalted status of being the grandchild of al-Muezz badeen Illah – was crowned Caliph at the age of 11! He ruled between the years 996-1021, but due to his tender age, in practice it was the child-Caliph's ministers (*wazirs*) who wielded the actual power behind the thrown for some time. They gave the young Caliph power to influence religious matters only, and they appointed him as Imam.

When the Caliph was 24 years old (1009), the extremists among his ministers gained the upper hand. They led to a series of decrees against Christians and Jews. In 1012 the pressure on non-Muslims in Eretz-Israel reached unprecedented heights: **In the name of al-Hakem, non-Muslims in Eretz-Israel were ordered either to convert to Islam or leave the country!** That is, every non-Muslim in the country faced the choice: **'Leave the faith or leave the country.'**

The al-Hakem Edict became a decisive turning point in the demography of Eretz-Israel. In contrast with the small number who converted to Islam prior to the decree, <u>those among the People of Israel who accepted the Islamic faith rose as a result of the al-Hakem Edict to 90 percent!</u> The number who continued to abide by the Religion of Israel became a tiny minority of the People of Israel in Eretz-Israel. **Among the Christians**, the results were even more far-reaching. <u>A huge majority of Christians</u> who had clung to their homeland until then through countless trials and tribulations, <u>left Eretz-Israel</u>.

Those Christians who left in the wake of the al-Hakem Edict included the majority of the Descendants of the Roman Army, almost all the Christian Arabs and all the members of the Small Nations who had become Christians during the Byzantine period. The tiny minority of Canaanites and Philistines who still held on to the pagan ways of their ancestors, also for the most part left Eretz-Israel, and only a few hundred remained, hardly enough to attract the attentions of the authorities.

The inhabitants who remained in Eretz-Israel underwent a complex transformation. In contrast with the exodus of the Christians, that for the most part took place within a narrow time span, the Islamization of those who remained took place gradually, both in scope and degree of strict observance of the commandments of Islam that authorities exacted from New Muslims. **The percentage of the overall population that was not Muslim originally but chose to remain in Eretz-Israel and convert to Islam peaked at 90 percent.**

In 1044, the Edict was revoked. Approximately a fourth of the New Muslims returned to their original faiths as soon as they were permitted to do so. In light of the complexity of the data for so many population groups over such a short period, only the demographic profile that emerged after the Edict was revoked is presented here.

After the large exodus as a result of the Edict, among the Christians who were not members of the People of Israel, 180,000 remained. Among them, by the end of the process, 170,000 had converted to Islam, most of them Descendants of the Roman Army. Only some 10,000 Christians who were not members of the People of Israel remained in Eretz-Israel. They were Christian Arabs. **The Arabs who had been the largest ethnic group in Eretz-Israel after the Bar Kokhba Revolt, gradually became a marginal minority group.**

The al-Hakem Edict created serious and complex changes for the People of Israel. The varied sub-groupings that comprised the People of Israel in terms of religious affiliation and (i.e., ethnic groups and individuals each practicing multiple religions) became so jumbled that realities on the ground went beyond what could be imagined in one's wildest dreams. The following survey seeks to present the sub-groupings fully in an orderly fashion to enable readers to fathom the full ramifications of the Edict.

To gain the full picture of the changes among Christians in Eretz-Israel, the situation among Christian members of the People of Israel will be dealt with first. The majority (they encompassed 72,000 prior to the Edict) distanced themselves one way or another from Christianity and only a tenth of the original 72,000 remained faithfully devoted to Christianity – that is, openly and solely Christian.

Another group of Christians among the People of Israel openly embraced two faiths. They publicly followed the practices of both Islam and Christianity. This was an acceptable option since the Edict required inhabitants to accept Islam, but did not require that they abandon other religious practices. Yet, due to the difficulties in practice of maintaining two religions simultaneously, only a very small minority chose this 'dual path.'

Another group of Christians – Christians who in the past belonged to the People of Israel and had interlaced Christian and Jewish practices – followed the Edict by integrating the practices of all three religions. These were the **Alawi**, the smallest sub-grouping among the Christians who were part of the People of Israel. A larger group of Christians who belonged to the People of Israel became crypto-Christians – Muslims outwardly, while continuing to follow Christian practices clandestinely in their homes.

For the majority of the remaining Christians among the People of Israel who had outwardly submitted to Islam, their original religious ties and faith weakened over time, and they became distanced from their Christian roots. Outwardly they behaved like Muslims but in their homes they either maintained some Christian practices, or became entirely secular.

For over 400 years following the Muslim Conquest, members of the Jewish People in Eretz-Israel increased their numbers through natural population growth (including the Christians among them). By the end of the 11th Century they numbered 600,000. More than half of the non-Christians (54 percent) continued to follow the Jewish religion publicly, even after passage of the al-Hakem Edict, including 17 percent who openly practised two religions – Jewish and Islam. The rest of the Jewish People (46 percent) were Muslims outwardly and crypto-Jews – continuing to follow the Jewish commandments clandestinely.

Among the Jews, a minority of the Moabites and Edomites continued to practise Judaism exclusively. Most of the members of this group publicly became dual religionists – both Jews and Muslims at the same time. The outcome was that **unlike all the other groupings within the People of Israel, among the Edomites and the Moabites adherence to the Jewish religion remained** complete even outwardly, even if their majority took upon themselves Muslim practices. **In this manner, the Edomites and Moabites continued their traditions going back to the days of the Great Revolt, of supreme devotion to their Judaism, devotion that excelled that of the rest of the People of Israel.**

Despite the deaths and expulsions the Abbasids inflicted on the Samaritans, natural population growth enabled them to maintain a stable population from the year 640 up to the advent of the 11th Century, but the al-Hakem Edict led most of them to convert to Islam, joining the small minority of their brethren who had done so while continuing to secretly practise the Religion of Israel.

In general, during the period that the edict was in effect, it was fulfilled on a large scale. A large number of non-Muslims left the country (47 percent) and the overwhelming majority of those who stayed in Eretz-Israel (90 percent) became Muslims at the beginning. These New Muslims constituted 48 percent of those who were non-Muslims originally. Only about 5 percent of the non-Muslim inhabitants succeeded somehow in avoiding the edict's sweeping directives.

After the edict was rescinded, many (27 percent) inhabitants who had originally been Jews and had accepted Islam under duress, returned to practise Judaism openly. Thus, 'at the end of the day' the number who publicly left Judaism dropped to 46 percent while the number of openly practicing Muslims among those who had originally been Jews by religion totaled 63 percent.[14] The rescinding of the edict was not significant for the majority of those who had already embraced Islam. They were primarily the poorest populations who for 32 years had gotten used to living free of the heavy taxes imposed on non-Muslims, and were in no hurry to give up the exemption which had improved their standard of living.

Even following the rescinding of the Edict, the Muslim regime continued to heavily discriminate against non-Muslims. This led to a large percentage of the population which had up until then avoided accepting Islam to finally outwardly accept Islam. It should be kept in mind that for most of those who became Muslims over this long period, they accepted Islam for appearance sake only. As for the People of Israel, those who remained in Eretz-Israel were primarily tillers of the soil in the mountain regions. This was the primary path chosen in order not to be forced to leave the country and not entirely to leave their faith. Thus there was no massive 'transfer' as far as the People of Israel was concerned, although the threat of expulsion served as an overshadowing threat that led to mass adoption of Islam for appearance sake, a phenomenon that spread over time.

The expulsion Edict was the fourth **significant depopulation point** in the number of inhabitants in Eretz-Israel since the Great Revolt. But unlike all the previous waves that depleted the population, this one did not affect the People of Israel, who for the first time in the period under study significantly increased their

---

[14] 46 percent, together with 17 percent of the original Jews who openly practiced both religions – Judaism and Islam.

portion in the overall demographic profile of Eretz-Israel due to the departure ('transfer') of the Christians.

1012 - The El Khaken Edict		
Ethnic Group	No. of Inhabitants	Percentage of Population
Jews	570,000	62%
Samaritans	70,000	8%
Edomites & Moabites	30,000	3%
Total People of Israel	670,000	73%
Roman Army	170,000	18%
Arab Citizens	16,000	2%
Arab Army	68,000	7%
Total	**924,000**	**100%**

Table 8: The Population after the Departure Due to the al-Hakem Edict.

Without the Muslim rulers intending to do so and without the authorities directing events in this direction, what transpired in Eretz-Israel was that **the People of Israel again became the clear majority in Eretz-Israel**, although the majority of the People of Israel had become Muslim 'on the surface.' **Seventy-three percent of the inhabitants** (including the Arab Army) who remained were sons of the People of Israel, in all its shapes and forms. The second largest grouping, far behind the People of Israel, was the Descendants of the Roman Army (18 percent). The remainder was primarily Arabs (9 percent, including the Arab Army).

For the population breakdown after the expulsion, see Table 8 above. For details on religious affiliation after the Edict was revoked, see Table 9 in Appendix 5. (Readers should take note that in Graph 2 that follows and in subsequent graphs, the darker line presents the percentage of the People of Israel within the overall population of Eretz-Israel according to the percentage scale to the right of the graph. The lighter line presents population growth, according to the numerical scale in millions of inhabitants, to the left of the graph.)

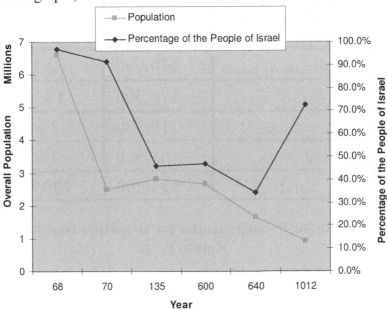

Graph 2: Continued Depopulation and Changing the Trend in the Share of the People of Israel.

Inter-denominational Developments in the 11th Century

Due to Christian and Muslim beliefs that the Day of Judgment would come in the 11th Century, this period was rife with religious commotion and violence. Christians believed that the year 1000 –

74

a millennium after the birth of Jesus, would usher in the Second Coming (Armageddon and the End of Days) while the Muslims held to Mohammed's prophecy that a Day of Judgment would come no later than the year 1100.

When nothing happened in the year 1000, the Muslims jeered the Christians and argued that the absence of a Second Coming in the year 1000 proved that Islam was the true faith. The Muslims told the Jews, who had experienced hundreds of years since the destruction of the Second Temple and the Arab Conquest – without the appearance of the Messiah – that their lack of Redemption was a sign of the truth of Islam. This was the prevailing milieu and mindset at the time the al-Hakem Edict and other steps were taken by al-Hakem.

The zealous extremism of the Caliph al-Hakem first appeared in the year 1009. Fueled by expectations that the Day of Judgment was at hand and growing belief among Muslims that there was no longer any room for Christianity or Judaism, al-Hakem's ministers urged the young Caliph to view himself as the redeemer of humankind. They used the atmosphere of religious fervor to torch the Church of the Holy Sepulcher in Jerusalem, in the name of the Caliph.

Setting fire to the holiest site for Christians was part of a wider attack on churches and synagogues throughout Eretz-Israel. The deeds of the Fatimids against the Jews of Egypt were far worse. Following a host of degradations that targeted Jews, in 1012 Muslims razed the Jewish Quarter of Cairo and annihilated its inhabitants.

The religious zealotry of Muslims towards Christians can be understood against the backdrop of religious tensions at the time between the two largest world religions, as described above. The rise in persecution of Jews had another source:

At the same time there was tension between Shi'ite - Ismailian Fatimids, and Sunni Abbasids. The Shi'ites had always contended

75

that they represent true Islam and challenge Sunni Islam's legitimacy. The Fatimids claimed to be the descendants of the Prophet Mohammed and therefore named themselves after Mohammed's only daughter – Fatma. The Abbasids responded by undermining the Fatimids' legitimacy by claiming they were of Jewish origins. In the year 1011 the Abbasids escalated the rivalry and the schism within Islam by formalizing this accusation of the Fatimids' origins in the **Baghdad Proclamation**.

In fact, both sides were correct. It was a well known fact among Muslims that the grandfather of the founder of the Fatimid Caliphate (Ubayd Allah bin al-Hassin al-Mahdi) was a Jew who was adopted in childhood by a childless Fatimid family. What they didn't know was that Ali, Fatima's husband and the son-in-law of the Prophet Mohammed, was a Jew who had converted to Islam! (Ali was among the first persons to become a Muslim).

The Fatimids – in a 'holier than the Pope' counter-response – felt they had to demonstrate their loyalty to Islam and distance themselves from the Jews by persecuting the Jews – maltreatment that reached its height in 1012.

The ethnic linkage to Judaism of the founders of Islam does not end with Ali. Ali was a second cousin of the Prophet Mohammed while Mohammed's paternal grandfather and Ali's maternal grandfather were brothers. Both brothers, Ali's two grandfathers, were Jews. In other words, a quarter of the founding prophet of Islam's bloodline was Jewish. Ali's two grandfathers-siblings and he himself converted to Islam, although Ali's parents did not become Muslims. Thus, it isn't surprising that in the formative years of Islam, when Islam was still close to Judaism, rumors spread among the Jews of Eretz-Israel that a Jewish prophet had arisen in Arabia.

The Caliph al-Hakem himself did not support the actions taken in his name. As he matured, al-Hakem sought to wrestle control from his all-powerful ministers to end their repressive policies. In 1017,

76

he declared freedom of religion throughout the Caliphate. But his ministers took steps to torpedo the proclamation in practice. Frustrated that his entire world was being limited to religious matters, al-Hakem naively tried to get his ministers to obey him by declaring himself a divine ruler, appointed by Allah. Ultimately in 1021, al-Hakem gave up efforts to control his ministers and decided to abdicate his office. He went out to the desert to meditate. A delegation that went out to search for him only found his belongings, and his clothes – arranged in a fashion that left the impression that his body had vaporized.

The destruction of the holiest church in Eretz-Israel parallel to the Edict designed to forcibly convert or expel non-Muslims targeted Christians in particular. The Edict almost depopulated the Holy Land of Christians entirely – and fanned hatred of Muslims among Christians throughout Europe – feelings that further along led to the Crusades, a unique phenomenon in history.

The same Fatimid Caliph who rescinded the al-Hakem Edict, rebuilt the Church of the Holy Sepulcher in 1046 in an attempt to contain Christian animosity towards Muslims. But the **Seljuq Turks**, who were Muslims, and who succeeded the Abbasids in control of the Abbasid Caliphate, rekindled religious rivalry.

The Seljuqs conquered Eretz-Israel in the year 1075, and added it to the Abbasid Caliphate. They were not cognizant of the heightened sensitivity of events in the Holy Land for Christians, and fueled further Christian hostility by forbidding Christian pilgrims from visiting Jerusalem, including the Church of the Holy Sepulcher.

Prevention of Christians from conducting pilgrimages was viewed as a very serious matter, particularly when it came on the heels of weakened governance in Eretz-Israel that preceded the Seljuq's conquest, and the negative impact of the chaos on Christian pilgrims. The most serious incident took place in 1065, when bandit gangs attacked a large contingent of Christian pilgrims from

Germany. Only 2,000 among the 7,000 pilgrims survived and returned to Germany.

Calls among Christian leaders in Europe to save the Holy Places that began soon after the measures taken by the Caliph al-Hakem, gathered strength, reaching a peak in the closing days of the century. In 1095, **Pope Urban II** called upon Christians to launch a Crusade to protect the Holy Places. This, the First Crusade, set out shortly afterward, culminating in 1099 with the conquest of Jerusalem by the Crusaders. Mohammed's prophecy of a Day of Reckoning came true, but in a totally different form from Muslim expectations.

The Musta'arbim

Members of the People of Israel who had converted to Islam under the Muslim regime were called *Musta'arbim*. They were the Islamic (in Eretz-Israel and in Babylon) equivalent to the Spanish and Portuguese Marranos during the Inquisition: 'Islamic crypto-Jews.' The *Musta'arbim* passed on their original identity from generation to generation, and most continued to secretly practise Jewish customs. Their name is derived from *"mustar ke-Arvi"* ('concealed as an Arab') in Hebrew and the Arabic term *musta'areb* in Arabic: connoting 'one who became Arabized.'

Initially, the *Musta'arbim* were Muslims outwardly, only for appearance sake. But over the generations economic hardships and new forms of persecution led to a waning of the tie to the Religion of Israel and the use of Hebrew and Aramaic of their forefathers. Linkage of *Musta'arbim* with Jews in the Diaspora – a tie that even when they were full Jews had been exceedingly weak due to the low educational level and limited business acumen of the local Jewish community in Eretz-Israel – dissipated entirely. On one hand, maintaining a tie with brethren in the Diaspora was liable to expose the *Musta'arbim's* latent Jewish identity to a hostile regime and endanger their lives. On the other hand, there was a definitive economic advantage to continuing to act as Muslims. Moreover,

78

the Jews of the Diaspora were not keen to maintain a relationship with distant brethren who had left the fold and openly espoused Muslim practices or the rituals of any other faith, whom many Diaspora Jews considered apostates.

In Eretz-Israel, the name *Musta'arbim* was also applied to Christians forced to become Muslims, in contrast with other places where 'crypto terminology' applied to Jews only. This was the case not only for Christians among the People of Israel in Eretz-Israel, but also the Christian Descendants of the Roman Army.

Slowly, over hundreds of years of conquest, and a host of ongoing and intensified pressures of which the al-Hakem 'transfer' Edict was the apex but not the end, the overwhelming majority of the population, lacking leadership and subject to unending suffering, submitted and became *Musta'arbim*. That included a large majority of those who had remained Jewish or Samaritan up until the Arab Conquest – such as was the case among most of the villagers, and also most of the Jews and Samaritans that had become Christian willingly or had been forced to convert to Christianity earlier.

The Islamization process did not pass over the minority of Descendants of the Roman Army. Following the conversions of 1012 when most of the Descendants of the Roman Army left Eretz-Israel, those among the remaining Christians who refused to become Muslim gradually declined in numbers up until the Crusaders' takeover of the Holy Land. Their numbers dwindled due to epidemics that took their toll on the population and others who opted to emigrate in the face of continuing persecution by Muslim authorities that made life unbearable in general, and raised serious questions about the sustainability over time of secretly observing Christian practices.

Among those of the Christian faith among the People of Israel who remained devoted to their beliefs, no substantive change took place in the period following the al-Hakem Edict period. Of those who openly practised two religious faiths simultaneously – Christianity and Islam – the majority joined the Alawi, and the others became Christian *Musta'arbim*. The *Musta'arbim* among the Christian members of the People of Israel slowly became distanced from Christianity and most became Muslims outwardly and secular in their homes.

The Alawi

One of the groups in Eretz-Israel that suffered at the hands of the Muslims, were members of the Alawi sect. (Their descendants today hold key positions in the Syrian and Moroccan regimes.) The number of Alawi at the dawn of Islam numbered some 10,000 souls who originally were Christians belonging to the People of Israel. Their origins were in a small grouping of messianic Jews whose roots go back to the year 23 CE. They organized themselves in Judea, and a small minority resided in the Galilee. Their numbers in the Jewish community in Judea in the aftermath of the Bar Kokhba Revolt dwindled, and the group's center shifted to the Galilee.

Members of the group continued to practise certain Jewish commandments despite adopting some of the customs of Christianity. Under the influence of Islam and Muslim hegemony, against the backdrop of the Alawi's inclusive-pluralistic approach to religious belief, they incorporated some of the commandments of Islam as well.

The Muslim regime in Eretz-Israel put great pressure on the Alawi due to their non-Muslim facets and beliefs. The fact that the Alawi only adopted a part of Islamic practices bothered the regime which feared they would undermine the faith of other newly-converted inhabitants. That is, in addition to their Islamic-ness, the Alawi were also Jews and Christians. Muslim hatred of the Alawi was, therefore, far greater than their intolerance towards Jews and the Christians. This was not only due to the above, but also because they carried the impediments of both the Jews and the Christians.

80

As a result of pressures, most of the Alawi left Eretz-Israel in the 8th Century. They migrated to the Christian Byzantine Empire, to areas that today are part of Turkey. A tiny minority remained in Eretz-Israel as part of the People of Israel.

After three hundred years, the Alawi who had migrated to Byzantium were forced to uproot from their place of exile due to the antipathy that Christians had developed towards Muslims, sparked by the actions of the Caliph al-Hakem towards Christians in Eretz-Israel. They were forced to leave. Due to their small numbers, there was no logic to staying in such a hostile environment and in the course of the third decade of the 11th Century, the Alawi moved to Morocco in order to distance themselves as much as possible from the focus of the clash between Christians and Muslim.

In the period following al-Hakem, most of the Christians among the People of Israel, who during the reign of al-Hakem had outwardly become Christians and Muslims, joined the Alawi sect. As a result of this move, prior to the Crusader's Conquest the size of the Alawi community in Eretz Israel grew back to its original size at the dawn of Islam (some 10,000 strong).

The Period of Unrest

During the period between the abolition of the al-Hakem Edict in 1044 and the Crusaders' Conquest in 1099 the process set in motion by the al-Hakem Edict continued. This was a period of considerable ferment among those inhabitants who at the beginning, as a result of the Edict, outwardly abandoned their original faith, and then after its abolishment returned openly to Judaism.

Many communities in Eretz-Israel were divided between those who openly re-embraced their original faith and the *Musta'arbim*. Even families were split asunder. Under the harsh economic conditions prevailing in Eretz-Israel, those who remained loyal to their original religion 'through hell and high water' were keenly aware of how harsh their lot had been for defiantly maintaining their religious beliefs openly, compared to the relatively easy lives their brethren the *Musta'arbim* enjoyed – both those who opted to remain *Musta'arbim* in order to continue enjoying the economic advantages of Muslims and those brethren who so easily 'slipped back into openly professing their Jewish faith' after the Edict was rescinded. The *Musta'arbim* did not seem to have paid any price for their 'accommodation.' Exemption from taxes was a significant boon, and at times was accompanied by other perks such as the ability to sell their agricultural products to the authorities, or gain employment in the government machinery.

In retrospect, the 'accommodation tactic' of the *Musta'arbim*, which those who defiantly adhered to the Religion of Israel viewed at first as the worst of all evils, was subsequently viewed in a more positive light – as perhaps a shrewd survival tactic, particularly among the younger generation whose determination to 'cleave to their religious beliefs at all costs' was undermined by the fact that the *Musta'arbim* had not left the fold and seemed to enjoy a win-win solution – economic gains without losing their roots. There seemed to be no logic in open and rigid resistance.

The younger generation in families who had remained openly loyal to their Jewishness and were proud of it, baited their peers whose families were *Musta'arbim* for their lack of loyalty. The baiting, however, worked as a boomerang.

When *Musta'arbim* youth asked their elders to explain their lack of loyalty, their parents cited economic factors and argued that maintenance of Jewish customs in the home was sufficient, charging that their more rigid brethren were stupid and their children were unfortunate victims of unnecessary zealotry. The sons of the *Musta'arbim*, lacking a decisive reply to their tormentors, chose to bait their tormentors in return, jeering at their peers' poverty and parents' stupidity. The offspring of the 'loyal Jews' responded in kind, but the negative message that the price

82

they had paid for their loyalty may have been unnecessary – remained, draining any sense of pride in such 'heroic acts of resistance.' When these youth ultimately established their own families and faced the realities of making a livelihood, growing economic hardships led many to join the ranks of their *Musta'arbim* neighbors.

Likewise, the resoluteness of those who openly practised two religions was also eroded. It was not easy to fulfill the commandments of two religions such as Judaism and Islam, both putting great demands on the lives and the time of their adherents. The younger generations looked with envy at their peers – neighbors and relatives from *Musta'arbim* families who had a much easier time of it, relatively speaking, in terms of religious observance.

This internal ferment and erosion, parallel to persecution by Muslim authorities and discrimination against non-Muslims, soon had an impact. From the year 1044 up to the conquest of the Holy Land by the Crusades in 1099, the large number who continued to espouse their Jewish faith in public succumbed to pressures and became *Musta'arbim* themselves, including those who up until then had exercised both Jewish and Islamic practices in public.

In the year 1044, some 300,000 out of 670,000 members of the People of Israel of all persuasions, most of them members of the Jewish People, continued to openly espouse the Religion of Israel. Ninety-five thousand of them embraced Islam parallel to this. On the other hand, in 1099, out of 680,000 members of the People of Israel (an increase due to natural population growth and the influx of Yemenite Jews) only 110,000 remained outwardly faithful to the Religion of Israel. Only 30,000 among them continued to embrace both Judaism and Islam at the same time. Tables 10 and 11 in Appendix 5 present the ethnic and religious composition in the year 1099.

The upshot of relentless pressures and persecution to abandon their faith led 80 percent of the members of the People of Israel to become *Musta'arbim* by the close of the 11th Century. Together with those who accepted Islam parallel to their original religious faith, a full 86 percent had become outwardly Muslims. This magnitude of acceptance of Islam was close to the numbers who had converted to Islam *prior* to the repeal of the al-Hakem Edict – that is, the impact of the lifting of the Edict was transitory, at best.

At this time, a different kind of *Musta'arbi* identity emerged among the population of Eretz-Israel that quickly became the largest grouping in the demographic composition of the country. The majority of *Musta'arbim* belonged to the Jewish People, and therefore the *Musta'arbim* considered themselves first and foremost Jews. The Samaritans who had become *Musta'arbim* lost their Otherness as Samaritans and the only identity that remained was *Musta'arbi*. The Samaritans' common fate with Jewish brethren who had become *Musta'arbim* diluted and dissipated the differences between Jewish *Musta'arbim* and *Musta'arbim* who originally had been Samaritans in comparison with the differences that for generations had set Jews and Samaritans apart.

To the same extent, the common denominator of Christian *Musta'arbim* among the Jewish People with *Musta'arbim* who had previously been Jews who openly embraced their faith grew, as well. Even a portion of the *Musta'arbim* who were descendants of the Roman Army developed a closer affinity over the years with the other *Musta'arbim* in the country.

In essence, identification with one another among *Musta'arbim* of different origins forged a strong *Musta'arbi* identity. The shared experience of oppression and mutual need to hide their beliefs from the authorities while outwardly pretending to be practicing Islam overrode the differences.

Over time, the *Musta'arbi* public nurtured a sense of oneness that transformed into a kinship with all the trapping of a community, a

84

Musta'arbi people. Most of the members of the *Musta'arbi* public – the majority of the population for a lengthy period – preserved over time cognizance of their Jewish-Israelite identity. Even today, many of the descendants of this public are aware of their origins.

The Period of Conquests of Eretz-Israel and of the Crusades

Beginning in the second half of the 11th Century, Eretz-Israel witnessed a series of conquests, but only some left any significant mark. Therefore, only the main ones will be discussed. Even in earlier periods, Eretz-Israel underwent a substantial number of conquests and invasions beyond what has been presented in this work. The high incidence of such events stem not only from Eretz-Israel's stature as a Holy Land to so many religions, but also its geopolitical position as a crossroads between Europe and Asia, and even more so a strategic land bridge between Europe, Asia and Africa.

The Crusades, which began in 1096, played an important role in the complex series of conquests Eretz-Israel endured. The height of the First Crusade was the conquest of Jerusalem and liberation of the Church of the Holy Sepulcher in the year 1099. The name of the church – whose destruction together with the barring of Christian pilgrims and banishment of Christian inhabitants from the Holy Land kindled the Crusades – was added to the name of **Godfrey of Bouillon**, the commander of the Crusader forces that conquered Jerusalem. Bouillon, who was subsequently crowned the first Crusader monarch of Jerusalem, was also titled "Defender of the Holy Sepulcher."

The Crusaders who conquered Jerusalem slaughtered about two thousand Jewish Jerusalemites who had remained devoted to their faith through thick and thin, and had fought shoulder-to-shoulder with the *Musta'arbi* and the Muslim defenders of the city. The prohibition on Jews to reside in Jerusalem imposed by the previous

(Roman-Byzantine) regime, was reinstituted by Crusader rulers. In the course of their conquest of Eretz-Israel, Crusaders massacred some 5,000 members of the Jewish faith (including defenders of Jerusalem.)

A unique and interesting phenomenon took place a short time after the Crusader takeover of Eretz-Israel. Some 7,000 inhabitants who practised both the Muslim and Jewish faith, who after the Christian conquest were able to abandon Islam without fear of reprisal, indeed did so and returned to exclusively espouse Judaism. Some 75,000 Jews at this point espoused solely the Jewish faith. Among the Samaritans, 2,000 returned to the Religion of Israel exclusively. In this case as well, there were Samaritans who had previously publicly espoused two religions.

Jews from Europe immigrated to Eretz-Israel during this period, assisted by the well-developed maritime transportation lines the Crusaders established between Europe and the Holy Land.[15] But most did not remain in the country; those that did were not of any magnitude capable of changing the demographics of Eretz-Israel. In fact, the number of Jews in Eretz-Israel at the close of the Crusader Period dropped significantly.

The lack of a return to Judaism among the *Musta'arbim* – those whose forefathers two or three generations earlier had converted to Islam under duress – was the product of a messianic milieu that seized the country. A messianic cult organized on the Carmel called *"Ca'eloha"* attracted many adherents, both elderly and young, among the *Musta'arbim*. The cult focused on analysis and understanding of past events upon which, it was believed, the future of Eretz-Israel could be decoded. According to the *Ca'eloha* forecast, the Muslims were destined to return and re-conquer the

---

[15] Development of maritime transport was the result of the blockage by the Muslims of the land route by which the Crusades had originally reached the Holy Land, and the fact that the Muslims were inferior to the Christians on the seas.

country. In light of the large following that the *Ca'eloha* cult attracted, the majority of the *Musta'arbim* community chose to remain as they were.

Another factor in the decision to remain *Musta'arbim* was economic: the *Musta'arbim* in Eretz-Israel received assistance from the Arabs in the Arabian Peninsula.[16] The support, which locals labeled **Mazor**, continued even after the end of the Crusader Conquest and even increased as a counterbalance to the fact that Muslims lost the economic edge they had held in imposition of taxes. Unlike those with dual faiths who reverted to fulfilling only Jewish ritual, most of the *Musta'arbim* did not return to Judaism fearing the loss of the *Mazor* that would entail.

In contrast with the negligible return to their roots among Jews and Samaritans, among Descendants of the Roman Army the phenomenon was much more widespread. But one should keep in mind: Unlike the People of Israel, they were returning to the dominant ruling faith in the Holy Land at the time, a move that carried marked advantages.

At the outset of the Crusader Period, some 50,000 Descendants of the Roman Army who had outwardly converted to Islam returned to the Christian fold. The others, out of 130,000 who were *Musta'arbim* prior to the Crusaders' conquest (that is – 80,000) had become truly believing Muslims – primarily under the impact of the *Mazor* and the messianic cult. These 80,000 continued to be called *Musta'arbim* due to their past, although they had ceased to practise Christian rituals within the privacy of their homes. The ethnic and religious composition of Eretz-Israel after the Crusaders Conquest is presented in Tables 12 and 13 in Appendix 5.

Another small grouping that deserves to be mentioned, only because in the 20th Century it underwent tremendous natural

---

[16] Similar to the economic support Saudis provide Hamas in the period of Israeli rule.

population growth, are the Soldiers of the Arab Army from the year 638 (the Arab Conquest); some 300 remained on the Mount of Olives in Jerusalem after the Crusader Conquest. These people will be labeled henceforth – **Descendants of the Arab Army**.

Throughout their rule, the Crusaders persecuted non-Christian inhabitants of Eretz-Israel. The ones who suffered most were *Musta'arbim* among the Descendants of the Roman Army who did not return to Christianity. The Crusaders viewed their behavior as a sign of disloyalty and in response, killed many of them. As a result of this killing, their numbers dropped by the end of the Crusader Period to a mere 23,000. Those of the Jewish faith were also persecuted by the Crusaders and their numbers dropped as a result of killings and flight so that by the end of Crusader rule, only 56,000 Jews who exclusively practised their original Jewish faith remained.

By contrast, those among the *Musta'arbim* of Israel who were not devoted to Islamic faith suffered relatively less, since they had internalized the 'art of outward accommodation' and were used to telling the authorities what they expected to hear. In any case, they were for the most part dwellers in the mountain regions who the Crusaders rarely encountered.

Parallel to the harm inflicted on inhabitants of Eretz-Israel during this period, there was also some settlement. Following the conquest of Jerusalem and the mountain regions of Eretz-Israel from Crusader forces by **Salah a-Din,** the Kurdish military commander brought 3,000 Kurds to Eretz-Israel and settled them for the most part in Jerusalem, and a smaller number in Hebron.

Mameluk Rule – the Breaking Point for Judaism in Eretz-Israel

With the expulsion of the Crusaders from Eretz-Israel by the **Mameluks**, most other Christian inhabitants departed as well. Of the inhabitants who remained in Eretz-Israel, most were Muslims. While a small number were Arabs and other minorities, the majority were Muslims for appearance sake – the *Musta'arbim*.

With the destruction of the Crusaders' Kingdom, almost all of the *Musta'arbim* who were Descendants of the Roman Army that had returned to Christianity after the arrival of the Crusaders, did not want to live under Muslim rule. Their decision to leave Eretz-Israel came after the conquest of Akko – when in the course of taking the city the Mameluks massacred Christians and Jewish defenders of the city. Consequently, Christian Arabs who had remained in Eretz-Israel after the al-Hakem Edict at this point also chose to leave. All of them left the country together with the defeated Crusaders.

Only a small number of the Christian Descendants of the Roman Army chose otherwise: Several thousand Christian Descendants of the Roman Army whose forefathers had converted to Islam and returned to Christianity with the conquest of Eretz-Israel by the Crusaders preferred to stay under Mameluk rule, and again became *Musta'arbim*. In this manner, the number of Descendants of the Roman Army dwindled with the departure of those who clung to their Christian faith. Only 26,000 *Musta'arbim* who were Descendants of the Roman Army remained, and even these, like the Arabs, became a small minority among the inhabitants of Eretz-Israel. The former-Europeans included some 500 Crusaders who converted to Islam and remained in the country. These Crusaders are the source of the smatterings of blond haired and blue-eyed Palestinians one witnesses today. Other Crusaders who remained in Eretz-Israel after the fall of the Crusader rule were some 300 Armenians who remained in Jerusalem and continued to practise their Christian faith openly.

89

The only Christians who remained in the country and within the fold of their original religion were a small minority among the ethnic Jews who continued to remain faithful to Christianity. Due to the hatred the Mameluks harbored towards the Crusaders, their attitudes towards them, including Christian pilgrims, who continued to visit the Holy Land, was even worse than their attitude towards Jews.

Most of the non-Muslims in Eretz-Israel at this point were Jews who remained Jews by faith. The re-conquest of Eretz-Israel and its full subjugation by the Muslims had a depressing chilling effect on those who up to this point had remained Jews by religion. Within a short time of Muslim repossession of control, 10,000 who openly practised Judaism joined their *Musta'arbim* brethren. A similar number of Jews joined those practicing two religions simultaneously – most of them the descendants of those who had held two religious faiths previously, and had left Islam with the Crusader Conquest.

The most prominent phenomenon from a demographic standpoint was that the People of Israel – despite the religious and political changes taking place around them – again constituted an overwhelming majority of the inhabitants of Eretz-Israel – 94 percent. The relative weight of the People of Israel among the overall population in 1291 approached that of before the Great Revolt (96 percent).

Yet, contrary to the hegemony of People of Israel as an *ethnic* group, the number of members of the People of Israel embracing the *Religion* of Israel dropped. The defeat of the Crusaders and the return of Muslim rule to Eretz-Israel broke the spirit of part of the minority who outwardly remained Jews even after the Edict of the Caliph al-Hakem and the period of unrest that followed. The religious composition of the population in 1291 is set forth in Table 14 in Appendix 5, while the ethnic composition follows, in Table 15.

90

1291 – Under Full Mameluk Rule		
Ethnic Group	No. of Inhabitants	Percentage of Population
Jews	674,000	81%
Samaritans	80,000	10%
Edomites & Moabites	30,000	4%
Total People of Israel	784,000	94%
Roman Army	26,000	3%
Arab Civilians	10,000	1%
Kurds	3,000	0%
Crusaders	400	0%
Mameluk Army	12,000	1%
Total	835,400	100%

Table 15: The Ethnic Composition in Eretz-Israel after Completion of the Mameluk Takeover

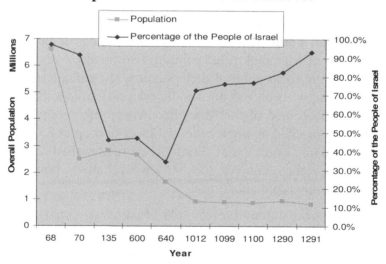

Graph 3: Continuation of the Trend of Increase in the Share of the People of Israel

91

Depopulation of Eretz-Israel towards the Close of the Mameluk Period

Beginning in the year 1453, the overall population of Eretz-Israel rapidly dwindled. In this year, internal divisions began to disrupt Mameluk rule leading to neglect of its holdings and its inhabitants. The situation was further exacerbated by a series of epidemics that began in 1438, two earthquakes and the scourge of locust. A large percentage of the population died of hunger or disease – from among the *Musta'arbim*, those who had fully preserved their Jewish religion, and the rest. A good percentage of the losses were due to a mass exodus to neighboring countries towards the end of this terrible period of man-made catastrophes and mainly natural disasters.

The results of such horrific events were rapid. By the time the country fell into **Ottoman Turk**ish hands in 1517, the civilian population of Eretz-Israel that remained was a mere 150,000 inhabitants.

The end of the Mameluk Period became the **fifth significant depopulation point** in the number of inhabitants in Eretz-Israel. This period of Mameluk rule spanning two hundred years did not have a specific focal point of depopulation. Nevertheless, most of the depopulation occurred during the 64 years following the year 1453. In the course of the Mameluk Period, the depopulation of Eretz-Israel reached an unprecedented level (a drop of 83 percent!) – from 940,000 souls (year 1290 – before the final fall of the Crusaders in the country) to the lowest known point in the country's demographic history.

A small minority among the 150,000 Muslims remaining in Eretz-Israel included 24,000 *Musta'arbim* who were Descendants of the Roman Army. The overwhelming majority of the inhabitants still dwelling in Eretz-Israel were *Musta'arbim* who were Descendants of the People of Israel.

The dramatic drop in population had a number of causes: Negative natural population growth due to the harsh conditions; the death of many from epidemics and primarily from famine as a result of extended and heavy drought; and the fact that a good portion of the breadwinners were 'neutralized' by epidemics. In addition, widespread hunger led many to leave the country and immigrate to surrounding countries – mainly to the Arabian Peninsula.

Among the emigrants, most of the Moabites and Edomites left at the beginning of the 16th Century due to the famine that prevailed in their ancestral homeland east of the Jordan. In the year 1517, only a few thousands remained in Eretz-Israel east of the Jordan. Most went to Persia, but a minority of Edomites and Moabites headed south, to Sudan, to the Arabian Peninsula, including Yemen – and a very small number to Egypt. As will be described towards the conclusion of this chapter, the communities in exile in Persia later lost all ties to their ancient origins and identities. Thus, one can view their offspring only as **Descendants of the Edomites and the Moabites**.

This grouping of Descendants of the Edomites and Moabites later was transformed into a key entity in the history of Eretz-Israel in modern times. As a result, in order to abbreviate their designation in this work, the **Descendants of the Edomites and Moabites have been assigned** the label **Brethren of Israel**.

Due to the tremendous depopulation in Eretz-Israel (and the number of Samaritans in particular), and taking into account the fact that the Samaritans ceased to view Samaritan *Musta'arbim* in their midst as having religiously become 'non-Samaritans,' there is no point in continuing to make a distinction between *Musta'arbim* **who are Descendants of Jews** and *Musta'arbim* **who are Descendants of Samaritans.** Therefore, all will be labeled henceforth – **Descendants of Israel**.

Due to the schism in the fate of the Brethren of Israel and the fate of the Descendants of Israel, the term Descendants of Israel/

Descendants of the People of Israel in the simple sense will not include the Brethren of Israel. When one does merge the two together, a new term becomes necessary: **Descendants of Israel in the Broader Sense**, or **Descendants of the People of Israel in the Broader Sense.**

Tables 16 and 17 in Appendix 5 detail the ethnic and religious components of the population-at-large in the year 1517. In order to distinguish between Jews by faith and *Musta'arbim*, and in order to bring this into line with conventional historical thinking, the ethnic distribution in the tables for this year and henceforth differentiates between Jews by faith (and Samaritans by faith) and Descendants of Israel, although all belong to the same *ethnic* grouping. This is necessary, for after the 16th Century the population tables will not detail the population composition by religion.

The other important point to note about Table 17 is that the smallest drop in the number of inhabitants, relative to the onset of Mameluk rule, was among the Roman Army's *Musta'arbim*. Drought and hunger were the primary stressors in the drop in inhabitants, whether due to death or emigration. All the Descendants of the Roman Army resided in the prosperous lower regions where yields in periods of drought were better than in the mountain regions.

Moreover, in years of intense and unrelenting drought, it was possible to use wells in the lower regions to raise food at a subsidence level. Inhabitants of the mountain country could use only cisterns and some spring water, but these essential water sources were totally depleted or dried up after extended drought.

Ottoman Rule in Eretz-Israel

The Ottoman Empire was friendly to the Jews at the outset. The regime encouraged Jews from Europe to come settle within its territory and assist in its development – particularly from a

94

commercial standpoint. No small number of exiles from Spain (following the expulsion of Jews in 1492) took advantage of the opportunity to settle in Asia Minor (today's Turkey), in Eretz-Israel, in Syria, in Egypt as well as in Greece – which at the time was part of the Ottoman Empire.

This trend that began outside Eretz-Israel in the late 15th Century intensified and expanded from the year 1520 to include Eretz-Israel in response to the ascendancy to power of the sultan **Suleiman the Magnificent**. During this period the Ottoman Empire prospered and exemplified itself as a competent centralized government.

Suleiman's aspirations to provide his subjects with security led, among things, to restoration of the walls of Jerusalem. Sections of the walls had been destroyed by various conquerors since their erection by the Turkish Emir at the outset of the Fatimid regime. In the period of desolation during the 15th Century, the importance of the city declined and its population was greatly diminished. Work on the wall, which remains standing unchanged to this day, was carried out very slowly due to the small number of workmen that could be had in the area. Consequently, the renovation took eight years (1536-1544) to complete.

After the death of Suleiman the Magnificent in 1566, the Turkish Empire declined and the central government weakened. Attitudes towards the Jews gradually worsened when local governors (*pashas*) targeted the Jews far more than the central government did.

After the Ottoman Empire consolidated its hold on Eretz-Israel and restored order and security, the number of inhabitants in the mid-16th Century doubled – reaching 300,000. The end of the prolonged drought and the arrival of more plentiful rainfall was a contributing factor to this trend.

The growth in population was largely the product of the return of *Musta'arbim* from neighboring countries. During this period,

Eretz-Israel was not attractive to non-Jewish immigrants and the religious question was not a prominent issue. Thus, most immigration to Eretz-Israel consisted of longstanding original inhabitants who returned home out of a deep tie to their ancestral homeland, out of their will to reclaim the land they personally owned and because of familial kinships with those who had remained. Immigrants to Eretz-Israel from earlier periods who had left towards the close of the Mameluk Period, along with new immigrants, had little reason to immigrate to Eretz-Israel during this period.

The original inhabitants, *Musta'arbi* tillers of the soil who were Descendants of Israel, had a historical link to Eretz-Israel and abiding loyalty to its soil. Thus, some 120,000 returned to Eretz-Israel at this juncture in time. All told, the number of Descendants of the People of Israel during this period (not counting those who were openly Jewish) reached 220,000.

Those who arrived in the country during this period included a small Bedouin minority whose origins stemmed from *Musta'arbim* who had also returned to their lands of origin, as well as a small number of Mameluk exiles who had fled to Egypt. Parallel to the Judham Tribe, the latter increased the number of Eretz-Israel Arabs by a small degree.

The Turkish regime, in contrast with the Arab and Crusader regimes, did not bring Turks or other settlers to establish themselves and lord over local inhabitants who could have served as a source of revenue from taxes and maintenance of the Turkish Army. The only Turks who came to Eretz-Israel were military personnel, several thousand in number.

In comparison to the trickle of other immigrants who came to the country during this period, the number of Jews who immigrated was not insignificant. The Turkish regime in Eretz-Israel was initially open to Jews and allowed them freedom of religious expression. Such conditions of relative tolerance on the heels of the expulsion of the Jews from Spain led to the influx of some 37,000 Jews to Eretz-Israel.

A good portion of the Spanish exiles that had been forced out of Spain continued to harbor a great love for their original homeland – Eretz-Israel – while they had not yet succeeded in putting down roots in the countries where they had found shelter. They were cognizant that with the end of Arab control over Eretz-Israel, it was now possible to again live as Jews in Eretz-Israel. This, in essence, prompted some to set out for Eretz-Israel.

Among the exiles that arrived in Eretz-Israel was no small number of Jews originally from Morocco. Approximately half of the 3,700 Maghrebians who arrived in Eretz-Israel from North Africa (the Maghreb or 'west' in Arabic) were Jews. The other half was Muslim Arabs. Most of the Maghrebi Arabs and most of the Maghrebi Jews who came to the country did not stay. Ultimately, they left the country.

Another group that did the opposite of the dominant immigration pattern of the period included thousands of *Musta'arbim* from the Galilee who were members of the Alawi sect. In contrast to the immigrants who were returning to Eretz-Israel, the Alawi immigrated to Syria during the corresponding period. While some of the group returned to the Galilee at the end of the 17th Century, the importance of those who remained in Syria is greater than their numerical strength: They constitute today the Alawi minority (under the leadership of the Assad family) that has ruled Syria for some time.

There were only several thousand Christians in Eretz-Israel in the mid-16th Century, all of them Descendants of Israel. Tables 18 and 19 in Appendix 5 detail the ethnic and religious composition of the inhabitants of Eretz-Israel in the mid-16th Century.

The Flourishing of Judaism in Safed

The Jewish community was concentrated at this time in Safed. In addition, there were other places in the Galilee – all told, 13 points of settlement (most of them villages) where Jewish families lived side-by-side with Muslims. The most logical explanation for Jews living alongside Muslims in the same village is that, in fact, members of the Muslim families were offspring of *Musta'arbim* – some of whom had previously converted to Christianity before they became *Musta'arbim.*[17] Later, under pressure from the Turkish regime – pressure similar to those exerted by Arab-Muslim rulers – some of these Jewish families disappeared. It is logical that they chose the path taken by the *Musta'arbim.* The others remained in small numbers in the Galilee and even the mountain country in the vicinity of Hebron until 1936. For example, in 1931 in the Galilean village Peki'in there are accounts of the presence of 52 Jews whose families had remained Jewish since the time of the Second Commonwealth.

Jewish hopes of Redemption ushered in by the end of Arab rule over Eretz-Israel were even stronger than similar expectations at the end of Byzantine rule. The same disenchantment took hold when it again became apparent that Redemption was illusionary. Yet, the period when hopes of Redemption and a Return to Zion were growing was in 'perfect timing' with the Expulsion from Spain, prompting tens of thousands of Jews to go to Eretz-Israel, settling primarily in Safed which then became a center of Jewish mysticism (Kabbalah). Villagers in the Galilee moved to the city to make there living from services to the Jews, who in turn sustained themselves through weaving and contributions from Jewish brethren in the Diaspora.

---

[17] Historically, the dominant pattern of settlement is homogenous villages, while cities and towns may be divided into separate ethnic/religious quarters and neighborhoods.

98

Yet, Safed witnessed very strange demographic shifts in the mid-16th Century that demand elucidation: According to one report, the number of Jews in Safed and the vicinity in the year 1560 was 70,000; according to another – only 12,000. Ironically, the source of both reports was the same individual– the Turkish scholar Chelbi, following two separate visits to Eretz-Israel. According to one report, there were 40,000 Jews in the entire Galilee. In 1568 it was reported that there were 2,000 Jews in Safed, mostly elderly individuals who had come to the Holy Land to die. A short time afterward, it was reported that there were 14,000 Jews.

Even if one assumes that the number 70,000 cited for Safed actually referred to the entire Galilee, the number of Jews in the country with the Turkish Conquest – 5,000, as well as all those who immigrated to Eretz-Israel afterwards – 37,000, add up to 42,000, not 70,000. The discrepancy in the estimates and apparent 'lack of consistency' or 'logic' in the data actually has a reasonable explanation: After each wave of hopes and expectation of Redemption, many *Musta'arbim* identified with expectations of Redemption and 'recalled' their Jewishness; then when Redemption failed to materialize, or due to other troubles, or following the appearance of tax authorities (faced with the marked advantage of being a Muslim), countless Jewish inhabitants again reverted and 'retreated into' their traditional *Musta'arbi* lifestyle.

There is documentation of controversy over issues of Jewish Law (*Halacha*) within the Safed Jewish community during this period – between exiles from Spain who had settled in Eretz-Israel and veteran Jewish inhabitants of Eretz-Israel who are labeled in these documents *Musta'arbim*! That is, some of the *Musta'arbim* – the villagers who came to Safed and whose numbers peaked at an estimated 30,000 – returned openly to practise Judaism.

The large Jewish immigration to Safed that took place at the beginning of the Ottoman Period, in essence, enabled many rural *Musta'arbim* to migrate to the city to make a living from serving the new residents. From this point onward, they ceased to be peasants; consequently, they were exempt from the burden of land taxes placed on non-Muslims, although they had returned openly to Judaism. This (as well as the improved standard of living inherent in the transition from village to city) paved the way for many *Musta'arbim* to return to the Jewish faith of their forefathers.

Newly-arrived Turkish authorities were not yet familiar with the inhabitants of Eretz-Israel, and their attitudes towards the Jews were positive, at first. Thus, an open return to Judaism did not carry any danger that returnees would be viewed as traitors to Islam or would be punished for duplicity.

A Major Change in the Meaning of Musta'arbim

Despite the return to Judaism of a portion of the *Musta'arbim*, they continued to be called *Musta'arbim* since the term had been in practice for hundreds of years. The *Musta'arbim* had never considered themselves non-Jews and therefore did not view this term as something counter to being Jewish. The Jews who came from the Diaspora and encountered those who openly practised Judaism but called themselves *Musta'arbim,* mistakenly assumed that the term referred to Arabic-speaking Jews who had assimilated into Arab culture. The Spanish exiles even coined a Spanish term for the Hebrew *Musta'arbim*: "Mooriskos," after Spanish Jews who had acculturated to Muslim culture during the Moorish Conquest of Spain, without losing their Jewish identity.

The Jews who came from the Diaspora did not know the background of most of the Jews they encountered in Safed whose forefathers had been Muslims outwardly in previous times. The *Musta'arbim* were not exactly proud of their deceptions, nor did they go out of their way to share their family history with 'Jewish brethren from abroad' fearing they would be ostracized. For the same reason, the existence of many tens of thousands of *Musta'arbim* who 'remained in the closet' was concealed – out of fear that this might jeopardize the wellbeing of *Musta'arbim* who had not returned openly to Judaism, should the Turks learn of their 'duplicity' and take offense.

100

The several thousand Jews in Eretz-Israel who had refused to become *Musta'arbim* and whose forefathers had never abandoned their Jewish faith through thick and thin were pleased by the decision of some of their kin to return openly to Judaism, but they hid this from newly-arrived Jewish brethren from abroad, fearing their kin who had recently re-embraced Judaism openly would be ostracized. The number of *Musta'arbim* who became openly Jewish was so great that inhabitants who had always remained Jews by religion became a small minority within the community. **Since the latter spoke Arabic and had assimilated into Arab culture the Jews who came from the Diaspora failed to note the difference between the two groups[18] and considered all the outwardly 'Arabized' veteran population to be** *Musta'arbim*.

Following a change for the worse in governance (the appointment of an oppressive pasha or regional governor in the Turkish province to which Safed belonged), the Jewish center in the city disintegrated. A portion of Safed's Jewish residents, including former *Musta'arbim* who had returned to practise Judaism openly, as well as the Maghrebi Jews, moved to Jerusalem where the local government was less harsh towards the Jews. From this period onward, Jerusalem became a Jewish center in Eretz-Israel, despite the small size of the community at the time.

Following the influx of Safed *Musta'arbim* to Jerusalem – both those who had returned to Judaism after a period in which they hid their faith from the Arabs, and the Arabic-speaking minority who had remained Jews throughout – the term *Musta'arbim* came to signify all Jewish Jerusalemites who had never left Eretz-Israel. Maghrebians and other Jews who came to Jerusalem at a later date erroneously used this designation for such long-time Jewish Jerusalemites and the area in Jerusalem where they resided was dubbed accordingly – the *Musta'arbi* neighborhood.

---

[18] Several thousand continuous adherents to Judaism, in contrast to 30,000 *Musta'arbim* who had only recently returned openly to Judaism.

Likewise, the area where those from North Africa resided was called the **Maghrebian Neighborhood** – until its destruction in the 1990s in the course of new construction. In the course of time, when hopes that Redemption was imminent failed to be fulfilled, the few Maghrebians who remained in other parts of Eretz-Israel were forced under pressure of the authorities and surrounding culture to convert to Islam. The remaining Jews in Safed moved for the most part to neighboring countries, or returned to the Diaspora. The remaining *Musta'arbim*, most of them offspring of Galilee villagers who had moved to Safed, returned to their native villages, disappointed that the promised Redemption had dissipated before their eyes.

Far more serious, the *Musta'arbim*, according to the term's original connotation, were largely broken in spirit by the fact that their messianic expectations had not been fulfilled. While they continued to publicly act like Muslims, their devotion in fulfilling their Jewish *religious* commandments in private faded; with this spiritual collapse, <u>the original connotation of the concept *Musta'arbim* disappeared.</u> **Despite this, the *national* affinity of these Muslim inhabitants of Eretz-Israel to the People of Israel did not disappear, and narratives of their national origins continued to be passed on from father to son.**

The term *Musta'arbim* in its new connotation was no longer limited to Eretz-Israel. The term was used for longstanding local Jews in Egypt and in the **Haleb** (Aleppo) province of Syria to differentiate between themselves and Jews who immigrated to these countries during the Ottoman Period from Europe and the western part of North Africa. These Jews, who lived in Egypt and Syria were, in part, the descendants of *Musta'arbim* who had left Eretz-Israel towards the end of the Mameluk Period and never returned. Some of these *Musta'arbim* returned to practise Judaism openly in the milieu of religious tolerance that typified the beginning of the Ottoman Period, but they continued to designate themselves *Musta'arbim*, since they had never abandoned their

102

Jewishness and did not view their dichotomous 'accommodation' as abandonment of membership in the People of Israel.

Migration to the East

From an overall demographic standpoint, following the disintegration of the Jewish center in Safed and up until the dawn of the 19th Century, the population-at-large in Eretz-Israel remained unchanged. This fact indicates that previous movement into Eretz-Israel was, first and foremost, the return of former inhabitants who had left due to local conditions but an abiding loyalty to their former roots and ancestral land brought them back – as long as this kind of 'reservoir' of potential immigrants existed. While during this period there were small variations in population, such shifts were primarily the result of environmental factors and natural increase, and there was no influx into Eretz-Israel of any magnitude worth mentioning.

One migration that nevertheless took place in Eretz-Israel in the course of the 17th Century was the departure, in a slow trickle, of most of those Brethren of Israel who still remained after most of their kin had left for Persia at the outset of the 16th Century. When they joined their brethren in Persia where the economic situation was better than in Eretz-Israel, the new departees left the areas they had inhabited in the east of Eretz-Israel totally depleted of population. Only in the first half of the 19th Century did this population return to its ancestral lands in Eretz-Israel, as will be detailed further on in this chapter.

In the 18th Century, the Ottoman Empire atrophied to a large extent. The tax burden demanded of the peasant class who tilled the soil was tremendous. The collection machinery was placed in the hands of subcontractors who lent money at usurious interest rates and paid Turkish authorities in advance for what they were committed to collect. Then, the subcontractors demanded larger sums, milking the population for everything they were worth – particularly the peasants – and raking in handsome profits.

103

The calcification of the Ottoman regime was not limited to negative actions by the authorities. There were acts of omission, not just acts of commission: The primary role of the regime, any regime – to provide its subjects with security – was not carried out. Lawlessness spread, with Bedouin[19] pillaging and robbing villagers, although the situation in the cities was better than on the roads or the periphery. If heavy taxing and insecurity were not enough, an extended period of drought followed, making the lives of villagers simply unbearable.

By contrast, not far away, east of the Jordan River the economic situation was much better. Over a lengthy period of time this region was unpopulated after the Brethren of Israel left the country. Opportunities for commerce emerged, and the climate was more amenable than in the west. There was another attraction, as well: Settlement east of the Jordan allowed inhabitants to dodge tax collectors who did not visit this area due to its sparse population. Prosperity from developing commerce enabled more than a tenth of those who moved eastward to live in the cities, which were fortified against Bedouin marauders.

In the course of the 18th Century, due to the factors cited above, most of the inhabitants of western Eretz-Israel abandoned their homes, particularly a large majority of the inhabitants of the mountain country (who were Descendants of Israel) and settled east of the Jordan. Some of them 'inherited' the neglected households and holdings left by the Brethren of Israel. Most viewed the migration eastward as a temporary measure until conditions back home improved. In any case, areas east of the Jordan River were considered part-and-parcel of Eretz-Israel, and for the offspring of the *Musta'arbim*, the move was not viewed by any measure as a betrayal of their own longstanding loyalty to Eretz-Israel and its soil.

---

[19] Bedouin is used in this book as in the Arabic language – for plural.

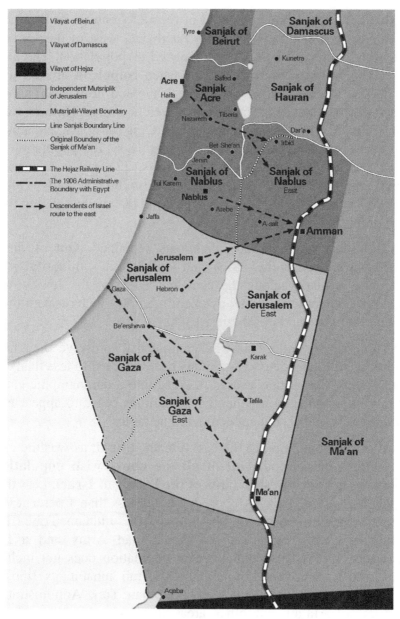

Legend:
- Vilayat of Beirut
- Vilayat of Damascus
- Vilayat of Hejaz
- Independent Mutsriplik of Jerusalem
- Mutsriplik-Vilayat Boundary
- Line Sanjak Boundary Line
- Original Boundary of the Sanjak of Ma'an
- The Hejaz Railway Line
- The 1906 Administrative Boundary with Egypt
- Descendents of Israel route to the east

Tyre ● Sanjak of Beirut

Sanjak of Damascus

● Kunetra

Acre ■
Haifa ●

Safed ●

Sanjak Acre

Nazareth ● Tiberia

Sanjak of Hauran

Dar'a ●

Bet She'an ●

Irbid ●

Jenin ●

Sanjak of Nablus

Sanjak of Nablus East

Tul Karem ●

Nablus ■

● Arebe

● Jaffa

A-salt ●

■ Amman

Jerusalem ■

Sanjak of Jerusalem

● Gaza   Hebron ●

Sanjak of Jerusalem East

Be'ersheva ●

■ Karak

Sanjak of Gaza

Sanjak of Gaza East

Tafila ●

Sanjak of Ma'an

Ma'an ■

Aqaba ●

Map 1: The Sanjaks East of the Jordan after Passage Eastward

Visitors to Eretz-Israel at the end of the 18th Century, whose focus of interest was naturally the Holy Land (i.e., west of the Jordan), found a country almost entirely depleted of population. The most outstanding sign of desolation was when **Napoleon** arrived with his army in Eretz-Israel in 1799: Napoleon found an almost deserted country, and only encountered a small Turkish force garrisoned in a limited number of cities along the coast, and almost no local civilian population. In the year 1800, the population on *both* sides of the Jordan was 8,000 Jews, 22,000 Christians and approximately 250,000 Muslims – a total of 280,000 souls. Out of 270,000 non-Jews by faith, close to 210,000 resided at this time *east* of the Jordan.

To the west, only 70,000 inhabitants remained. Out of these, 55,000 dwelled in the cities and only a tiny minority were villagers, primarily along the coastline. Most of the Jews, some 3,000 in number at the time, dwelled in Safed. In Jerusalem there were 2,000 Jews and in Tiberias, 1,000.

The number of Samaritans who continued to preserve their faith and were still considered Samaritans had dwindled to less than 150 souls. Thus, Samaritans ceased to constitute a demographic entity of any importance; consequently, Samaritans cease to appear as a sub-grouping in subsequent demographic tables.

Most of the population to the east remained rural, as was the case in the previous period. **Out of all the non-Jewish population, 84.5 percent were Descendants of the People of Israel.** Less than 5 percent were nomadic Arab Bedouin and less than 1 percent was veteran Arabs – primarily offspring of the Judham Tribe. The remainder was Descendants of the Roman Army and a few thousand Kurds. This breakdown in population does not include the Turkish Army, and some 50,000 Arab inhabitants (mostly nomadic Bedouin) in the Sanjak (Ottoman Turk Administrative District) of Ma'an and other areas that today are part of the Kingdom of Jordan that did not belong to any Sanjak since they contained no permanent settlements.

106

The inhabitants who migrated across the Jordan gave the villages they established in the east the same names as their native villages to the west. When Turkish census takers came to their villages, they presented themselves as temporary residents in the east, who belong to the western Sanjaks. One of the reasons for this was to prevent a loss of possession of their homes and lands in the west. As a result, however, a process was set in motion of '*de facto* expansion' of the western Sanjaks eastward, nibbling away at the western part of the original Sanjak of Ma'an whose official (*de jure*) border was the Jordan River.

The unofficial borders between the Sanjaks in the east were delineated according to the inhabitants' original ascriptions to Sanjaks in the west. Over time, regional designations in the east were formally 'assigned' to their corresponding western Sanjaks – but official records did not precisely follow the demographic self-ascription of the inhabitants vis-à-vis their origins. Rather, the borderlines were based on natural borders – on the latitudinal watercourses in the east that emptied into the Jordan River. Thus, the official border between the Hauran Sanjak and the Nablus Sanjak was the **Yarmuk watercourse**. The Nablus Sanjak was separated from the Jerusalem one by the **Yabuk watercourse** (Wadi Zarka), and the Jerusalem Sanjak was separated from the Gaza Sanjak by the **Arnon watercourse** (Wadi Mujib).

All elements of the population in the year 1800 in the western Sanjaks and throughout the country are presented in Tables 20 and 21 in Appendix 5.

Beyond the Descendants of the People of Israel in the eastern part of Eretz-Israel, one particular phenomenon complicated matters and left an impact on what later transpired in Eretz-Israel, primarily west of the Jordan: a series of complex internal migrations – from the east to the west, and vice-versa.

This series of moves, together with immigrants who arrived from abroad, both Jews and Arabs, resulted in a mélange of origins and

107

identities that became so intermixed and confused that recognition of historic linkages and kinships became almost impossible. This confusion became the primary factor in the breakdown in kinship and affinity between Descendants of the People of Israel that remained in Eretz-Israel and the Jews who returned to Eretz-Israel.

The Sojourn of the Brethren of Israel in Persia

The confusion had its beginnings at the outset of the 19th Century, with the return of the Brethren of Israel from Persia. **As is the case in Iran today, at this time as well, Muslim Persian rulers were extremists and very aggressive, and played a core role in events.**

In the year 1502, at the time when the Brethren of Israel arrived in Persia, Persia had again become an independent country for the first time since the Arab Conquest. The Shah Ismail I liberated Persia from Ottoman Sunni rule.

The Shah was both the political and religious leader, whose powers were similar to those wielded by Iranian Ayatollahs today. Ismail's followers viewed him as an incarnation of the divine. Ismail I transformed Shi'a into the state religion and established an Islamist Shi'ite state that forced its inhabitants to accept this form of Islam.

The Persian population did not oppose such religious coercion; the Ottoman Turks had previously imposed Sunni Islam on their Persian subjects. Among those Persian Muslims who had not been Shi'ite previously were many descendants of the *Musta'arbim* among the Jews of Babylon, and many 'closet' Druze. They took little interest in the differences between Sunni and Shi'ite doctrine and simply followed whatever form of Islam the authorities dictated, as they had done under the Ottomans.

The situation among non-Muslims was different. Non-Muslim regions were considered by Persian Shi'a to be a "**Defilement of**

Non-Believers." The Jews who still practised their religion openly, like those who continued to follow the indigenous Persian religion – Zoroasterism – and adherents to other religions, became the target of harsh persecution.

The situation worsened in the mid-17th Century, when life in Persia began to resemble life during the Spanish Inquisition. **Ki'tav Anusi** (The Book of the 'Forced Ones' – 'Marranos') describes the harsh edicts of the period directed against Jews. Jews and others who were coerced to change their religious beliefs during this period – similar to the New Christians or *Conversos* in Spain – were dubbed 'New Muslims' (**Jdid al-Islam**) by the Persians.

The Persian Shi'a regime was aggressive towards its neighbors, as well. Persia attacked and conquered territory in every possible direction, subjugation that led to attacks and counter-attacks that at times reached the heart of Persia itself. The primary enemies of Persia were the Ottomans to the west and the Russians to the north. The primary area of dispute was Iraq, eastern Turkey and territories of countries north of Iran, including the Caucasus territory that up until recently belonged to the Soviet Union. The regime aspired to restore Persia's former glory and power during the Persian-Parthian Empire.

On the eastern front as well, things were far from quiet. Towards the end of the rule of the **Safavid** Dynasty of shahs, the Afghans threw off the Persian yoke and even conquered a significant portion of Persia itself. The founder of the next dynasty of Persian shahs, **Nader**, reoccupied Afghanistan and his conquests extended as far as Delhi in India.

In 1795, the **Qajar** Dynasty came to power in Persia. This dynasty was even more extreme than its predecessor in persecuting non-Muslims (the 'Unclean') and annihilated entire communities. Followers of Zoroaster, who during this period were still a significant part of the population in Persia, were harshly treated and were debilitated and worn-down by unrelenting persecution.

They feared the upsurge in the influence of Islam in their country, particularly among members of their community. As a result, followers of Zoroaster rose up and attacked their Muslim neighbors, particularly those who were considered 'foreigners' and lacked protection. In particular they targeted Arabs – who had brought Islam to Persia in the first place. Other Persians had no great love for the Arabs either, for having taken away their independence in the past.

The Brethren of Israel who were considered Muslim-Arabs were one of the groups that suffered greatly from the Persian pogroms. When *Musta'arbim* Brethren of Israel first arrived in Persia at the beginning of the 16th Century, they preferred to continue to be considered Muslims, in order to avoid becoming a target of prosecution by the Muslim majority, and to avoid the economic discrimination that Jews were subjected to, that *Musta'arbim* had dodged even when they were residing in Eretz-Israel.

In terms of national identity, belonging to the Jewish nation would have given away the Jewish faith of the Brethren of Israel, at least in their past, and generated distrust among the authorities. The latter were already skeptical of the devotion to Islam of local Jewish *Musta'arbim*. The Brethren of Israel couldn't even claim to be Persians, because when they arrived they didn't know the Persian language. With no other choice, and given that their native tongue was Arabic, they presented themselves as Arabs.

In the wake of such a lengthy sojourn in foreign surroundings, that over the years became highly hostile, while numerically the Brethren of Israel remained a small minority, towards the end of this period the Brethren of Israel were forced not only to hide their 'Jewishness' but also their 'Arab-Sunni' identity.[20] They had to appear outwardly as locals without a defined religious affiliation. At times, in the company of Muslims, they appeared to be Shi'ite

---

[20] During the Parthian Period the *Musta'arbim* in Eretz-Israel had to appear in public as Shi'ites, and during the Mameluk Period, as Sunnis…

110

Muslims. In the company of members of the Zoroaster faith, they tried to hide any religious affiliation and claimed they were, in fact, forced converts to Islam who, like members of the Zoroaster faith, had been persecuted in the past by the Muslims.

In addition, due to the complexity of their predicament, of their fear from the external extremism, a portion maintained households that were secular, a portion Jewish and a portion Arab-Muslim without differentiating between Shi'a and Sunni doctrine, and the rest instituted a mélange of family rituals influenced by multiple streams of ritual and belief.

The *Musta'arbi* Brethren of Israel were already used to the duality of one set of rules in public, one set of rules in private, each time circumstances in Eretz-Israel had called for this, accommodating their behavior according to who was the hostile party at the time. But the situation in Persia was more complex: They had to play two contradictory games of deception against two different parties who rivaled one another!

In mixed surroundings the *Musta'arbi* Brethren of Israel had to use two conflicting game plans, in tandem. Such a task could be accomplished by artful use of cunning and evasion, but often this was simply an impossible mission. Brethren of Israel caught in this 'double play' suffered the consequences – including families that were murdered for their 'duplicity.'

They were now 'caught in the middle,' forced to hide their 'Arabness' due to the animosity of Persian Muslims who were hostile because of the *Musta'arbi* Brethren of Israel's Otherness as 'Arabs,' parallel to needing to hide both their religion and 'Arabness' from the threatening-and-threatened followers of Zoroaster. Thus, *Musta'arbi* Brethren of Israel in Persia were thrust onto the horns of a true dilemma as to how to define themselves: They began to tell their children in secret about their hidden 'true' Arab identity, out of loyalty to and desire to somehow preserve their 'original' identity.

111

The narratives of hidden Arab-Muslim origins, together with all the explanations about the cunning required to conceal this identity, parallel to the alternate identities in the public domain they had to assume were complex enough. It did not need to be further exacerbated by adding that their Arab-Muslim identity had, in essence, been forced upon their forefathers when they were Jews, and that their Jewish identity had, in fact, been forced upon their people when they were Edomites and Moabites...

In order to preserve their Otherness, and in order to keep inherent contradictions at a manageable level, Brethren of Israel in Persia clung to their Arab-Muslim identity. Over time, all earlier different identities were pushed into the shadows.

The small group of Brethren of Israel who migrated to Persia in the course of the 17th Century and joined their established kin who had arrived earlier, told the veterans about the despair into which their kin still in Eretz-Israel had sunk, how the motivation to continue to live a 'dual existence' and preserve their Jewish identity in secret had waned. Due to a constellation of causes, the tie with early Judaism and its leadership slowly dissipated and ultimately disappeared entirely.

In the end, relentless and increasing persecution against the Brethren of Israel in Persia, together with the complexity, confusion and dangers inherent in living there, along with improvement in the economic and climatic situation east of the Jordan River, brought the Persian chapter of the Brethren of Israel to an end: With the advent of the 19th Century, gradually the Brethren of Israel left Persia and returned, for the most part, to eastern Eretz-Israel.

112

The Return of the Brethren of Israel and Its Ramifications

The generation of Brethren of Israel who returned to eastern Eretz-Israel, remembered the stories told by their fathers that their homeland was Eretz-Israel, but nothing more. After their return they re-embraced their Arab-Sunni customs – fully and publicly. But all traces of their previous history – including having been *Musta'arbim* – was totally lost from collective memory, both due to everything that had ensued up until their return ...and due to subsequent traumatic events that gave birth to new narratives that took the place of the old ones, that will be discussed further on in this book.

The Brethren of Israel were relieved to be liberated of the burden of dualities and subterfuge of their former lives in Persia and whole-heartedly embraced their new identity. Only a minority took pains to fulfill all the commandments of Islam. The majority was not particularly interested in religion. Yet, they fully and faithfully embraced their 'Arabness,' ignorant of the other aspects of their past.

The complexity of life in Persia, juggling so many identities for generations and the attributes necessary for survival in a hostile environment, had a creative side: the Brethren of Israel became the most sophisticated, savvy and experienced sub-grouping among the Palestinians.

During the same period in which the Brethren of Israel returned to their homeland, the Descendants of Israel had already ceased behaving as *Musta'arbim*. All – even the *Musta'arbi* Descendants of the Roman Army – had ceased to be called *Musta'arbim*. Despite this, among the Descendants of Israel – particularly within the close family circle – stories about the Jewish origins of the family were passed on, and a few Jewish customs were preserved. Under such conditions, although the Brethren of Israel viewed the Descendants of Israel as their brothers back in history, there was

113

nothing in the behavior of the Descendants of Israel that could remind the Brethren of Israel of their shared *Musta'arbi* past.

This state of affairs was the product of the fact that once the Descendants of Israel saw that the Brethren of Israel had forgotten their Jewish origins and become devoted Arab-Muslims, the overwhelming majority of the Descendants of Israel were reluctant to tell them about their shared Jewish ancestry. They hid from the Brethren of Israel the Jewish customs they still upheld primarily in the privacy of their homes, so that word would not reach Muslim authorities, knowledge that was liable to be detrimental, at least in terms of discrimination in taxes.

In this manner, the return to the homeland of the Brethren of Israel did *not* become a founding event that could have rekindled cognizance of their *Musta'arbi* past as Jews and their legacy as Edomites and Moabites – a past they did not share with the Descendants of Israel. Moreover, their return to the homeland was a turning point in 'Palestinian consciousness,' and it led the Descendants of Israel among the Palestinians to further conceal and hide their Jewish-*Musta'arbi* past, even more than before.[21]

Out of fear that their children or young people would spill their secret and the family would suffer, a tradition developed among the Descendants of Israel that the source of unusual [Jewish] customs was not explained to the young, who were merely told that these customs their family followed were a time-honored tradition; only when a father was elderly did he transmit the story of the family origins secretly to his grown sons.

Of course there were families where the father died at a relatively early age or died suddenly before he could pass on knowledge of the family's true origin to his sons. Other fathers did not pass on

---

[21] Only at a later stage did some of the Descendants of Israel dare to reveal their secret – confidentially, to some of the Jews returning to Zion.

114

the story, fearing the fate of their own offspring. As generations passed, the number of cases where the Jewish-Israelite origins were lost and forgotten increased. In other cases memories faded naturally and details of the narrative narrowed.

Secrecy was very widespread to start and grew to encompass almost all members of the community since the Brethren of Israel returning from Persia encountered at the beginning many Descendants of Israel east of the Jordan. Later on, as will be discussed further on in this work, they met more Descendants of Israel west of the Jordan.

It seems that from this point to this very day, the Brethren of Israel don't know a thing about their true origins except that they are the offspring of intermarriage with Descendants of Israel. At the same time, among the Descendants of Israel, hardly any of the young people knows anything about their ancient origins, and there are families that have lost this knowledge entirely.

In places where this kind of knowledge is known, transmission from generation to generation is done as discreetly as it was under discriminatory Muslim regimes in the past, all the more so today, under the Islamic terror regime that now controls the Palestinian Authority and lords over Palestinian society. Because of the ignorance of their family origins (along with the weakening of parental authority in any case in modern life) many Palestinian youth – unaware of their own historical bond with the Jews – are vulnerable to the anti-Semitic hate ideology spread by terrorist leadership!

In examining the course of events, one perceives how Persian Shi'ite extremism (although this was not its intention) caused the estrangement between Palestinians and Jews – estrangement that led to the rise of the conflict in the Middle East.

115

The Brethren of Israel returning from Persia, quite naturally migrated to their ancestral lands in the southern quadrant of Eretz-Israel east of the Jordan. Yet, the prosperity that existed in eastern portions of the more westerly Sanjaks encouraged Brethren of Israel to migrate to these areas. The returnees, however, also settled in the southern part of the Sanjak of Ma'an, the ancient homeland of the Edomites.

Friction was high because most of the more choice land in the easterly sections of the westerly Sanjaks was by now occupied by the Descendants of Israel (who had come from the west and migrated eastward due to climatic change and economic advantages). Most of the returnees from Persia were forced to live and eke out a livelihood in the Sanjak of Ma'an, and some were even pushed into the northern sector of the Arabian Peninsula. These areas were relatively inferior in quality to the westerly Sanjaks – both in the fertility of the land and annual rainfall. It was for this reason that the arid Sanjak of Ma'an had been unpopulated even in early times.[22] The population density that developed, particularly in the ancestral lands of the Moabites, led small groups among the last Moabites to leave Persia, to reconsider returning to the homeland; they migrated to Syria, Lebanon and Egypt instead.

All in all, the Brethren of Israel that resided in eastern Eretz-Israel in 1840, after most had returned from Persia, was close to 60,000. The Sanjak of Ma'an was populated by 30,000 Brethren of Israel; another 24,000 managed to squeeze into other sanjaks, and 5,000 established themselves in the Arabian Peninsula. Over a period of years, additional Brethren of Israel returned from Persia, from Yemen and from Sudan – some 20,000 in number. The total population of Brethren of Israel in Eretz-Israel at the close of this 'repatriation process' of the Brethren of Israel reached more than 80,000. The returnees from Sudan included descendants of the Edomites who were now dark skinned and Bedouin.

---

[22] That is, 23,000 inhabitants in 1800.

116

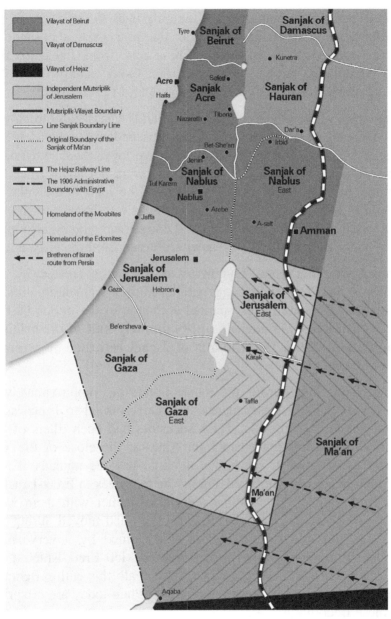

Map 2: The Friction Created between Descendants of Israel in the East and Returning Brethren of Israel.

The Brethren of Israel were not the only ones to settle east of the Jordan River during this period. In the year 1820, thousands of Druze arrived from northwest China and from Lebanon, and moved into the Sanjak of Hauran (i.e., today mainly the Golan Heights, which was not considered then part of Eretz-Israel).

The return of the Brethren of Israel to lands east of the Jordan was not the only event that troubled the Descendants of Israel in the east, at this time. The tax collectors, who prior to this had harassed only inhabitants of western Eretz-Israel, were not about to be left without revenue. They moved eastward in the wake of the villagers who had abandoned their lands in western Eretz-Israel and crossed the Jordan to escape the drought and dodge heavy taxes, also lured by a 'new' source of profits – newly-returned Brethren of Israel.

The above migrations, together with pressures created by the return of the Brethren of Israel parallel to improvement in climatic conditions in Eretz-Israel, sparked a change in the milieu east of the Jordan River. As a result, **approximately half of the original population of the Descendants of Israel returned to western Eretz-Israel.**

Parallel to this, during the same timeframe, approximately a thousand Bedouin Descendants of Israel returned to Eretz-Israel from the Sinai Peninsula. Their ancestors had been tillers of the soil who had left Eretz-Israel for Sinai at the close of the 15th Century, and due to conditions in Sinai became nomads. These Bedouin were not numbered among the returnees to Eretz-Israel at the beginning of the Ottoman Period. Together with them were some 700 Bedouin Brethren of Israel who had moved during the same period into the Sinai Peninsula (joined by a very small number from Egypt), after their forefathers left Eretz-Israel at the beginning of the 16th Century. Almost all the entire Bedouin population of the Negev and the Coastal Plain today are offspring of these Bedouin.

The Inhabitants of Eretz-Israel in 1840

In the year 1840, there were 10,000 inhabitants who were Jews by faith – most in Jerusalem, 25,000 Christians, and 270,000 Muslims (a total of 305,000 (not including the Sanjak of Ma'an). The population growth of 25,000 relative to 1800 was the result of the return of Brethren of Israel from Persia and Sinai. The number of returnees was greater (60,000) but a large number were not counted since the Sanjak of Ma'an was not included.

From the standpoint of the division between east and west, the fact that the Descendants of Israel returned, for the most part, to the west, altered the settlement pattern in Eretz-Israel. A little more than 130,000 of the overall population of Eretz-Israel in 1840 were still residing east of the Jordan River. The rest, 175,000, the majority in the country, including Jews, were already west of the Jordan River.

Out of the population-at-large close to 230,000 were the Descendants of Israel – not including the Brethren of Israel – whose numbers were similar to the number of Descendants of Israel in the mid-16th Century. Returnees to the west from east of the Jordan settled in the mountain country, their ancestral lands. **The Descendants of the People of Israel in western Eretz-Israel, Muslims and Christians alike, constituted some 80 percent of the 165,000 non-Jews by faith in the west.**

The remaining inhabitants of western Eretz-Israel included the Descendants of the Roman Army, Kurds, hundreds of Bedouin who were Brethren of Israel and Arabs who were divided into three groupings – each numbering a few thousand persons: pastoral Bedouin, veteran members of the Judham Tribe and Descendants of the Arab Army, and Others (to be delineated). In addition, there were dozens of Samaritans and dozens of idol worshippers of Canaanite and Philistine extraction and approximately 100 Armenians (e.g., the rest of the Armenians were expelled by the Turks).

119

East of the Jordan, inhabitants who originated in the west (who at this point were scattered among the mountains and valleys) numbered some 100,000 – 95,000 of them Descendants of Israel. The tiny remaining minority of inhabitants of the east included in the population census was made up mostly of Brethren of Israel, and a few pastoral Bedouin Arabs. **The data indicates that in 1840, 73 percent of the population in the east (*not* including the Sanjak of Ma'an) were Descendants of the People of Israel in the Narrow Sense.**

What is significant in the statistics is that in terms of overall population in 1840, there was almost no change since the mid-16th Century and up to the year 1840. The primary changes over this three hundred year period were: the spread of Descendants of Israel to both sides of the Jordan; the return of most of the Brethren of Israel to east of the Jordan after their numbers rose relatively to the period when they left the country; the number of the original Jews by faith was diminishing (even further than their small numbers to begin with), but compared to the year 1800, the number of Jews had risen as a result of the influx of some 2,000 Jewish immigrants to Jerusalem.

Between the years 1831-1936 the first railroad was built in Eretz-Israel.[23] This construction process itself marginally contributed to the size of the population, in addition to the changes described above. Thousands of railroad workers were brought from Egypt by Muhammad Ali. Two thousand five hundred members of the railroad construction gangs, most from Egypt and some from

---

[23] The building of the railroad in Eretz-Israel initiated by Muhammad Ali was envisioned to connect Jaffa and Port Said, to establish strong commercial ties between Eretz-Israel and Egypt; however, Muhammed Ali only completed the section between Jaffa and Gaza. The project came to a halt after the defeat of Muhammad Ali by the Turks and their allies. Later, the Bedouin dismantled the track and sold the raw materials to the Ottomans, and it took some 50 years until the first railroad line was laid – connecting Jaffa and Jerusalem in 1892.

Libya, were originally peasants who remained in Eretz-Israel after work on the railroad was stopped. They established neighborhoods in Jaffa and settled in a number of villages,[24] some of them new villages which they founded. These villages were the first settlements established in Eretz-Israel by a Muslim government since the building of Ramle in the year 715 CE.

The railroad was built because in the year 1831 Muhammad Ali took Eretz-Israel from the Turks. Although the Egyptian regime was considered a successor of the Mameluks, it was more progressive and enlightened than the crumbling Ottoman Turkish Empire. Muhammad Ali's rule in Eretz-Israel rectified longtime discrimination against Jews and Christians. As a result, Christian missionaries began to arrive in Eretz-Israel from Europe.

Muhammad Ali was an Albanian Muslim who was brought by the Turks to Egypt in order to assist them in their war with the French. He brought an end to the original Mameluk Dynasty in Egypt and due to his good ties with the Turkish regime became the Viceroy (*Wali*) of Egypt. Further on, Ali liberated Egypt from Turkish rule and from there went forward to conquer Eretz-Israel, Syria and Lebanon.

Abolition of Muslim superiority and levying of a new head tax on all inhabitants regardless of ethnic origin or faith, and introduction of compulsory labor and compulsory military service generated fierce animosity among Muslims. This led to a *falakh* or "peasant revolt" that failed, primarily due to internal division between various Muslim sub-groupings.

The Egyptian government's primary opponents were rich *effendis* (i.e., the large landowners) who for the first time were required to pay taxes and whose clout had been curtailed by Muhammad Ali's reforms. Later, another uprising took place in Hauran (the Golan

---

[24] This included **Salameh, Sumeil** and **Sheik Munis**, and the villages **Kubeiba, Melabbes, Jaljulia, Kalanswa, Kfar Kasem, Taibe, Ara, Ara'ara, Kfar Kara** and **Um el-Fakhem**.

121

Heights) by Druze (who were considered Muslims) that was far more serious than the peasant revolt, and was barely put down.

In 1840 Turkish rule was resumed in Eretz-Israel. The Turks were assisted in retaking the Holy Land by the western powers who viewed Turkey as a stabilizing element against Russian expansion. With the aid of the British Navy, the western powers pressured Muhammad Ali to give up the territory he had conquered.[25] Despite Muhammad Ali's relinquishment of control of Eretz-Israel, the aura of religious tolerance brought by his regime, together with the growing influence of the European powers that followed, set the stage for the arrival of the first Jewish immigrants to Eretz-Israel – an influx that marked the beginning of the revitalization of the Jewish community in Eretz-Israel.

One of the most interesting events of the period took place in the village of Sakhnin in the Galilee. Following the institution of freedom of worship in Eretz-Israel by Muhammad Ali – the first time there was freedom of faith after 1,500 years of persecution and prohibitions – the Descendants of Israel in Sakhnin raised their heads. In 1837, local residents built a synagogue in their village and returned to practise Judaism. However, after the Turks reintroduced their own repressive regime, Turkish authorities were angered by what appeared to be Muslims abandoning the dominant faith, and in 1867 they destroyed the synagogue.

Another interesting case was the initiative of **Sir Moses Montefiore** (1784-1885) and Muhammad Ali to establish a Jewish state in the territory between Gaza and **Ramallah**. Moses Montefiore tried to obtain British approval for this initiative. Muhammad Ali's support was due to two factors: His anger with

---

[25] The intervention of the western European powers in determining the regime in Eretz-Israel at the time was the first time in modern times that the Europeans assisted shady forces to control the Holy Land. Intervention of this sort had become a tradition 150 years later, when most western Europeans began consistently backing Yasser Arafat's terror regime.

122

the Muslims in Eretz-Israel for their disloyalty, and his aspirations to develop the territory in his control. In the framework of the initiative, wealthy Jews from the Diaspora bought land in Gaza, opened a port and a commercial center. The enterprise died with the re-establishment of Turkish rule.

1840 - The Sanjaks of the West						
Ethnic Group	Inhabitants in the West		Inhabitants in the East		Inhabitatnts in Both Sides	
	Number	Percentage	Number	Percentage	Number	Percentage
Descendants of Israel	131,000	75%	95,000	73%	226,000	74%
Roman Army	21,500	12%	2,500	2%	24,000	8%
Arabs	9,000	5%	9,000	7%	18,000	6%
Jews	10,000	6%			10,000	3%
Kurds	3,000	2%			3,000	1%
Brethren of Israel	700	0%	24,300	19%	25,000	8%
Total	175,200	100%	130,800	100%	306,000	100%

Table 22: The Population in the Western Sanjaks in 1840

The overall number of Descendants of Israel, including all the Brethren of Israel (including the Sanjak of Ma'an and the small minority in the Arabian Peninsula) was close to 290,000 or 75 percent of the non-Jewish population in all of Eretz-Israel (both sides of the Jordan). Table 22 above, details the composition of the population in the Western Sanjaks.

Table 23 in Appendix 5 details the composition of the population in all of Eretz-Israel. The difference between the 1840 data and data from 1800 was primarily the result of the return of the

Brethren of Israel to eastern Eretz-Israel. The data demonstrates that **in the year 1840, 72 percent of the inhabitants of the <u>entire east</u> of the Jordan (including the Ma'am Sanjak) were Descendants of the People of Israel (i.e. including Brethren of Israel, or 44 percent without them.) Eighty percent of the <u>non-Jewish</u> inhabitants <u>west</u> of the Jordan were Descendants of the People of Israel! The percentage of Arabs in western Eretz-Israel was a mere 5 percent of the entire population.**

Chapter Four

Eretz-Israel in Modern Times from a Demographic Perspective

The Druze

According to tradition among the Druze of the Levant (Syria, Lebanon) and of Israel, the Druze are the descendants of the **Midianites** – the people of the prophet-priest **Jethro** (Moses' father-in-law – the father of his wife Tsipporah, and Moses' mentor following his flight from Egypt after killing an Egyptian). Jethro is called by the Druze **Nebi Shoo'aib**. Their ancestral lands were in the desert, adjacent to Egypt. According to Genesis, **Midian** was the son of Abraham, born after the death of his wife Sara, and of the patriarch's new wife **Keturah** (who according to Druze tradition was the daughter of the Druze tribe).

The Greek historian **Herodotus** mentions the Druze in his writings as one of the Arian-Persian tribes, a portion of whom migrated from India-Persia westward, while part remained in Persia. Today, the Druze in Iran number five million souls, and are called *Mu'akhidun*.

The Druze religion is one of the oldest secret religions. According to Druze beliefs, the souls of Druze are reincarnated as other Druze, and are never reincarnated as members of other groups. This kind of 'closed circle' form of incarnation does not extend to other groups according to Druze belief, nor does it exist in any other religious belief system. Druze belief holds that incarnation is, in essence, an 'inherited soul' – that is, the soul of the deceased continues to exist even after it has been incarnated in a newly-born Druze. Up until recently, acceptance of new scholars in the Druze religion was reserved solely for members of the community above the age of 40. During the period of the Muslim Empire, both original Druze and Midianites were forced to convert to Islam.

125

The Midianites behaved outwardly as Muslims, but in their homes – particularly in places where the community's sages congregated – they secretly practised their own religion. The Midianites who resided in Egypt were among the residents of Cairo after it became the capital of the Fatimid Caliphs. In the al-Hakem caliph's intractable pursuit of religious wisdom, al-Hakem encountered in his own capital the secret religion of the Druze. Midianite sages told al-Hakem that he was considered the second incarnation of Ali, the husband of Fatima (the daughter of Mohammed) and the father of Shi'a Islam.

Since al-Hakem had emerged from within the Ismailian sect (which founded the Fatimid Caliphs' dynasty) which was part of the Shi'ite faction of Islam, and since al-Hakem's rivals – the Abbasid Caliphs – claimed that he was not related to Ali, the Druze claim that al-Hakem was related to Ali according to the Druze religion was very appealing. Therefore, in the year 1017 towards the end of his reign, al-Hakem allowed the Midians to practise their religion openly, leading other Muslims to take interest in the Druze religion, and even become Druze.

The Midians who lived in Egypt, who had been forced to become Muslims, were considered as belonging to the dominant religious stream in Egypt – the Ismailian sect. Under such conditions, exposure of their religion and permission to practise it openly left the impression that the Druze in Cairo were an offshoot that had split from the Ismailian sect. Al-Hakem, who had made belonging to the Druze permissible and exposed the existence of this clandestine faith for the first time, was considered the founder of the Druze religion. One of the prominent Midian leaders of the period was named **A-Darazi**. The mistaken impression that this faith had emerged as a separate religion only at this time lead to the Midians also being called 'Druze.'

Al-Hakem's endeavors to spread the Druze religion continued even after his death. In the year 1027, his emissaries arrived in the Galilee, and led some 4,000 residents to join the Druze religion.

126

Most of the new converts were Assyrians, who had previously fled to the Galilee to escape Islamic coercion under the Abbasid Caliphate and then were forced to submit to Islam under the al-Hakem Edict. Approximately a thousand of the converts were Jewish Musta'arabim.

After the rule of al-Hakem, gradually the attitude of the Fatimids towards the Druze religion changed, and in 1043 joining the Druze religion was prohibited. Henceforth, members of the Ismailian sect viewed the Druze faith as heresy. From the year 1073 the Druze were forced to leave Cairo due to persecution by the Ismailians. Neighboring regions in the Levant and Eretz-Israel were under Fatimid rule, then Crusader rule. Islamic streams in other regions were equally hostile: Shi'ite Muslims ostracized the Druze, and the Sunni Muslims considered them to be rival Shi'ites. As a result most Druze fled and found shelter in far-off northwestern China. Other Midians who lived in the Arabian Peninsula, which was also under Fatimid control, moved to settle south of Beirut and near Damascus – areas that at the time were sparsely populated – and for a period, these areas were dominated by the Druze. In the Western Galilee most of Druze converts became *Musta'arabim* and only a small minority remained Druze – in Yirka and the vicinity.

A smaller number of Druze who lived in Lebanon had migrated some 400 years ago to the Carmel, joining the 600 Druze who had remained in the Western Galileee from the 11th Century. In the 19th Century, part of the Druze who had lived in China returned and joined their brethren who had remained in the Levant. First, some reunited with those Druze in the Hauran region, afterward mostly with the Druze community in Eretz-Israel. The returnees brought with them the large colorful Druze head covering that, in fact, is typical of Central Asia; it is still worn by the older generation of Druze to this day. The Druze who remain in China today continue to live a secret existence. They are considered by their brethren in the Levant and in Israel to be a potential reservoir that could demographically strengthen them, while enabling these Chinese 'closet Druze' to finally live openly as Druze.

The Beginning of the Return to Zion in Modern Times

The period of Mohammed Ali's rule and European involvement in Eretz-Israel marked the beginning of resettlement of western Eretz-Israel.

Many Jewish sages believed that the year 1840 – according to the Hebrew calendar *Heh-Taf-Resh* - would mark the **Beginnings of Redemption** (*Atkhalta de-Ge'ula*, in Aramaic). This had led, over the previous century, to the immigration of hundreds of Talmudic scholars and a number of renowned sages to Eretz-Israel. This immigration increased, spurred by the freedom of religion under Mohammed Ali's rule, and some of the Jews that came to Eretz-Israel believed the year 1840 would bring full Redemption itself.

Among devout Christians as well, the importance of Eretz-Israel grew during this period. Both Christian settlers and pilgrims began to go to Eretz-Israel in the belief that a Second Coming was imminent. Among them were missionaries who believed Redemption hinged on the Jews accepting Jesus and converting to Christianity – and who actively engaged in attempts to proselytize the Jews of Eretz-Israel. Further on, groups of foreigners of various and sundry types (half of them Christians) began to arrive in Eretz-Israel, each group numbering a few thousand settlers each.

In addition to the railroad workers that Mohammed Ali settled in western Eretz-Israel, there were also military personnel from Mohammed Ali's army who were left permanently in western Eretz-Israel, forced to remain in Syria and Eretz-Israel after part of Ali's army became detached from Egypt as a result of Mohammed Ali's departure from the Levant and Eretz-Israel under pressure.

128

Already in 1840 the Egyptian soldiers left behind took revenge on the Druze for their revolt against Mohammed Ali. They destroyed the Druze villages on the Carmel. Most of the villagers fled to Syria, but also to the Galilee and Lebanon. Later on, these Egyptian soldiers, joined by additional personnel who had been left in Syria, went to live in proximity to their brethren – the railroad workers. Since the military personnel were not farmers, most lived in the cities – primarily Jaffa. Those who had come from Syria preferred the more northern city of Nazareth.

Termination of Egyptian rule in Eretz-Israel – which appeared to echo events at the time of the first redemption of Israel at the hands of the Egyptians during the Exodus from Egypt – was not the only 'repeat performance' in history that appeared to be at work in preparation for the a third Redemption of the People of Israel. As in the case of the fateful meeting between Moses and Jethro, the first to arrive in Eretz-Israel after the departure of Mohammed Ali were the Druze. Over a decade, between 1840-1850, several thousand Druze repatriated to the Carmel to rebuild and even expand the destroyed villages of their predecessors who had come from Lebanon. The new arrivals were Druze who had come from western China to the Hauran twenty years earlier and had not put down roots there.

Due to this increase, the 1870 census in Eretz-Israel (without the Sanjak of Ma'an) encompassed 350,000 inhabitants. Data summarized by Elon Yarden in his volume, in Hebrew, *Zion shall be Redeemed with Judgement* (*Tzion ba-Mishpat Tipadeh*[26]), shows the distribution between the inhabitants of the mountain regions, Descendants of Israel, and inhabitants of the low lying areas, populated by various gentile nations. Yarden reports that according to censuses taken at the time, 250,000 persons inhabited the mountain regions. In the numeration of the 250,000 dwellers in the mountain country, there were some 15,000 Jewish

---

[26] See source 8.

Jerusalemites who constituted the majority of Jews in Eretz-Israel that year. Thus, according to the data, 235,000 of the dwellers in the mountain country were non-Jews by religion.

It is striking that this calculation of the non-Jewish inhabitants of the mountain regions is almost identical to the number of Descendants of Israel – not counting the Brethren of Israel (230,000) cited for the year 1840 and earlier – in the mid-16th Century. The affinity between the two statistics validates Elon Yarden's argument that, even today, dwellers of the mountain country in western Eretz-Israel are almost all Descendants of Israel.

Before discussing the details of settlement in Eretz-Israel during this period, it is important to make a distinction between internal and external immigrants. **Internal immigrants** are people whose forefathers originate in Eretz-Israel who migrated from place to place within Eretz-Israel – particularly between western Eretz-Israel and eastern Eretz-Israel, or immigrants whose forefathers had gone from Eretz-Israel to neighboring countries (primarily Syria and Lebanon) and ultimately returned to their native soil (sometimes generations later). **External immigrants** are foreigners, including Arabs, whose forefathers did not originate in Eretz-Israel and who came to Eretz-Israel from elsewhere.

Internal Population Exchange

While the increase in the number of non-Muslim setters in Eretz-Israel between various periods was primarily the result of the arrival of Christians and Jews from distant lands, the growth in the number of Muslims was the product of migration of Brethren of Israel from the Sanjak of Ma'an across the Jordan into western Eretz-Israel. This shift began to take place after 1840 – internal migration that would be a decisive event in the fate and the face of Eretz-Israel.

130

The movement westward of the Brethren of Israel from the Sanjak of Ma'an raised the number of Muslims within the territory whose inhabitants were included in the Ottoman's Eretz-Israel census. A small part of the growth in Muslim population during this period was the result of Druze whom the Ottoman's counted as Muslims.

Brethren of Israel moving into western Eretz-Israel was not limited to the Sanjak of Ma'an. Some came from the parts of the western Sanjaks in the east. However, these areas were already considered part of the population of Eretz-Israel, and their migration did not affect the size of the overall population. In addition there were also small groups of Descendants of the Moabites who upon leaving Persia had settled in Egypt, Syria and Lebanon and now moved into western Eretz-Israel. This migration, which was for the most part internal, constituted the primary change in the demography of non-Jews in western Eretz-Israel up until 1914.

Parallel to this, other Brethren of Israel returned after 1840 to areas east of the Jordan, completing the homecoming of this community from Persia to Eretz-Israel. They replaced those inhabitants who had moved from east to west – primarily from the Sanjak of Ma'an which had been far more sparsely populated than any other Sanjak in the east. Brethren of Israel migrated from east to west in response to difficult conditions during this period in the Sanjak of Ma'an – the friction with Descendants of Israel who had settled in the best lands within the eastern Sanjaks. This was the first time in modern times that a 'return to Zion' by any party was disrupted by more veteran residents.

Experience had taught Brethren of Israel to recognize the potential of the western part of Eretz-Israel. This part was considerably empty. The amount of fertile soil was much greater than in east of the Jordan, and generally received far more rainfall – particularly compared to the Sanjak of Ma'an. The arrival of Christians and Jews to the west led Brethren of Israel to believe that their future would be better in western Eretz-Israel than in the country's eastern part. Among the inhabitants of eastern Eretz-Israel who had a similar perspective of the future were the Druze from the Hauran (which is also east of the Jordan – on the Golan Heights), whose migration westward was fueled by similar motivations.

When Brethren of Israel returned from Persia to Eretz-Israel they knew that their ancestral homelands were situated east of the Jordan, but they had lost ties with their past, including their original identity as Edomites and Moabites. They found no difference between themselves and their brothers – the Descendants of Israel. Consequently, all of Eretz-Israel was considered a shared homeland. All parts of Eretz-Israel were viewed as their homeland, and they did not consider their migration to western Eretz-Israel to be a matter of significance beyond the opportunities for improving their living conditions and the desire to avoid conflict with the Descendants of Israel who had already occupied the choicest lands in the east.

The Brethren of Israel who arrived from the east demanded that the Ottoman Turk government give them agricultural land in the relatively empty western portion of Eretz-Israel as compensation for the lands that had originally been theirs in the east. In 1856, the Turkish regime adopted a program of agrarian land reform and allocated land to the new immigrants.

The new settlers, a large proportion of whom hailed from the economically-backward Sanjak of Ma'an, constituted a source of cheap labor and cheap agricultural products – competing with more veteran residents and driving down the standard of living. The changes in the labor market and in the value of agricultural commodities in the west was further exacerbated by diminishing part of the land that was available to the Descendants of Israel, as well as poor climatic conditions[27] and a harsh tax system. These hardships combined to spark additional shifts in population in the opposite direction – this time, from west to east.

---

[27] At the time climatic conditions in the east, except for the Sanjak of Ma'an, were less severe than in the west.

Up until 1914, the Descendants of Israel who had remained in the east were joined by more than a third of their kin that had resided in the mountain regions of western Eretz-Israel, but who again moved eastward. Movement to the center of the eastern portion of Eretz-Israel was easier for the mountain dwellers in the west since they had economically established kin who could absorb them who had lived in the center of the east since the 18th Century. In addition, economic conditions in the east (not counting the Sanjak of Ma'an) were better than those which had developed in the west following the influx of poor Brethern of Israel from the Sanjak of Ma'an.

The harsh climatic conditions, and particularly the lack of rainfall and heavy taxing of agricultural land current in the western part of the country in previous periods – primarily in the 18th and 19th Century – led to the depletion of villages. This was reflected not only in the migration of Descendants of Israel eastward, but also villagers moving closer to urban centers in the western parts of Eretz-Israel where they could compensate for low yields and increasingly smaller (i.e., unsustainable) plots, due to the division of fields among offspring, by offering their labor, services and products to city dwellers in order to pay tax collectors and landowners.

Many villagers who were unable to withstand payment of high taxes were forced to sell their land to tax collectors, although after calculation of their debts, few assets remained – leaving the farmers destitute *and* landless. They faced three options:

1. To migrate eastward where they had more affluent kin – a step that would allow the displaced peasants to recover economically;

2. To move closer to the cities, where there were alternative paths for earning a livelihood, besides agriculture;

3. To become tenant farmers and rent their former lands from tax collectors who had taken ownership of their lands in exchange

for erasing their debts – yet, ironically, the rents they now faced were often greater than the taxes they had been forced to pay as landed peasants.

This state of affairs not only led part of the Descendants of Israel to abandon their villages; it also enriched the tax collectors. While the 1856 land reform lessened the effect of this 'land grab,' this process continued and left its mark on society. In western Eretz-Israel a class of rich *effendis* emerged who slowly gained control of a large portion of the land and most of the country's financial assets.

Most of the non-Jewish immigrants by religion who entered western Eretz-Israel at this time were internal immigrants. They moved closer to areas of Jewish settlement in the coastal plain and the valleys, from various regions both west and east of the Jordan. A large portion of the internal immigrants of the period were peasants (*falakhim*) whose livelihood rested on working their village plots or who settled on the periphery of the cities. The rest were pastoral Bedouin who were also Brethren of Israel.

Waves of immigration continued in both directions. As a result, by 1914 most of the Brethren of Israel who had lived in the more westerly Sanjaks east of the Jordan moved west of the Jordan. Most, together with a considerable percentage of cohabitants of the Sanjak of Ma'an who also joined them, completed their move into western Eretz-Israel before the year 1882. Subsequently, other Brethren of Israel moved westward, boosting the numbers of this group in western Eretz-Israel by 1914 to 79,000.

The situation in western Eretz-Israel at this time from the standpoint of population size, commercial conditions and climatic conditions was inferior to the situation in the center and the northern sectors east of the Jordan. Only the Brethren of Israel in the southern part of eastern Eretz-Israel where climate was bad, or in the central part of eastern Eretz-Israel where they were subject to pressure from the Descendants of Israel moving into the east, were worse off, and preferred to move westward. The situation in the west, on the other hand, led a significant[28] portion of the inhabitants of the Galilee, descendants of inhabitants who originally were *Musta'arbim* who were Christians prior to outwardly accepting Islam, and those who were still Christians (all of them Descendants of Israel), to emigrate to Syria and Lebanon.

Thus, the overall balance in internal migrations almost cancelled out one another: Some 78,000 Brethren of Israel arrived in western Eretz-Israel, and 81,000 Descendants of Israel left. Yet the movements of populations generated a great change in the *composition* of inhabitants who were non-Jewish by faith. Later on, this situation was rectified to a certain extent. But the loss of historic memory among Brethren of Israel as to their Jewish past led to most of the complications regarding the composition of the Palestinian population west of the Jordan. Moreover, as will be discussed further on, this internal change in the composition of the population is the primary reason for continuing conflict in the Middle East.

New Settlers in Eretz-Israel

The internal migrations of Brethren of Israel to western Eretz-Israel, throws into relief the external immigration of tens of thousands of Arabs from the Arabian Peninsula who joined the Descendants of Israel, landing in various parts of eastern Eretz-Israel. Natural population increase among inhabitants of eastern Eretz-Israel, fueled by improvements in the standard of living there, led to an increase in the overall population in the east.

In contrast to events in the east, up until 1914 very few Arabs immigrated into territory west of the Jordan River. Except for the railroad workers, a few thousand other Arabs came – half of them soldiers of Mohammed Ali who had remained in the area. The others were Arab laborers who came to make a livelihood from

---

[28] 28,000.

Jews arriving in the country. All these joined the other Arabic-speaking foreign element: the Druze.

Narratives of the period describe Muslim laborers who came from various lands to settle adjacent to Jewish pioneers and offer the Zionists their labor. Many other narratives describe heroic Jewish settlement in malaria-infested areas, and the difficulties the Jewish pioneers encountered in becoming farmers and working the soil.

But the number of Jews in agricultural settlements of the period was not particularly large. Since most of the Yishuv at the time was concentrated in Jerusalem, the number of Jewish farmers was not significant – nor was the number of foreign immigrants great, even in the relatively sparsely-populated state of the country at the time. A relatively large number of Muslim immigrants indeed arrived, but they were mostly internal immigration from among Descendants of Israel.

Significant Arab immigration to western Eretz-Israel began only later on, after the First World War, when Jews began arriving in larger numbers. The Jews settled in large numbers in new settlements they built and developed, creating employment opportunities on a scale beyond the abilities of the local labor pool to meet. But until 1914, Arab immigration was very limited.

Among the Christians in Eretz-Israel, a large part of the growth in their numbers in the year 1870, compared to 1840, was the result of non-Arab external immigration that settled primarily west of the Jordan. Beginning in the mid-19th Century, some 12,000 foreigners arrived in western Eretz-Israel – European Christians and Muslims. The Christians established churches, monasteries and other religious institutions, pilgrims' hostels, and medical institutions.

The most prominent group among the Europeans was several thousand **Templars**, who built a number of new settlements or separate neighborhoods such as Sarona (which in 1948 became the "Kiriya" complex, where the Tel Aviv branches of Israeli government offices and an extension of adjacent IDF headquarters

136

are situated) and Wilhelma (near Ben-Gurion Airport), and the German Colonies in Haifa. Other members of the Templar Society settled in existing cities and towns such as Bethlehem, Jerusalem (the German Colony), Jaffa and Nazareth. The Templars were devoted Christians who came to the Holy Land propelled by a belief that the Second Coming was approaching.

In addition to the Templars, other Christian Europeans also came from various places, most of them Christian clergy. Other Christian foreigners followed. Their total numbers were in the vicinity of several thousand, all told – and included **Lovers of Eretz-Israel**[29] who came from Europe. This group also included the Armenians who had stayed after the Crusader period. The European Christians' impact on the character of life in Eretz-Israel at the dawn of the modern era went far beyond their numerical strength. East of the Jordan also held an attraction to Christians from Europe, and several thousand Greeks settled there.

Along with the Christians who came from afar, there were also Muslim **Circassians** who arrived from the Caucasus. Thousand of Circassians had joined the Turkish Army during the Turk rule of their country. After the conquest of the Caucasus (northeastern Turkey today) by Russia, the Circassians were persecuted in their homeland by Christian Russian rulers. After their release from military service, a portion of the demobilized soldiers were settled in parts of Eretz-Israel by the regime that allotted them land. The families of the persecuted soldiers who remained in the Caucasus homeland were encouraged by the Turks to join their soldier-kin in Eretz-Israel, and the Caucasus was emptied of inhabitants. Approximately 2,000 were settled east of the Jordan in 1902, and about 1,000 to the west of the Jordan beginning in 1878.

---

[29] Christians and others from distant lands who settled in Eretz-Israel out of religious devotion and love of the Holy Land – due to their devotion to the Bible and the belief that their presence would help bring the Redemption of humankind, a Second Coming that would come out of Zion.

Parallel to the Circassians, during the same period additional former personnel in the Turkish army settled in the western part of Eretz-Israel. This included Bosnians and Turks. The demobilized soldiers built settlements in the Galilee and in the Jordan Valley. Also in the case of the Bosnians, the reason for their settlement far from their homeland was the wars between the Turks and the Russians that contributed to the disintegration of the Turkish Empire and sparked persecution of Muslim Bosnians by their Russian occupiers. The Turks felt responsible for their former Muslim subjects and encouraged them and provided incentives for them to go to areas that were still within the Empire, including Eretz-Israel. In addition, Lovers of Eretz-Israel in Albania and Macedonia also came to Eretz-Israel at this time. They were Muslims and some internally assimilated Muslims and Christians. The number of foreign Muslims and assimilated Christian foreigners west of the Jordan was a mere few thousand.

The biggest increase in Christians was among longstanding Christian Descendants of Israel. Their relatively high birth rate was fueled by two factors: intermarriage with Muslim women and a significant rise in the standard of living, relative to their Muslim brethren, due to the Christians' ties with Christian Europe, which raised levels of sanitation and medical care among them.

In order to simplify discussion of the process that followed, which becomes more and more complex, the foreigners discussed above, regardless of religious association, are called in the rest of this book: **Distant Foreigners** and **Foreigners of Distant Origins**. Use of this nomenclature will relate to all the Christians of foreign origins, but also will include other foreigners from distant lands (i.e., regardless of religious ascription): Circassians, Turks, Bosnians and Albanians. To these, one needs to add the Kurds, whose numbers grew up until 1914 through natural increase to some 5,000.

Among the Jews, the year 1882 marked the beginning of the First Aliyah – the first wave of Zionist immigration that brought tens of

138

thousands of Jews from Eastern Europe, including the **Biluim**. The same year, the agricultural village **Rishon le-Zion** was founded. The term 'First Aliyah' is a bit misleading. Already in 1881 the first groups of new Jewish immigrants arrived from Yemen; it is possible that they were influenced to do so by a group of hundreds of Descendants of the Moabites from Yemen who had come to western Eretz-Israel earlier in the course of the settlement activity of the Brethren of Israel. Apparently the latter kindled the spirits of Yemenite Jews and led them to sense that the time had come for a Return to Zion.

Four years prior to the beginning of the First Aliyah one can already see signs of renewed Jewish agricultural settlement in Eretz-Israel, marked by the actions of a group of Jerusalemites who left their city to found the first agricultural village or *moshava* – Petach Tikva, which became known as the 'Mother of all the *Moshavot.*'[30]

All Jewish waves of immigrations from the First (1882) to the Fifth Aliyah (1933-39) were, in fact, preceded by a slow influx of Jews to Jerusalem. But this phenomenon was of individual families and not groups of significant size that constituted discernable 'waves' of thousands and even tens of thousands of people. In 1904, the Second Aliyah began to arrive, a wave of Jewish immigration that continued up to 1914. This influx was also from Eastern Europe, primarily Russia. At the outset of 1914 – just prior to the outbreak of the First World War – there were 100,000 Jews who had settled west of the Jordan out of an overall population of 700,000 souls. In the course of that year, once the war had started, the Turks began to expel a portion of the Jews

---

[30] The *moshava* was established in 1878 near the Arab village **Malabes**, where the railroad workers from Egypt had settled some 45 years earlier. In the course of time the *moshava* became a city. The Arabs of Malabas later changed the occupied part of their village to Faja. Under this name, the village became one of Petach Tikva's neighborhoods with the settlement of Jews there after Arab residents fled in the 1948 war.

who were nationals of enemy countries, and the number of Jews dropped by 10 percent.

Composition of the Population in Numbers, for the Year 1914

In the course of the period between 1840 and 1914, the standard of living in Eretz-Israel improved, including sanitation and health. As a result, natural population growth was no longer marginal as it had been in the preceding period. Improvement intensified in later periods. The composition of the Palestinian population in 1914, including the impact of various immigrations and natural population growth, is detailed in Table 24 below.

1914 – In the Entire Country						
Ethnic Group	Inhabitants in the West		Inhabitants in the East		Inhabitants in the Entire Country	
	Number	Percentage	Number	Percentage	Number	Percentage
Descendants of Israel	97,000	41%	167,000	46%	264,000	44%
Brethren of Israel	79,000	33%	32,000	9%	111,000	19%
Descendants of Israel in the Broader Sense	176,000	74%	199,000	55%	375,000	63%
Roman Army	24,000	10%	3,500	1%	27,500	5%
Arabs	16,000	7%	151,000	42%	167,000	28%
Distant Forieginers	17,000	7%	6,500	2%	23,500	4%
Druze	4,000	2%			4,000	1%
Total	237,000	100%	360,000	100%	597,000	100%

Table 24: Non-Jewish Inhabitants of Eretz-Israel in 1914.

Since on the eve of 1914, and even more so afterwards, the number of Jews who came to settle in Eretz-Israel constituted a considerable portion of the inhabitants of western Eretz-Israel, the number of Jews by religion are not included in Table 24 and subsequent tables in order to focus on Palestinian data.

From a demographic standpoint, one can observe how the Descendants of Israel, despite the drop in their numbers west of the Jordan due to migration east and north of the Jordan, continued to constitute the largest component in the population west of the Jordan. But in contrast with the situation in 1840, a new reality arose: The Brethren of Israel, who in the previous period did not reside at all in the western side of Eretz-Israel, became the second largest group in 1914 – just short of the number of Descendants of Israel.

The Arabs continued to constitute a relatively small group (7 percent) in western Eretz-Israel. They belonged primarily to four groupings, each a few thousand persons: members of the veteran Judham Tribe, Egyptians, Bedouin and Others.

If one subtracts the Druze and the Foreigners of Distant Origins who are not Palestinians or Arabs, one finds that **81 percent are Descendants of Israel in the Broader Sense** (as was the case in 1840). However, in the narrow sense, the scope of Ethnic Descendants of Israel in western Eretz-Israel in 1914 dropped to 45 percent of all Palestinians (approximately half their weight in 1840).

As for the number of inhabitants east of the Jordan, in 1914 the inhabitants east of the Jordan had already been officially added to the Eretz-Israel census, and therefore the changes that one notes in their numbers since 1840 was the result of immigration, inhabitants of newly-added areas and natural population growth.

This particular period was one in which areas east of the Jordan blossomed. In addition to the Descendants of Israel who migrated to the east from west of the Jordan, additional immigrants also

141

arrived – many Bedouin and Arabs from the Arabian Peninsula. In addition, many longtime inhabitants from areas that were not counted in previous censuses were added.

The Brethren of Israel continued to return to the East during this period, but most left the east for western Eretz-Israel. Part lived in areas that had been included in the previous census, and part resided in areas that only in 1914 were added to the census for the first time. The data from the east in the 1914 census is included in Table 24 above. The statistics show that the growth of Descendants of Israel in the east since 1840 was not significant (see Table 23 in Appendix 5 for comparison).

The most significant change in the east was that there, as well, the second largest group was the Arabs, whose numbers approached those of the Descendants of Israel. Another prominent change was the status of the Brethren of Israel, who at this point constituted a mere 9 percent of the population of the east.

Beginning of the Conflict

Due to the increase in internal migrations of Jewish immigrants, and later during this period of Arab immigrants as well, a new reality emerged primarily in western Eretz-Israel. The Jews did not find any common ground in terms of language and culture with the permanent residents and internal immigrants who were not Jewish by faith. There were very few Jews who were able to bridge the differences, who studied their neighbors' background, thus learning of the permanent inhabitants' origins. These Jews called for strengthening ties with them, yet the overwhelming majority of Jews rejected this notion and distanced themselves from them.

The language and culture of these permanent inhabitants was primarily Arab-Muslim or Arab-Christian. They found a common language with Arab immigrants. The latter began to arrive in western Eretz-Israel during this period and their influx continued – primarily from Egypt, Saudi Arabia and from east of the Jordan.

142

Thus, the collective *Musta'arbi* identity, which had diminished over the years, was lost to a large extent, and a new Palestinian-Arab identity began to crystallize. With the Descendants of Israel hiding their original identity, the new Palestinian-Arab identity has set the tone among Palestinians since then to this day, despite the fact that most of the Arabs who immigrated to Eretz-Israel left long ago.

What added fuel to the flames was the large number of internal immigrants, Brethren of Israel, who by this time for the most part, were already in western Eretz-Israel. In addition to the fact that the Brethren of Israel considered themselves Arabs, they had no inherent attachment to Eretz-Israel or any commonality with the Jews. The alienation between Jews and Brethren of Israel worsened due to the fact that in 1914 the Brethren of Israel became a very large group among Palestinians west of the Jordan.

The situation among the Brethren of Israel contributed greatly to the sense of distance and estrangement between Jews and the majority of Palestinians at this time. The presence of a rival other – the Jews – only deepened the roots of the new Palestinian-Arab identity in Eretz-Israel.

The way relations were played out in the end led to the tragic circumstances Eretz-Israel faces today. This was because of the relative weight of the Brethren of Israel in the western part of Eretz-Israel subsequently dropped due to the return to the west of the same Descendants of Israel who had left up until 1914, and the flight of the 1948 refugees. As a consequence, the relationship between Palestinians, and Jews returning to Eretz-Israel was shaped and crystallized at a time when the relative weight of the Brethren of Israel in the western part of Eretz-Israel was at its peak.

While the Brethren of Israel considered themselves native sons of the land, they still harbored the insecurity of immigrants: They sensed that their entitlement to their place of residence in the western part of Eretz-Israel and hegemony over their holdings was still vulnerable. As a result, they were open to incitement by parties with vested interests who incited them to consider Jews arriving in Eretz-Israel at the time as an element that planned to take over the country and as a threat to their own title to Eretz-Israel. Hostility towards the Jews grew because the points of contact and friction between Palestinians and Jews were primarily between Brethren of Israel and Jews, both due to the large number of Brethren of Israel and because the Brethren of Israel resided in the coastal plain and the valleys, side-by-side with the Jews.

What also contributed to bad blood was the fact that the Brethren of Israel were forced into exile in Persia in the 19th Century, resulting in them leaving their ancestral homelands east of the Jordan. The uprooting experience became a trauma for this group, and consequently they were extremely adversarial, with a low threshold for provocation – real or imagined. The last thing the Brethren of Israel 'needed' was the demographic challenge inherent in Jewish immigration. Moreover, during their sojourn in extremist Persia, the 'culture' of the temperament of the Brethren of Israel had acquired an aggressive if not violent edge.

Fear that additional immigration of Jews would be a tipping point and endanger their hegemony led the Brethren of Israel to launch terror attacks on the Jews in the coastal plains and the valleys of western Eretz-Israel to drive them out before it would be too late. Like the Descendants of Israel to the east, the Jews limited the land the Brethren of Israel held in the western parts of Eretz-Israel. The Brethren of Israel found themselves, for the third time in a little over 100 years, in the predicament where their neighbors began crowding them out, jeopardizing the Brethren of Israel's very future in western Eretz-Israel.

The worst fears of the Brethren of Israel, indeed, became a self-fulfilling prophecy when they chose terrorism as the tool to strike back. Their own terrorism (and the Jewish response), ultimately led the majority of this population to leave their homes and even flee western Eretz-Israel entirely – as occurred in the wholesale flight of Palestinian refugees in 1948.

The situation at the outset of the 20th Century was a tinderbox. Only one spark was needed to set the Middle East on fire – a blaze that has only gained in fury to this day. As a result, relations between Jews and Palestinians have, in many instances, been exceedingly hostile almost from the first point of contact between the two immigrant populations.

Hostility has only grown over the years. The denser the population became, the greater the rivalry over lands became, and with it the intensity of the Brethren of Israel's terror tactics to uproot the Jews. It was during this period that the seeds of hostility that continue to undermine relations between Palestinians and Jews germinated.

The label 'Palestinians' had been partially used for 1,800 years to designate the local population. Since most of the world (except some of the Jews) called Eretz-Israel "Palestine," as it was called in Europe for 1,800 years following the Bar Kokhba rebellion, giving the name 'Palestinians' to longstanding inhabitants was natural, although the term did not indicate their essence, not to mention their 'Arabness.' Moreover, this name clearly signaled the Palestinians' link to Eretz-Israel and to the People of Israel. Only their *Musta'arbi* nature in general and the complexities of migrations and changing identity, particularly of the Brethren of Israel detailed above, prevented a positive link being forged between Palestinian permanent residents and Jews returning to Zion.

Among the Palestinians there were also those who viewed Jewish immigration to Eretz-Israel as a threat to their wealth. A tiny minority of wealthy *effendi* families (landowners) held title to a large percent of the privately-owned land in western Eretz-Israel. The *effendi* economic elite rented out land to Palestinian peasants, charging oppressive prices that bled the tenant farmers dry.

The Socialist milieu that Jewish settlers 'imported' with them – championship of 'oppressed workers throwing off the chains of capitalist bondage' – was a source of worry for the *effendis* most of whom were key figures in Palestinian society's leadership. The first waves of immigration of Jews were based almost exclusively on young people from Eastern Europe whose worldview had been shaped by Socialist streams of thought revolutionizing Europe, including those that served as the foundation for communism. Not surprisingly, the Palestinian leadership branded the Jews 'Bolsheviks.'

The *effendis* were far from happy with the fact that Palestinian peasants now had the option of making a livelihood as laborers because of the Jews, free of their own control over most land, a factor that drove down the price of leasing land and the revenues of Palestinian landed 'gentry' and absentee landlords.

While the *effendis* sold the Jews marginal lands that were very problematic to farm, at inflated prices, increasing their wealth, at the same time they feared that in the long run, this lucrative business would come to an end. It was almost inevitable that the *effendis* would incite the Palestinian public against the Jews as the source of their troubles when Jews came to take possession of lands the peasants no longer owned but considered 'their own,' while pressuring authorities to close the doors to Jewish immigrants, charging that they were a dangerous element. As discussed above, there were sectors of the Palestinian public who were more easily incited, serving as the initial kindling that fueled animosity between the sides.

One of these wealthy families was the al-Husseini family – the clan that gave birth to the extremist anti-Semitic Mufti of Jerusalem, **Haj Amin al-Husseini**, as well as Yasser Arafat's mother. The Mufti was the leading Arab to collaborate with **Adolf Hitler**, but he was also (details follow) **the primary force behind the Nazi's preference of a Final Solution, rather than expelling European Jewry to Eretz-Israel.**

146

The al-Husseini family, whose ancestry is a mixture of Descendants of the Moabites with Descendants of Israel, achieved its exalted status as a leading Palestinian family after one of the family's forefathers, who sought to become a tax collector, told the Ottoman authorities that his family descended from the Prophet Mohammed.

Even before the atmosphere in Eretz-Israel between Palestinians and Jews reached a boiling point, intervention from the Arabian Peninsula had already begun to add fuel to the fire. The transformation of the only wall of the Temple Mount still standing – the Western Wall – into the holiest site for the Jews, together with budding Jewish immigration during this period, mostly to Jerusalem, were thorns in the side of Arab-Muslim leadership even outside Eretz-Israel.

Due to the Jerusalem Jewish community's lack of continuity of the Yishuv, and the desire to 'hold on to' some physical remnant of the Second Temple, Jewish immigrants (beginning with the arrival of the illustrious Jewish sage, the Ramban in 1267) associated the existing wall to the west of the Temple Mount with the 'walls of the Holy Temple' although they are, in fact, merely the foundations of the retaining wall of the Temple Mount.

In order to undermine the morale of Jews returning to Eretz-Israel and squelch the attraction of Jerusalem, the Muslim leadership in the Arabian Peninsula sent a four-man delegation to Jerusalem in the year 1872 to dismantle the walls of the Temple Mount. With the assistance of local laborers hired to carry out the work, and with the blessings of the Turkish government (whose support was also fueled by religious fervor), the delegation destroyed the southern wall of the Temple Mount, a wall whose construction, irony of ironies, had been primarily the work of past Muslim rulers.

There were deceased Jews who were memorialized by engraving their names on the stones of the southern wall. The wall was

147

dismantled down to its foundations; not a remnant remains, except vintage photos that have survived. The Western Wall was spared a similar fate due to the fact that the structural integrity of the mosques on the Temple Mount would have been jeopardized by any attempt to dismantle the western ramparts of the Temple Mount!

Prior to the destruction, the Jews imparted the same importance to both the southern and the western walls. (The northern and eastern walls had been destroyed by the Crusaders in the course of taking Jerusalem in the year 1099.)

Further along, there were 'local' Palestinian initiatives against the Jews: already in 1891, one witnesses the first political activism against Jewish immigration, which increased beginning in 1908, climaxing in the establishment of anti-Zionist media and organizations that put pressure on the regime to harass and 'discourage' Jewish immigration.

At first, the Turks stopped Jewish immigration entirely for a full year, then prevented new Jewish immigrants from buying land. After the League of Nations handed governance over to Great Britain, Palestinian-Arab leaders pressured British Mandate authorities to put limitations on the number of Jewish immigrants permitted to enter the country. Despite initial British pro-Zionist sentiments, Arab pressures ultimately brought further limitations to the number of Jewish immigrants allowed to enter the country. Far more serious, such attitudes towards Jewish immigration were responsible for bloody uprisings against the Jews of Eretz-Israel launched by some of the Palestinians.

The Birth of Palestinian Terrorism

The first bloody incidents began in a trickle – in 1886, gained momentum in the 1920s, and reached their peak in the 1930s with the 1936-1939 Arab Revolt. It began when Jewish immigration reached new peaks (parallel to significant Arab immigration into

148

Eretz-Israel, it should be noted). The attacks on Jews marked the beginning of terrorism against civilians as a phenomenon of the Eretz-Israel conflict.

These events mark the beginnings of Palestinian aggression against Jews, aggression that continued over many years, in part in certain periods with the assistance of the Arab countries. At a certain point, this aggression began to be met by an assertive response on the part of the Jews, even an aggressive one that turned the Palestinians themselves into the chief victims of the vicious circle of violence that occurred. This Palestinian aggressiveness stemmed from the fact that part of the Palestinians had lost the link to their own Israelite origins. The loss of this link is responsible for all the difficulties in Eretz-Israel in the course of the past one hundred years and most of the problems of the Middle East.

This portion of the Palestinians was hostile to the return of Jewish refugees to their land. The Jews' only 'crime' was that they dared return to the ancestral homeland from which they had been expelled by the Roman Empire some two thousand years prior, in order to cease being refugees. But according to the logic behind the behavior of Palestinians who had lost the link to their own origins and attacked the Jews, just as there are 'statutes of limitation' in patent laws, after a two thousand year absence, the rights of Jews returning to Eretz-Israel have lost their validity.

In weighing the legitimacy of such an argument, on one hand, it should be noted that the Jews in the Diaspora never gave up their desires to return to their homeland and when this first became feasible after the Ottoman Conquest, they found themselves facing a hostile regime that undermined their efforts to return, at every turn. Thus, one cannot claim any 'statute of limitations' applies to the rights of Jewish entitlement in Eretz-Israel since Jews never gave up this entitlement and it remained an unfailing, driving force and central pillar of Jewish identity and existence throughout the Exile. On the other hand, and most important, it was the majority of Palestinians themselves, the offspring of the People of Israel of the various kinds, whose very presence in Eretz-Israel so definitively substantiates that this was the homeland of the Jews, who remained in Eretz-Israel in significant numbers, both relative to other groups and in absolute numbers.

The application of terrorism – violence against citizens – as a vehicle is categorically illegitimate in principle, then and now, and the Koran as well forbids it. Nevertheless, one can understand the reasons for its existence. In the worldview of Palestinians who have lost the link to their past, the Jews came to rob them of their homeland, and a portion of these Palestinians wanted to take action, to strike out against this perceived threat. On one hand, reality was that at the time Jews in Eretz-Israel did not have an army that Arabs could attack or engage in battle. On the other hand, the Arabs hardly excelled at organization in any case, and did not have the force to fight the army of a ruling superpower such as Great Britain. The only option they had was to apply terrorism against Jewish civilians, and try to intimidate the Jews and weaken their resolve to immigrate to Eretz-Israel.

Thus terrorism became a norm among a portion of the Palestinian public. Later, the lack of ability to organize effectively in the face of an Israeli fighting force led to the use of terrorism against Israeli civilians even after there was an Israeli army. If terrorism prior to this carried some justification, this became null and void once the Jews had their own armed forces – considered 'fair game' and a legitimate target for engagement in the annals of armed struggle. Parallel to this, the inability of Palestinians to organize at this time was the result of being scattered among many nations, the majority living under Israeli rule. Since they received funding from abroad to underwrite their actions, and they were unequivocally devoted to remaining in their homeland, Palestinians believed that their weaknesses were no justification to passively accept their fate; rather, it gave them the legitimate right to continue using terrorism.

Wholesale terrorism began to take root in Eretz-Israel even prior to the First World War when there were cases of individual Jews

150

murdered by Arabs, including attacks fueled by nationalist sentiment. Beginning in the 1920s, however, certain Palestinian circles began to target Jews as a community for wholesale attacks. In April 1920, following incitement organized by Haj Amin al-Husseini, Arab mobs in Jerusalem carried out the first Palestinian rampage, leaving six Jews dead and hundreds more injured.

The next major terrorist attack was more organized: the slaughter of some 40 Jews in Jaffa in May 1921; the victims include two Jewish writers – **Yosef Haim Brenner** and **Tsvi Shatz**. Terrorism against Jewish civil society materialized in other places as well, including an onslaught that led to the destruction of **Kefar Sava**.

At the end of August 1929, under orders from Amin al-Husseini (who by then had been appointed Mufti of Jerusalem by British authorities) Palestinian terrorism was intensified: 133 Jews were slaughtered, including 63 in one day in Hebron and 30 in Jerusalem. The Jewish community of Hebron, which prior to the massacre had numbered 600 inhabitants, was evacuated by the British and subsequently prohibited from returning to the City of the Patriarchs, one of the four holy cities to Judaism (Jerusalem, Hebron, Safed and Tiberias).

During what came to be known as the 1936-1939 Arab Revolt, 510 Jews were killed, most of them slaughtered by Palestinians. The number of casualties was much greater. Attacks continued over time, reaching a peak in the summer of 1938 when 162 Jews were killed. Haj Amin al-Husseini instigated and led this prolonged rampage of sniping, bombing and frontal attacks on isolated Jewish settlements and Jewish neighborhoods and traffic on the roads (and British targets). The British previously awarded Amin al-Husseini with an additional title and increased political clout as head of the **Arab Higher Committee**, a body organized by British authorities to create a united Palestinian leadership.

Despite its name, the Arab Revolt was not a popular uprising of Palestinians against the British and the Jews. At the height of the rampage, the number of insurgents numbered fewer than 2,000 persons, or 0.2 percent of some one million Palestinians and Arabs living in Eretz-Israel at the time. At the outset of 1936 Palestinian leadership rejected a British offer to establish a legislative council based on proportional representation that would have given their people (i.e., Palestinian-Arabs, not Jews) majority control of the future of Eretz-Israel. Instead, they chose to stir up a bloody revolt to enhance their clout in negotiations with British authorities.

The Jews were not the primary victims of Palestinian terrorist gangs during these years. Due to internal conflict, resulting from the arduous economic straits brought by terrorist operations and harsh measures taken by British authorities against Palestinians in response, and vendettas among Palestinians, 6,000 Palestinians were killed by Palestinian terror gangs, causing Palestinian educated and wealthy classes and moderates to flee the country, further plunging the Palestinian economy into worse and worse circumstances.

The ferocity of the Arab Revolt caught the Jewish community by surprise. During the years 1936-1939, initially Jewish settlement activity in Eretz-Israel came to a standstill in the face of rising terrorism, but then was renewed – almost defiantly at a faster pace. To fend off terrorism, a new settlement strategy was adopted where new communities were established overnight, protected against Arab marauders by a pre-fabricated watchtower and a bullet-proof defense parameter of parallel wood panels filled with gravel. The vanguard for establishment of what became known as "Stockade and Tower" settlements were members of the Hashomer Hatzair Movement who insisted on settling in the Beit She'an Valley – establishing Kibbutz Nir David in an area that up until then had not been settled by Jews. In the course of these bloody attacks, between 1921 and 1936 Palestinians expelled Jews who had lived in mixed communities for generations – from Gaza and from villages in the vicinity of Hebron and villages in the Galilee. Only in Peki'in in the Galilee, one Jewish family remained.

British Rule – A Period of Significant Immigration

During the First World War, the situation in Eretz-Israel deteriorated. The Turks even worsened the situation by expelling some of the new settlers. As a result, the number of Jews dropped significantly, and some of the foreign laborers who had come to find work among Jewish newcomers dispersed and returned home.

Following the issue of the **Balfour Declaration**[31] in 1917, stating Great Britain's support for establishment of a national home for the Jewish People in Eretz-Israel, and the end of the First World War and establishment of a British Mandate over Palestine by the League of Nations to carry out this goal, in 1919 Eretz-Israel witnessed a third wave of Zionist pioneers, the Third Aliyah that continued until 1923. In 1924, the Fourth Aliyah began – a wave of immigrants primarily from Poland that lasted until 1929. Difficult economic straits in the country in 1928 led a portion of the Jewish population to leave the country. Yet in 1929 a new wave of immigrants the Fifth Aliyah commenced – lasting until the outbreak of the Second World War in 1939. The Fifth Aliyah set new records and was larger than all four waves combined.

The Fifth Aliyah included, for the first time, a majority of Jews who were middle class and non-Socialist, who were prompted to settle in Eretz-Israel by growing anti-Semitism in Europe and the rise of Hitler to power in Germany in 1933. These immigrants constituted the foundations upon which an Israeli Right-wing arose, after the influx of immigrants in previous waves served as the foundations for the Israeli Left. The Fifth Aliyah and the economic prosperity that followed in the wake of such a huge input of human resources and capital, prompted the influx of waves of non-Jewish immigrants from neighboring countries and the migration of additional inhabitants from eastern Eretz-Israel to western Eretz-Israel, attracted by the prospect of economic

---

[31] Lord Balfour was the British Foreign Secretary during the First World War.

153

betterment. By the year 1938, the number of non-Jews reached a million souls, compared to 300,000 Jews (i.e., this number of non-Jews and all references henceforth already include <u>all</u> the inhabitants east of the Jordan.) During this period immigration of Jews and non-Jews to Eretz-Israel peaked. The pressures and competition generated constant friction, which sparked an increase in Arab-Palestinian terrorism (the 1936-1939 Arab Revolt.)

Terrorism during these years led some 40,000 Jews to flee the country, primarily Jewish Jerusalemites. These Jewish refugees who left Eretz-Israel in the face of Palestinian aggression fled well before the flight of Palestinian refugees in 1948.

Parallel to the emigration of Jews due to terrorism, the influx of other Jews from Europe seeking refuge continued unabated, however, in response to Palestinian violence, the British chose to curtail the number of immigration visas for Jews ('Certificates') to 60,000 a year. Consequently on the eve of the Second World War, the official number of Jews in Eretz-Israel was merely 320,000.

The cutback in Certificates led to a massive effort to save Jewish lives in jeopardy in Europe by dodging Mandatory restrictions on Jewish immigration. Boatloads of undocumented Jewish immigrants were transported from Europe to Eretz-Israel clandestinely, circumventing ports of entry and a British blockade, to 'steal into the country illegally.' This endeavor was called in Hebrew *Aliyah Bet*, a compliment to *Aliyah Alef* or legal entrance with British-issued Certificates. The illegal entries that succeeded in reaching shore and 'disappearing' with the help of the local Jewish community were not accounted for in British records. Thus, the number of Jews in the country was significantly higher than official figures. At the outbreak of the Second World War the number of actual Jews in Eretz-Israel was 384,000 (a 20 percent increase).

After the Second World War, waves of Holocaust survivors began to arrive. Most came by sea – some legally with Certificates of Entry, most as illegal immigrants who succeeded in entering without documents or whose ships were caught and their human cargo transferred to British prison ships and the refugees incarcerated in special camps and only allowed to enter against British immigration quotas. The *Aliyah Bet* endeavor was largely responsible for the growth of the Jewish population which reached 660,000 when Israel declared its independence on May 14, 1948.

Prior to the outbreak of war in 1948, there were 1,323,000 non-Jews in all of Eretz-Israel on both sides of the Jordan, while in western Eretz-Israel (i.e., west of the Jordan) there were 636,000 non-Jews. Within the sectors where the Jews were concentrated, 393,000 non-Jews resided. The boundaries of these 'Jewish areas,' along with the Negev, were what became known as the **Green Line** (i.e., the Armistice Line that delineated the territory of the State of Israel at the close of the 1948 war).

Later, in order to inflate the number of Palestinian refugees, the Palestinians exaggerated the population of western Eretz-Israel by 100 percent, and claimed that at the outset of 1948 the number of Palestinians who had resided previously within the post-war Green Line (i.e., most of whom had been 'expelled by Israel') was 800,000.

The Palestinians were assisted in their subterfuge by the fact that all the population censuses and various estimates published at the time did not make any differentiation between east and west, since during the Ottoman Period just prior to the dawn of the Mandate Period both were one entity.

The various districts of Eretz-Israel during the Ottoman Period were named after cities in the west (Gaza, Jerusalem, Nablus and Akko) but Gaza, Jerusalem and Nablus included a very wide strip of territory east of the Jordan. Although already in 1914 the territory east of the Jordan as a whole was included in published figures, most of the actual inhabitants of the east resided in areas whose inhabitants prior to this were erroneously considered residents of the west. Adding all the residents east of the Jordan to the census generated no attention at the time and all the inhabitants of the east were considered inhabitants of the west.

To maintain statistical continuity, this was carried over and adopted by British authorities. The 1922 census of all of Eretz-Israel shows no jump in the number of inhabitants relative to Turkish times – a jump that would lead scholars to think the inhabitants of the east had been added to the census. Settlements in the east that had been given identical names to villages in the west when the villagers migrated eastward at an earlier time only prolonged the confusion. The British continued to view both sides of the Jordan as one entity. The mistake occurred, despite the fact that the British did not view the published data as referring to the western part of Eretz-Israel alone.

All these factors led to errors among many scholars as to what transpired in the Holy Land during the 20th Century. As will be discussed in detail, the Palestinians took advantage of this situation and the benevolence and naiveté of **UNRWA**[32] officials to inflate beyond all proportion the number of non-Jews residing inside the Green Line before the 1948 war – both to magnify the Palestinian refugee problem and the number of inhabitants in Judea, Samaria (West Bank) and Gaza after the war.

Components of the Non-Jewish Population on the Eve of the 1948 War

Between 1914 and 1948, 125,000 non-Jewish external immigrants entered Eretz-Israel west of the Jordan. This number included a small minority of Druze who hailed from the Hauran in Syria who

---

[32] The UN's special framework established in 1948 to aid Palestinian refugees. All other refugees in the world are handled by the UN's High Commission on Refugees.

came in 1934. Prior to that, in 1874, these Druze had arrived in the Hauran from north-eastern China, where they had settled following persecution in Lebanon.

These Druze – who joined veteran Druze brethren who had arrived after 1840 – received their name from the area from which they had come: the **Hauran**. This area was part of **Druze Mountain** (*Jabel Druze*) whose name bore witness to the fact that most of the Druze in the Levant resided in this mountainous area. The migration of the Hauranis west of the Jordan resulted from suppression of the Druze Revolt in the Jabel Druze region by French rulers of Syria.

As a result of external immigration there were Arabs who entered areas of Jewish settlement. They came from east of the Jordan, from Egypt, from Saudi Arabia, from Syria and from Lebanon. The Arab immigrants from Syria and Lebanon settled in the northern coastal plain of Eretz-Israel – the majority in Haifa. The city had grown with the building of a port in 1934, and served as a source of livelihood to many.

The above figures do not include most Brethren of Israel who until 1914 remained to the east of the Jordan and only later migrated west of the Jordan, primarily from the Sanjak of Ma'an. In 1948, only a few thousand Brethren of Israel remained in this governing district east of the Jordan.

In addition, there were some 75,000 Descendants of Israel who migrated from east of the Jordan to western Eretz-Israel. Most were inhabitants who had migrated east between 1840 and 1914, and they and their offspring were now returning after conditions in the west improved, a process that took place parallel to the influx of Jewish immigration. Although these returnees originated from the mountain regions of Judea and Samaria, they resettled for the most part in a geographical triangle at the foot of the Samaritan foothills and the coastal strip to the west – primarily in Haifa and Akko, adjacent to Jewish settlement areas.

157

The choice of location had two causes: The first, the fact that the original holdings of the returnees were now in the possession of other inhabitants due to natural population growth among the Descendants of Israel, and to a smaller extent Brethren of Israel who had arrived before 1914. The second reason was the attraction of growing economic opportunities to make a living close to points of Jewish settlement.

Additional returnees to the country were the majority of emigrants who had left the Galilee for Syria and Lebanon in previous periods. Economic prosperity prompted some 31,000 Descendants of Israel to return to their villages in the Galilee. Veteran Galilee villagers who had remained and knew of the genuine origins of the Palestinians viewed these returning brethren from the Levant as comparable to another group of newcomers – the Jews – whom they also viewed as former brethren returning to Eretz-Israel from the Diaspora. From the year 1934 the veterans began labeling these returnees from the Levant with more than a wink, **Yahud al-Arab** ('The Jews of the Arabs'). This designation took root, then gained broader usage – applied to Palestinians as a whole – both due to their sophistication compared to other Arab people, and the hardships of their lot.

In essence, the Descendants of Israel who returned to western Eretz-Israel from eastern Eretz-Israel, from Syria and from Lebanon pulled in their wake Arab and Druze immigrants. Since the movement of people was considerable and there was no reason to hide the rapid development of western Eretz-Israel, many inhabitants of neighboring countries who had no inherent tie to Eretz-Israel jumped on the immigration bandwagon.

The places of residence of those who had left holdings east of the Jordan and crossed the river westward proved very attractive to Arabs from neighboring countries who moved into the vacuum left, to take possession of these areas or get them for a low price. Prosperity west of the Jordan impacted positively on the situation east of the Jordan which witnessed economic growth as well, and

158

very quickly some 200,000 Arab immigrants supplanted those who had moved westward.

The majority who moved westward came from the central and northern half of eastern Eretz-Israel and settled in areas directly west on the same geographic latitude, along the northern coastal plane that extends north of Tel Aviv up to Haifa Bay, including Akko. They were primarily Descendants of Israel and Arabs. Due to the proximity of their former places of residence east of the Hauran, the newcomers along with Descendants of Israel who prior to 1914 were in Syria constituted a 'critical mass' that attracted Druze and other Arabs from Syria, particularly from the Hauran which directly borders western Eretz-Israel in the north. Although politically the Hauran belonged to Syria up until 1967, from a historic-demographic standpoint the Hauran could be considered an integral part of the east of the Jordan, and part-and-parcel of historic Eretz-Israel.

The southern sector of the coastal plain (from Jaffa southward) was settled primarily by Brethren of Israel, as well as Egyptians and Saudi Arabians. Most of these Arab settlers, except for the Egyptians, were pastoral Bedouin who settled in the Negev, as well. Prior to this, most of the Bedouin had inhabited the northern sector of the coastal plain and the northern valleys. Among the Descendants of Israel and Brethren of Israel who up until 1914 resided in the mountain country in western Eretz-Israel, there were also many inhabitants who moved closer to Jewish settlements for economic reasons.

These parallel population movements of external Arab immigration and internal migration took place without any interference from British authorities. Contrary to the Mandate it had received from the League of Nations to establish a national home for the Jews, Mandatory authorities placed no barriers to prevent the influx of Arabs and others to Eretz-Israel overland.

During Turkish times, the entire Ottoman Empire was considered one country, without any borders to hinder the movement of peoples. The British continued this tradition and allowed inhabitants residing east of the Jordan and residents of Syria and Lebanon to enter western Eretz-Israel freely. This was the case although the British in 1922 had already partitioned the original Mandate to create a special Arab country out of eastern Eretz-Israel (Trans-Jordan), where Jewish settlement was prohibited and, since 1919, Syria and Lebanon were entirely separate political entities governed by French mandates earmarked to become independent Arab polities.

Parallel to this, British Mandatory authorities did everything in their power to stem the influx of Jewish refugees from Nazi Europe trying to enter Eretz-Israel by sea – even after the close of the Second World War. Under pressure from the Arabs and the Palestinians, the British severely limited the number of Jews permitted to enter the country and expelled to DP camps in Cyprus those caught trying to enter without permits.

Under such conditions it is not surprising that the British, contrary to their promises expressed in the Balfour Declaration, chose to reverse their policies almost immediately after being appointed Mandators by the international community to execute the vision of a Jewish national homeland in Eretz-Israel, and severely curtailed the borders of the proposed Jewish state to western Eretz-Israel only. Their discriminatory immigration policy of unfettered movement of Arabs into Eretz-Israel parallel to strict control and limitations on Jewish immigration made it impossible to achieve a Jewish majority in Eretz-Israel on both sides of the Jordan or even west of the Jordan earmarked for a Jewish homeland.

During their governance of the Mandate for Palestine, the British also sought to carry out a second partition of Eretz-Israel, to divide western Eretz-Israel between Palestinians and Jews. They had come to the conclusion that their own limitations on Jewish immigration had created a large Palestinian-Arab concentration in

160

Judea and Samaria. In order to preserve the concentration of Jewish settlement in the coastal areas as a decisive majority, the British decided to limit the areas where non-Jewish immigrants could settle. Beginning in 1935, the British limited the terms of Certificates of Entry they gave Arab immigrants, Druze and Brethren of Israel to areas of Judea and Samaria only, including east Jerusalem. They planned that these new residents would utilize holdings that had been abandoned by more veteran inhabitants who had moved closer to Jewish areas of settlement for economic reasons. But most of the immigrants ignored the conditions and the British turned a blind eye and didn't enforce the prerequisite. Thus, most of the non-Jewish immigrants settled illegally in areas of the coastal plain and the valleys where Jews were settling, as well as the Gaza Strip. Most of these areas, at a later stage, remained inside what came to be known as the Green Line (inside Israel 'proper').

The data above, of some 393,000 non-Jews within the Green Line in 1948 includes 66,000 immigrants who resided there illegally, since they had received entry permits for Judea and Samaria only. Moreover some 70,000 Descendants of Israel came from eastern Eretz-Israel, Syria and Lebanon to settle in areas within the Green Line without any immigration permits whatsoever from British authorities, sneaking across permeable borders or gaining entrance at formal border crossings under false pretenses.

The authorities during the Mandate Period also turned a blind eye to some of the migrants from east of the Jordan because at one point both sides of the Jordan had been one entity. The Descendants of Israel, due to economic consideration, chose primarily to settle in Jewish areas which for the most part were not even in the vicinity of their prior ancestral holdings.

In 1937 the British Mandatory government officially adopted the concept of partition of western Eretz-Israel recommended by the **Peel Commission,** for two separate countries, one Arab and one

Jewish. In 1947, this concept served as the basis for the 1947 United Nations Partition Plan.[33]

Towards the close of the British Mandate, in the 1940s, the Templars were expelled from Eretz-Israel. A large percentage were expelled by the British in the course of the Second World War due to their status as enemy aliens, and sent to Australia. Most of the Templars supported the Nazi movement and constituted a potential Fifth Column in Eretz-Israel at a time when Rommel's Afrika Corps had advanced as far as **El Alamein** in Egypt in their campaign to conquer the Middle East. Some of the Templars even assisted Palestinian marauders during the 1936-1939 Arab Revolt. In response to the Holocaust, the Haganah (the main Jewish military organization of that time) expelled any remaining Templars parallel to the departure of the British.

Natural population growth and immigration in the period between 1914 and 1948 brought demographic changes as presented in Table 25 that follows. One can see how the Descendants of Israel, who originally were inhabitants of the mountain country, grew significantly in number in western Eretz-Israel by 1914, but this did not change their relative strength in the overall population.

If one removes from the population base foreigners from distant lands and the Druze, who are not Palestinians, it becomes evident that **70 percent of the Palestinians** are **Descendants of Israel in the Broader Sense** (i.e., including the Brethren of Israel) (compared to 81 percent in 1914). On this basis, it becomes evident that in 1948 **the Descendants of Israel in the Narrow Sense constituted 41 percent of the Palestinians in western Eretz-Israel** (on par with their relative position in 1914, 45 percent, on a similar basis).

The most significant change was the relative position of the Arabs, who now constituted 22 percent of the Palestinians in the west

---

[33] Which since then and to this day serves as a beacon for many.

(compared to 7 percent in 1914). In 1948, the Arabs became the third largest group among Palestinians, a group whose size was now significant. Another prominent change was the Druze, whose numerical strength grew significantly to become the fourth largest group among non-Jews west of the Jordan.

Ethnic Group	1948 – Prior to the Flight of the Refugees					
	Inhabitants in the West		Inhabitants in the East		Inhabitants in the Entire Country	
	Number	Percentage	Number	Percentage	Number	Percentage
Descendants of Israel	231,000	36%	187,000	27%	418,000	31%
Brethren of Israel	166,000	26%	7,000	1%	173,000	13%
Descendants of Israel in the Broader Sense	406,000	63%	194,000	28%	600,000	45%
Roman Army	41,000	6%	6,000	1%	47,000	4%
Arabs	126,000	20%	475,000	69%	601,000	45%
Distant Foreigners	25,000	4%	12,000	2%	37,000	3%
Druze	47,000	7%			47,000	4%
Total	645,000	100%	687,000	100%	1,332,000	100%

Table 25: Eretz-Israel Prior to the Flight of the Refugees in 1948.

On the basis of 360,000 inhabitants in eastern Eretz-Israel in 1914, some 200,000 Arabs had also settled in this area by 1948. In contrast, during the same period some 140,000 migrated from there to west of the Jordan. Taking into account natural population

163

growth, this period is summarized for lands east of the Jordan in Table 25 above. One observes that in absolute numbers, the Descendants of Israel in the east rose relative to 1914 due to natural increase, but this increase was very modest due to the departure of many Descendants of Israel for western Eretz-Israel. On the other hand, the number of Arabs rose significantly, and they became the decisive majority in the east. **In 1948, prior to the war, only 27 percent of the inhabitants of eastern Eretz-Israel were Descendants of Israel** (compared to 46 percent in 1914), and approximately **69 percent were Arabs** (compared to 44 percent).

The Significance of the Demographic Data on Eretz-Israel and the Fate of the Jews

Changes in the number of inhabitants in 1948 and the composition of the population compared to the situation in the year 1800, when the number of Jews by faith was marginal compared to others, throws into relief a very important fact: In the course of a century and a half, the number of non-Jewish inhabitants on both sides of the Jordan grew by a million[34] souls – compared to an increase to just above 650,000[35] among the Jews.

From the standpoint of absolute numbers, what becomes evident is that those who were considered Arabs increased greatly despite the process of a Return to Zion fueled by Zionism. In western Eretz-Israel alone there was almost a balance between the number of Jews and the number of non-Jews. **The situation in Eretz-Israel on the eve of the outbreak of the Second World War was even more serious:** At this juncture, even **west of the Jordan, non-Jews numbered 427,000, compared to 384,000 Jews.**

---

[34] 1,320,000 non-Jews in 1948 compared to 330,000 in 1800, including the populations in eastern Eretz-Israel.

[35] Approximately 660,000 in May 1948, compared to 8,000 in the year 1800.

164

The future of Eretz-Israel as a Jewish homeland was in great peril due to the inadequate numbers of Jews willing to respond to the Zionist call by actually immigrating to Eretz-Israel. At the other end of the ideological spectrum of Jewish life in the Diaspora stood the ultra-Orthodox (*haredi*) leadership who at the time, for the most part, were hostile to Zionism and considered it a rival force in Jewish life, and immigrating to Israel before the coming of the Messiah was an affront to the will of the Almighty. Their opposition was also based on experience and false Messianic hopes in the past. Since most of the leaders of the Zionist movement viewed nationality as the primary expression of Jewishness and turned their backs on religion, most of the *haredi* sector viewed them as heretics.

At the other end of the non-Zionist camp were many secular Jews who did not want to be considered Jews and sought to assimilate into the dominant culture, and viewed immigration to Eretz-Israel and establishment of a Jewish homeland as contrary to their own 'enlightened' outlook – a step backward into the past and 'fuel' for anti-Semites that would jeopardize all Jews. One cannot ignore that immigration embodied great sacrifices few were willing to take – the harsh conditions in what was largely a wasteland along with the hostility of the Arab majority. The last consideration, however, was the most decisive reason so few Jews answered the call: The overwhelming majority of Jews had not fallen exclusively under the spell of any of the three competing ideologies – the Zionists, the *haredim* or the assimilationists.

Only after the Holocaust did the majority of survivors come to the conclusion that Europe was not safe for Jews. Only the Holocaust brought the survivors of those interested in assimilation to understand that their fate would be no better than those Jews who openly professed their faith. Only after the Holocaust did a portion of those who followed *haredi* leadership realize that as a temporary substitute for the Messiah they had gotten Hitler.

Only the Holocaust led to an upsurge in the scope of Jewish immigration, led to acceptance of the 1947 Partition Plan by a majority of the UN General Assembly, and brought about establishment of the State of Israel, and the creation of a Jewish majority in the State of Israel and western Eretz-Israel as a whole! To this one needs to add the flight of Palestinian refugees in 1948 that greatly increased the margins of a Jewish majority west of the Jordan, and all the more so – within the Green Line and 'Israel Proper.' Only the Holocaust created among survivors the tremendous emotional vigor and determination needed to successfully repel Israel's adversaries in wars that pitted their small country against a coalition of enemies that, tragically, was driven and fueled by a mistaken Palestinian identity.

Divisiveness and conservatism among the Jews of Europe prevented significant immigration to Eretz-Israel before the Second World War. But the fault lay not only with the Jews. Besides the Nazis that bare by far, the main resposibility, there were other ugly and guilty parties. However, before exposing these other ugly partners it must be emphasized that no one can take away the main and complete resposibility of the German Nazis for the Holocaust. It is well known about the existence of many European collaborators with the Nazis that bare secondary guilt for parts of the Holocaust. But there were also other partners – especially one from the Middle East that is not so well known in this respect.

After the slaughter of Jews instigated by Haj Amin al-Husseini in 1929, the Palestinian leader dropped his aggressive policies for a time. The rise of the Nazis to power in Germany in 1933, however, and implementation of their anti-Jewish programs and escalating use of violence against Jews prompted the Mufti to embark on his own terror rampage against the Jews in the 1936-39 Arab Revolt.

The anti-Zionist terrorist behavior of Palestinian leadership, which reached its height in the 1936-1939 Arab Revolt, led British authorities to cut back Jewish immigration to a trickle. When

166

persecution of Jews in Germany began, the Jews had nowhere to flee. No country was willing to accept them, and the English prevented them from entering the place earmarked as their national home, the building of which Great Britain was duty-bound to execute as the appointed mandator on behalf of the League of Nations.

In 1937, well before the decision to embark on a Final Solution to the Jewish Problem (taken at the Wannsee Conference in January 1942 and chaired by Reinhard Heydrich) **Adolf Eichmann** was sent to Eretz-Israel to examine the alternative of transferring Jews to Eretz-Israel. In the German leadership there were proponents of two different approaches that appeared equally feasible for rendering Germany *Judenrein*: deporting the Jews to Eretz-Israel or exterminating them. The adamant opposition of the Mufti, Haj Amin al-Husseini, to deportation of Jews to Eretz-Israel strengthened the position of those who supported extermination. Surely the option of deportation was not taken due to any pro-Zionist sentiments; it was merely seen as a convenient avenue not only to get rid of the Jews but also for the Nazis to confiscate the assets of deportees.

If there is any doubt as to the degree of Haj Amin al-Husseini's influence among the upper echelons of Nazi leadership in regard to the Jews, one can learn much from the emigration papers that the Nazis gave Jews during the period when it was still possible to leave countries under their rule. The exit papers Nazi occupiers of Czechoslovakia gave Jews in 1940 – documents personally initialed by **Reinhard Heydrich** – gave the departees the right to go anywhere in the world **except territories of the Third Reich and Palestine!**

The influence of the Mufti on Hitler reached its peak in the Mufti's visit with the Fuehrer in Germany in 1941, prior to the Nazis' decision on a Final Solution. The Mufti of Jerusalem was considered a close ally of the Nazis in the Arab world. His collaboration included, for example, a motivational speech that al-

Husseini delivered before Muslims mobilized to serve in the Nazi Army in Tunisia.

It was not the Mufti's <u>direct</u> influence that led the Nazis to adopt the Final Solution path. **It was practical issues, the pressure of Palestinian terrorism under al-Husseini's leadership that prompted the British to prohibit large number of Jews from entering Eretz-Israel, left the Nazis no feasible alternative to expel Jews, prompting them to consider mass extermination as a solution.**

<u>The ramifications of the behavior of Palestinians' terror leadership and the British (i.e., the latter's surrender to the pressures of terrorism) was far reaching: Failing to carry out their duties according to the terms of the Mandate to realize the objectives of a Jewish homeland in Eretz-Israel and crowning Haj Amin al-Husseini as Palestinians' leader played a decisive role in the Holocaust of European Jewry.</u> <u>Eretz-Israel could have been a solution for more than six million European Jews who could have been forcefully transferred to Eretz-Israel even against their will, and contrary to the anti-Zionist opinions of a large percentage of established Jewish leadership, had Palestinian terror leadership not led the British to surrender to al-Husseini's anti-Jewish position and 'close the gates,' sealing the fate of six million Jews.</u>

Moreover, in 1941 the Mufti was among the heads of the revolt against the British headed by Rashid Ali al-Kaylani in an attempt to establish a pro-Axis regime in Iraq. Haj Amin al-Husseini hoped that in this manner, by expanding Nazi influence into neighboring countries, he could copy the Nazi's final solution vis-à-vis the Jews of the Middle East.[36] He established a Nazi youth movement among Palestinians whose members wore Nazi-style uniforms

---

[36] On part of the Mufti's expansive activities, including collaboration with the Nazis, see among others source 17 in the Bibliography.

168

bearing Nazi symbols, and even planned an **Auschwitz**-style extermination camp that he schemed to establish near Nablus.

In order to put things in proportion one must differentiate between motives and objectives on one hand, and the outcome, on the other. Conventionally, judgment of the actions of a given party is based on weighing together the motivations behind the person's actions and their objectives, with the actual results. In this context, in the face of the stark consequences, it is only fair to note that certainly the British, and, no doubt, even the Mufti himself, were not interested in European Jewry and had no desire to see its extermination. It was merely the situation in Eretz-Israel itself, exacerbated by the rise of the Nazis to power and their anti-Semitism, that brought the Mufti to act as he did in order to block, by any means at his disposal, a Jewish takeover of Eretz-Israel.

In general this volume, while trying to explain the motivations of the players in the conflict in Eretz-Israel, strives to be fair in its guilt-assigning – to present each side's culpability in all its severity so that both sides can learn to appreciate the grievous wrongdoing that lack of cognizance of the Palestinians' origins has led them to commit against one another, so that both sides can rectify their mistakes.

Up to the year 2005, the Holocaust was the first and the only victory Palestinian terrorist leadership could mark to their credit in their war against the Jews. While this victory was 'indirect,' the work of a third party, it eliminated six million Jews who could never become Zionists and immigrate to Eretz-Israel.[37]

---

[37] The second victory of the terror leadership was the Israel Disengagement from the Gaza Strip by a duly-elected Israeli government in August 2005. This act, a 'retreat' from a pattern of further Zionist settlement as the proper response to Arab violence that had characterized Zionism from its birth, was again an indirect victory, the work of others. Despite the tremendous differences in magnitude between these two 'victories' the notion that the Settler wear yellow stars as part of their

When one goes deeper into what was behind the series of events that created **the biggest calamity in the history of the People of Israel,** it becomes evident that **the most decisive albeit indirect factor that sparked this terrible process**, whose extremism brought, unconsciously, to the estrangement between Palestinian and Jews, **was none other than the Shi'ite Islamic leadership in Persia!** That caused the Brethern of Israel to forget their Jewish origins.

Such a far-reaching conclusion is voiced in order to put the words of the President of Iran Mahmoud Ahmadinejad in December 2005 into historic context when he said that Germany and Austria, due to their responsibility for the Holocaust that brought about the establishment of the Zionist state, have to earmark part of their territories in order to transfer the Zionist state there. Parallel to this, the Iranian leader spoke about the desire of the Iranian leadership to eliminate Israel, and denied the existence of the Holocaust.

Events in Eretz-Israel Prior to the 1948 War

Any survey of the British Mandate Period in Eretz-Israel cannot be concluded without mentioning that the Palestinian-Arab covenant at the time wasn't all-conclusive, just as it is not all-embracing today. During Israel's War of Independence there were many Palestinian villages and villagers who collaborated with the Israel Defense Forces. Many more sat quietly on the sidelines and did not participate in the fighting. They were the minority, but a significant minority which did not throw its lot in with Palestinian-Arab solidarity and preferred Palestinian-Jewish solidarity, or remaining neutral. With respect to this phenomenon, one should note that in 1936-1939 Palestinians from Samaria attacked Arab immigrants who came to their area.

---

protest movement (which was rejected) had substance that probably those who suggested it were unaware of.

170

There were also incidents of the opposite: Arab immigrants who attached veteran inhabitants – some 1,000 members of the Judham tribe who were murdered by Arabs in their midst between the years 1914-1948 because of disputes over land. The Arabs were hostile to the Judham tribe due to their longstanding sense of kinship with the Descendants of Israel.

In practice, most of the aggressiveness of Palestinians towards Jews was among the Brethren of Israel, who were from time to time joined by other groupings. One of the most outstanding phenomena in demographic-historical developments in Eretz-Israel was the flight of Palestinian refugees in the course of the 1948 War. Actually, realities were a bit different: Most of the Palestinian refugees fled prior to the 'official' outbreak of the war between the State of Israel and the Arab states that commenced on May 15th, 1948. The flight actually began in December 1947, immediately after the Partition Plan for western Eretz-Israel was approved by the United Nations, and limited warfare began. The Palestinians, who rejected the UN Partition Plan, launched a bloody battle against the Jews to prevent the partition implementation. The early stages of the 1948 War included clashes between organized units and terrorist attacks by armed Palestinian gangs on Jewish civilians in their places of residence and on the roads. Parallel to this, the two sides struggled to gain the upper hand by seizing militarily advantageous locations and strategic assets as soon as they were evacuated by the British – primarily army camps and fortified (Taggart) police stations.

The Arab states, that had announced in advance their intentions to invade Eretz-Israel after the departure of the British, actually began their invasions prior to May 15th. Syria and Iraq sent an army of irregular volunteers called the **Arab Liberation Army** (*Jaysh al-Inqadh al-Arabi*, henceforth, the ALA), under the field command of Fawzi Al-Qawuqji. The British did not interfere with the entrance of a foreign army. The Arabs threatened to send their

171

regular armies prior to completion of the British pullout if Mandatory authorities interfered with the ALA's movements.

The flight of the refugees was not a move planned in advance by the sides. It occurred due to a host of cascading events that preceded the outbreak of all-out war.

The most sensitive areas hit by Palestinian attacks were Jerusalem and the southern neighborhoods of Tel Aviv which were intertwined with the northern neighborhoods of Jaffa and partially surrounded by them. There were also raids on the Jewish neighborhoods themselves and torching of homes.

All these resulted, in addition to loss of life, in some 2,500 Jewish refugees who fled the southern neighborhoods for the center of Tel Aviv. The Palestinians also conducted a large number of terrorist acts in Jerusalem and on the roads to and from Tel Aviv – which reached their peak on February 22, 1948, when a car bomb in Jerusalem led to the death of 52 Jewish civilians and injury of countless others. This was a blow to the small Jewish community or Yishuv. The wounds of the 1936-1939 Arab Revolt – the loss of hundreds of Jews – had not yet healed. If the horrific losses in the war were not enough, during the 1948 War Jews faced the added horror of Palestinian mutilation of the bodies of Jews killed in action and the wholesale slaughter of POWs, behavior that is all too common in Arab culture. Such acts had two purposes: to embolden Arab combatants, and cause the public to join in the 'glorious victory,' and to scare and humiliate the enemy.

The Dir Yassin Incident

Because of the decisive role it plays in the Palestinians' founding narrative of their history, the Dir Yassin incident is dealt with here in great detail relative to the space given to other episodes in this volume. The incident was described as a great massacre that Jews perpetrated against Palestinians in a manner that led to the creation of the Palestinian refugee problem. In fact, there wasn't any

172

massacre to speak of at all, and the massacre described is based on false statistical data and manufactured news. On the other hand, actual massacres that were carried out by Palestinians, Arabs and Jews in the course of the war – including acts by Jews that were far more horrific than those purported to have taken place at Dir Yassin – (some of which will be described henceforth and in the appendix on refugees), hardly received any publicity.

Intelligence on the origins of perpetrators of terrorist attacks in Jerusalem and on the roads to and from the capital that the **ETZEL** (NMO – National Military Organization) headquarters had succeeded in gathering, parallel to news of the murder of wounded Jewish soldiers left on the battlefield at the **Castel**, pointed the guilty finger primarily at the inhabitants of **Dir Yassin**, a village on the outskirts of Jerusalem, not far from the highway that linked the coastal plain with Jerusalem.

Normally Dir Yassin was a tranquil village populated by Descendants of Israel. In the 1920s, Brethren of Israel residing in the village had participated in terrorist attacks in Jerusalem and on the roads to the city in 1921 and 1928. Later these Brethren of Israel left the village and established other villages in the Jerusalem corridor. At the outset of 1948, the *mukhtar* (village head) of Dir Yassin signed an agreement with Dir Yassin's Jewish neighbors to keep things quiet, promising to do whatever was required to keep the Palestinian gangs operating in the area from using the village as a base.

At the beginning of 1948, the area became the focus of battles and the Jews attacked villages of Brethren of Israel that had served as staging areas to attack Jews, particularly Jewish traffic on the road to Jerusalem. The inhabitants of these villages fled and some 70 settled in Dir Yassin as refugees. In addition 450 soldiers in the ALA moved from their concentration center in the area of **Ein Karem** to Dir Yassin. At this point the veteran villagers of Dir Yassin lost control of their own village, and some 30 marauders from armed Palestinian gangs succeeded in infiltrating the village.

All told, the 650 inhabitants of Dir Yassin found themselves in the midst of some 550 'uninvited guests' – most of them combatants.

Most of the combatants had no moral scruples and totally ignored any of the conventions of civilized war, behavior that has typified Palestinian violence since the beginning of the second *Intifada*, purposefully establishing their bases of operation among local civilians. The combatants at Dir Yassin built defense positions on the roofs of the villagers' homes in total disregard for the occupants' safety. The ETZEL received intelligence reports of activities within the village, on the presence of combatant forces and their intentions to use the village as a base to overrun the Jewish settlement **Motza** at a strategic point on the narrow road to Jerusalem, in order to totally cut off Jewish transport to Jerusalem.

The Jewish response to the growing threat to the city and Arab intensions to strangle the city's Jewish civilian population and defenders came swiftly. The results of the Jewish response and the impact it left on the Palestinian psyche were so deep that it is imperative to examine the details of the chain of events, if one is to lessen the hatred that events at the village kindled among Palestinians for generations to come.

On April 9, 1948, the ETZEL, together with the LECHI and in coordination with all other Jewish fighting forces (i.e., the Haganah) set forth to attack the Palestinian village to retaliate for attacks on Jewish convoys, and to put an end to the threat the village now presented. The attacking force encountered stubborn resistance from the foreign soldiers of the ALA and armed gangs hunkered down in the village who inflicted many casualties among the ETZEL, primarily wounded.

The ETZEL soldiers, witnessing mounting casualties among their comrades, had no choice but to liquidate the gun positions firing on them from above, and they blew up Palestinian houses on their occupants – after a Haganah vehicle with a loud speaker designed to call on the occupants to leave their homes got stuck outside the village and the order could not be heard within the village itself. In the course of the demolition, 60 non-combatants were killed among Dir Yassin's population. Subsequently, when the force came under fire from one of the houses, four other non-combatants were killed in the course of storming the building.

Towards the end of the battle, there was an incident in which a very small group of inhabitants surrendered to ETZEL forces. One of this group was a combatant disguised as a woman. When the 'woman' pulled out a weapon, one of the ETZEL soldiers opened fire on the group, fearing the surrender was a ploy to catch them off guard (as was the case in both the Six Day War and the Second Gulf War when 'surrendering' Arab combatants opened fire on their captors). The entire group was killed, including three non-combatants. Two other non-combatants were murdered in cold blood by ETZEL forces in the heat of the battle.

These two incidents and the large number of fatalities among non-combatants killed in the demolition of houses led to the mistaken conclusion among those who were unfamiliar with the details and the circumstances that a great massacre had taken place. In fact 69 non-combatants among the villagers were killed, most unintentionally in the chaos and confusion of the battle, as well as 23 Dir Yassin villagers who participated in the battle as combatants. All told, 92 residents of Dir Yassin were killed (a study by Bir Zeit University, which gathered testimonies from former residents of Dir Yassin, found between 92-110 of the village's residents were killed in the battle). In addition to these non-combatants, another 9 non-combatants among the refugees residing in the village were also killed.

The unavoidable product of an all-out attack on a fortified village left 210 Palestinians and other Arabs dead – 78 of them women, children and elderly persons, and 134 armed combatants, members of Palestinian gangs and ALA irregulars. The outcome was totally out of proportion compared to the toll Palestinian terrorism had exacted against Jews in their attacks prior to Dir Yassin which incurred painful losses but were not of the same magnitude as events at Dir Yassin. Yet, when one examines the broader picture including Jewish casualties during the 1936-1939 Arab Revolt which were *not* answered in kind, Dir Yassin appears in a quite a different light – as a reasonable response under prevailing circumstances.

On the surface, it would seem that the nine years separating the end of the Arab Revolt (1939) and the onslaught of local Palestinians on their Jewish neighbors following the UN's acceptance of the Partition Plan make any connection between the two irrelevant. The milieu, however, had changed, largely due to the loss of six million Jews in the Holocaust. And some of those who had survived the extermination camps had arrived in Eretz-Israel and joined the ETZEL.

Comprehension of the true magnitude of the Holocaust became evident to Jews in Eretz-Israel only towards the close of the Second World War (1945). The horrors of the Holocaust were still fresh in the minds of the Yishuv – both veterans and recent arrivals who had personally survived the inferno.

The ETZEL was by nature a military force that respected the rules of warfare and strove to avoid civilian casualties in use of its weapons (the principle of *tohar haneshek* in Hebrew, or 'purity of arms'). But the terrorist attacks perpetrated by armed Palestinian gangs, including murdering the wounded – combatants and citizens – left behind after their attacks, and mutilation of their bodies; the intentional targeting of women and children; and the ALA's disregard of moral restrictions in their low-intensity warfare against the Yishuv – all against the backdrop of the recent tragedies – sparked the uncompromising response on the part of ETZEL soldiers at Dir Yassin and their willingness to demolish houses where combatants were holding up, on the heads of all the occupants.

On the local level, what was mistakenly branded 'the Dir Yassin Massacre' sparked a genuine massacre by Palestinians on April 13th of a convoy of doctors and nurses en route to the Mt. Scopus campus of Hadassah Hospital, in which 62 Jewish doctors and nurses were murdered. The British, who had forces garrisoned nearby, did nothing to intervene and stop the carnage which lasted seven hours. By contrast to the ETZEL attack on Dir Yassin which was designed to combat marauders, the attack on the convoy – clearly marked as a convoy of medical personnel – was a deliberate attack against civilians, an 'act of revenge' that exacted a price of similar magnitude to those non-combatants killed, for the most part unintentionally, in the course of battle.

But the primary importance of the Dir Yassin incident was in the overall battlefront between Jews and the Arab states. The Palestinians took measures to spread the story of Dir Yassin far and wide – claiming there were no combatants in the village at the time of the attack and that all the dead were defenseless women and children who had been slaughtered. The secretary of the Arab-Palestinian Higher Committee specifically ordered refugees from the village to make up stories of an even higher death rate and every deed of massacre. The objective of spreading this lie was to hide from their own people their defeat in battle, to blacken the reputation of the Jews, and to lead the Arab states to respond forcefully. They were aided in this endeavor by some Jews – members of the Left, who sought to delegitimize the ETZEL and taint it with responsibility for a massacre. Members of the ETZEL, who wanted to give Palestinians some of their own medicine, to taste the bitter fruits of their own barbaric behavior and establish a deterrent, instill fear and awe and bolster the image of their prowess as a fighting force, intentionally inflated enemy casualties, claiming they had killed 254 Arabs at Dir Yassin.

The ramifications of events at Dir Yassin were far-reaching. On one hand, the Arab states were unaware of the atmosphere among the Jews at the time, and took no interest in the milieu within the

177

Yishuv. On the other hand, the Dir Yassin incident reverberated throughout the Arab world. Arab leaders were dragged into the conflict by Palestinian exaggerations and lies. The Arab states viewed the Jews' response in Dir Yassin through Palestinian eyes, and international media reports based on Jewish pronouncements distorted by vested-interests. As a result, they inflated civilian casualties even more, and hid the context of the ETZEL's actions to score political and public relations points.

The Arab states had already decided to invade western Eretz-Israel, a multi-pronged attack that was to take place immediately following the departure of the last British forces on May 14th, 1948. Due to the proximity of preparations for the invasion and events at Dir Yassin, the leaders of Syria and Lebanon (i.e., the most prominent being the Syrian head of state) called upon Palestinians in western Eretz-Israel to temporarily evacuate the country to avoid the perils of approaching war, and promised the inhabitants that they would return after the Arab armies had crushed the Jews.

These calls were issued via radio in neighboring countries whose broadcasts could be picked up in western Eretz-Israel and were heard primarily by those with closer ties to these countries. In other areas of Eretz-Israel only a small minority had radios that could receive the broadcasts on a regular basis. Palestinians in the center of the country, the majority of whom hailed originally from Egypt, tuned into the powerful signal of the Egyptian **Sa'ut al Arab** radio station that did not call for an evacuation.

The Arab-Palestinian Higher Committee also responded to the events at Dir Yassin in an exaggerated fashion, calling on Palestinians to abandon their homes and charging that those who stayed would be traitors to the cause. The head of the Arab League, **Azam Pasha,** went even farther, calling upon Palestinians to leave their homes to receive temporary shelter in neighboring states. The head of the League promised the Arab peoples that the Arab states armies' entrance into Jewish areas and Tel Aviv would be a

178

pushover, akin to a military parade. The Jews would be thrown into the sea and all their assets in Eretz-Israel attained during the Mandate Period would be inherited by returning Palestinians.

By contrast, King Abdullah of Trans-Jordan told Palestinians in the center of the country who appealed to him that they should stay put, but for the same reason: The Arab armies would come and crush the Jews. Once Abdullah also promised that the Jews would be defeated, there was no doubt in the minds of Palestinians that leaving their homes temporarily would not involve any serious damage. Moreover, the Palestinians feared that if they would not heed the calls to leave they would be placing themselves in harm's way. On one hand, they would be exposed to ALA shelling, on the other hand, by staying they would jeopardize being awarded the Jews' assets – booty that they had already decided how to allocate even before they left.

British Mandatory authorities encouraged Jews and Palestinians to leave mixed cities in which the other side had a decisive majority. While the Jews ignored the British calls and did not abandon Safed where Jews were a minority, Palestinians rushed to leave Tiberias.

The Flight of Most of the Palestinians in 1948

A large number of Palestinians panicked at the fierce Israeli response at Dir Yassin – fear propelled by the exaggerations in Arab media. **Most Palestinians whose roots in Eretz-Israel were not deep enough, and whose emotional tie with surrounding Arab countries was strong, responded to Arab leaders' and Palestinian leaders' calls, which they heard on Arab radio broadcasts.** In a period of several weeks following the Arab states' call to flee, in what became the **First Wave** of refugees, more than half the Palestinians residing west of the Jordan (i.e., a portion returned when they realized flight was a terrible mistake) took flight.

One could argue that in calling upon Palestinians to flee, the Arab states and the Arab-Palestinian Higher Committee created the Palestinian refugee problem. But on a deeper level, one could maintain that Palestinian devotion to aggression and terror, and adoption of illegitimate tactics in warfare and barbaric behavior sparked a harsh Jewish response while their endemic 'culture of lie-telling' provided the primary fuel that created the refugee problem.

Most of the flight was from three locations where the Jewish-state-in-the-making was forced to take defensive action in preparation for the invasion of the Arab armies. These activities transformed the Arab states' calls upon the Palestinians to leave their homes into a concrete issue that led Palestinians to follow their advice. The three were the cities of Haifa, Akko and Jaffa.

On the 21st of April the British announced that they were withdrawing their forces from the Haifa region to the Haifa Port area. In order to prevent the possibility that an invading Arab army would be able to join forces with the Palestinians in the city, the **Haganah** had to take control of the entire city within a day, including the Palestinian sector of the city adjoining the port. The Palestinians preferred to leave rather than surrender. They did so despite the entreaties of the Jewish mayor who called upon Palestinians to stay. The decision to leave was in the spirit of proclamations from the Arab states and those of their own Arab-Palestinian Higher Committee.

In essence, when the commander of Haganah forces called upon Haifa Palestinian leaders to surrender, the latter contacted Beirut to ask the advice of the Lebanese. The reply was almost immediate: "Leave the city. Don't fear for your property. Within a short time, you will return and receive the belongings of the Jewish residents, too." Except for a few thousand who chose to stay, 70,000 Palestinian left Haifa as refugees. Most were evacuated to Akko and to Lebanon by sea and overland via Nazareth.

180

Those evacuated to Akko and Nazareth later left Eretz-Israel. In Akko, crowding caused by the influx of so many refugees led to the outbreak of an epidemic that spread not only among the Haifa refugees but also local Akko residents, leading to the surrender of the city almost without resistance on May 16th (immediately after the invasion of the armies of neighboring Arab states). The takeover of Akko was designed to prevent the Lebanese Army from reaching Haifa. In the event of such an invasion, Akko would have been an important staging point and logistics base for attacking Haifa.

Most of the residents of Akko, including the refugees from Haifa, fled the city on the recommendation of the Arab states and due to the epidemic. The number of Palestinian refugees in the city was particularly large – some 100,000, a good percentage of the Haifa refugees. Akko was the most populated Palestinian city at the time, and even in earlier periods when Akko was the primary port in Eretz-Israel enjoyed economic prosperity as a city of commerce through which large quantities of goods and commodities passed. The port of Jaffa was not developed to the same extent. In the closing period of Crusader rule (1291) and particularly during the reign of Mohammed Ali's rule (1831-1840) Akko served as the seat of government of Eretz-Israel.

The economic-commercial prosperity that Akko enjoyed led to a tremendous growth in the number of residents of the city after the year 1914. Most of those who settled in the city were Descendants of Israel who came from east of the Jordan. Only the building of a modern port in Haifa in the year 1934 diminished Akko's hegemony over the region, though it didn't cause any significant reduction in the size of its population. On the other hand, the building of Haifa port greatly increased the number of Palestinian residents of Haifa.

Under the shadow of the approaching departure of the British army together with threats of invasion by the Arab states, the Jews feared that the Egyptian navy was liable to land in Arab Jaffa as a beachhead for mounting an attack on Tel Aviv.

In response to ongoing Palestinian attacks on Tel Aviv's southern neighborhoods bordering Jaffa, and to counter any plans of an Egyptian landing, the ETZEL entered Jaffa on April 25th, 1948. The ETZEL infantry units, accompanied by a relatively weak armored contingent compared to British tanks protecting the Palestinians, had little success. But ongoing mortar fire on Jaffa and the explosion of barrels of TNT that ETZEL sappers placed close to Palestinian sniper positions created widespread panic among residents of the city, beyond the military and civilian casualties they caused. Under cover of the chaos in the war-torn city, Iraqi volunteers from the ALA, who were supposed to defend the city, engaged in sacking the city and acts of rape. The price of food skyrocketed. Under the impact of the Arabs' and the Palestinian leaderships' call to take flight, most Jaffa residents decided to leave, and in their wake the gang members retired, as well. On May 13th, the minority who remained surrendered to Jewish forces.

Out of 60,000 residents of Jaffa, some 50,000 left. A small portion of the refugees – 14,000 – left the area that was included within the Green Line at the end of the war, including those who were evacuated by sea to Port Said and Beirut. Most of those who took flight initially took shelter in surrounding Palestinian villages on the environs of Jaffa (i.e. well within the Green Line) for instance **Yazur** (Azur, today) and **Beit Dagon**.

After the conquest of Jaffa, Israeli army forces approached these villages in the course of solidifying Jewish control of Tel Aviv's environs and securing the main road leading towards Jerusalem adjacent to Yazur and Beit Dagon. Conditions within the villages had deteriorated, swelled by the influx of so many refugees, prompting Jaffa residents to flee farther afield as the battlefront approached. Most fled to the Gaza Strip and further south. Their flight led to the flight of an additional 10,000 Palestinians villagers, as well.

Israeli positions established to block enemy troops from advancing towards Jewish areas also prevented supply of basic foodstuffs to such Arab villages scattered 'behind Jewish lines of defense,' contributing to the flight of these Palestinians.

Gradually, in a slow trickle, another 75,000 Palestinians whose villages one-by-one became a war zone picked up and left, often even before the arrival of Israeli soldiers. Some 4,000 were killed in the course of their flight, and another 9,000 left the Judea region due to severe food shortages. Approximately 7,000 were intentionally expelled by Israeli forces in what became the **Last Wave** of refugees. More details on the refugees can be found in Appendix 2.

After the first wave of refugees the Israeli leadership realized that the refugees' flight constituted a good solution to the problem of an Arab minority in the nescient Jewish state – by reducing its scope. As a result, the Jewish leadership embarked on a policy that later would be branded "ethnic cleansing" by its critics. In the course of 'priming' the exodus, the Israelis carried out a small number of massacres that were designed to spark the flight of Palestinian inhabitants. In the last wave, villages in the Jerusalem Corridor were razed and their inhabitants banished. Parallel to this, the Palestinians and the Arabs didn't refrain from carrying out their own atrocities, as noted above.

As the refugees took flight, the desire to expand the borders of the Jewish state beyond those designated in the Partition Plan without adding more Palestinian inhabitants took form. This aspiration led to very severe acts in the course of the war in which Israeli forces shot at refugees, primarily in the south, in order to empty the area and keep them on the move. As noted above, such acts led to the deaths of many Palestinians. This policy led to the demolition of many Galilee villages emptied as the residents fled, to ensure the inhabitants could not return. All the horrific acts committed by Jews must be examined against the backdrop of the invading Arab countries' promise to expel the Jews and to give their homes to Palestinians. The actions of the Jews pale by comparison with what the Arabs had in store, given a chance. More details on the refugee issue, including atrocities committed, are discussed in Appendix 2.

Summary of Refugee Figures from the 1948 War

All told, the number of Palestinians who fled their homes in the 1948 War and did not return on their own accord (based on details of the data in Appendix 2) was approximately 321,000. After calculation of those who fled and were killed or died of other causes in the course of their flight, some 315,000 arrived at their destinations. The number of Palestinians who survived the aftermath of the war was 312,000, after discounting those who subsequently died of hunger and other hardships – offset by births. Among them, 223,000 left western Eretz-Israel. Approximately 25,000 were left in Judea and Samaria, including 21,000 in refugee camps and some 4,000 who were residents of the Arab neighborhoods of west (i.e., Jewish) Jerusalem who settled in houses abandoned by refugees from east Jerusalem. Approximately 64,000 remained in the Gaza Strip – most in refugee camps. If one offsets those refugees who resided illegally in the places from which they fled, the number of genuine refugees drops to only 242,000.[38]

Out of 312,000 refugees remaining, 263,000 fled beyond the Green Line. Due to the urgings of the Arab states, the others fled in the First Wave from_Judea, Samaria and the Gaza Strip. Later due to hunger, others left these areas. Many others fled from there due to their calls, but later returned.

---

[38] Legally, one who claims refugee status has to be a legal resident of the place from which he or she took flight, and those who resided in western Eretz-Israel illegally prior to their flight certainly have no grounds for legal redress due to their plight.

The demographic data above challenges the number '660,000 refugees' officially claimed by the Palestinians. How Palestinians arrived at this inflated number that exceeds the entire Palestinian population residing west of the Jordan prior to the flight deserves explanation.

After the war, Israel agreed, within the framework of the Armistice Agreement with Jordan, to repatriate some 20,000 refugees who had fled to Trans-Jordan. As a **result the number of refugees from the 1948 War who left the territory that became the State of Israel and survived as refugees was 243,000. The total number of refugees in** 1948, after taking into account those allowed to return and negative population growth due to hardship and hunger among the refugees **was, in the last analysis, approximately 292,000.** The number of refugees who remained in western Eretz-Israel totaled approximately 203,000.

After the war, the Arabs admitted that 68 percent of the refugees fled without so much as seeing an Israeli soldier. And from Palestinian eye-witness reports of their flight from Jaffa and from the surrounding plains, it becomes evident that those fleeing did not encounter a single Israeli soldier before taking flight. The same was the case elsewhere when panic spread to epidemic proportions before the escapees could see the lack of effectiveness of the invasion of the Arab states, believing they were running out of harm's way and would return to claim their property. Some, mostly their offspring, still hope to do so one day, for their leaders adamantly demand the Right of Return.

In the name of accuracy, it would seem that the 68 percent that the Arabs claim left in the First Wave refer to the 71 percent of all 321,000 refugees. If one adds those who left due to hunger in Judea, the number who left due to reasons that have no direct link to this or that military action, it becomes evident that 74 percent of the refugees left of their own accord due to hardships of war, chaos and fear and false promises by their own leaders.

185

From an ethnic standpoint, 203,000 refugees who left Eretz Israel west of the Jordan River in the wake of the 1948 War and did not return or were not returned included 112,000 Brethren of Israel and some 13,000 Arab immigrants and a similar number of Druze. All told, 138,000 or 68 percent of those who left the country were foreign to western Eretz-Israel and therefore the Right of Return is irrelevant in their regard.

Total non-Jews prior to the 1948 Flight	636
In Judea and Samaria	176
In the Gaza Strip	67
Within the Green Line	393
Fled in the First Wave	230
Gradual, Flight	75.5
New Refugees who Left due to Hunger	9
The Last Wave	6.7
Total Number of Refugees who Left	321
Fled from Judea and Samaria	27
Fled from the Gaza Strip	23
Fled from Inside the Green Line	271
Perished in their Flight	-7.5
Total Number of Refugees who Arrived	315
Landed outside western Eretz-Israel	225
Landed in the Gaza Strip	64
Landed in Judea and Samaria	25
Negative Natural Growth	-3
Returned from Trans-Jordan	-20
Surviving Refugees	292
Refugees who remained beyond Western Eretz-Israel	203
Refugees beyond Eretz-Israel who fled from inside the Green Line boundary	152

Table 26: Number of Refugees (in thousands) by the stages of Flight and Arrival in Refugee Camps.

Of the remaining refugees who left western Eretz-Israel – all told 32 percent – they comprised some 56,000 Descendants of Israel, 8,500 Descendants of the Roman Army and 700 Kurds. In theory, the Descendants of Israel have the Right of Return to Judea and Samaria (a concept that becomes practical only if they accept the legitimacy of the concept of Return. The Right of Return in practical terms is dealt with in Chapter 9).

Only about 4 percent out of those fleeing western Eretz-Israel – the Descendants of the Roman Army – had the Right of Return in principle, on a personal level, to areas *within* the Green Line. In addition there are another 28,000 Descendants of the Roman Army who have a similar Right of Return from the Gaza Strip. The Kurds (3 percent) have the Right of Return to east Jerusalem.

Thus, out of all the refugees who survived the war and its immediate aftermath, and remained refugees in 1949, both within and beyond the borders of western Eretz-Israel, the scope of those from outside western Eretz-Israel who theoretically hold the Right of Return to Judea and Samaria is 19 percent. The scope of those with the Right of Return within the Green Line is only 11 percent.

Analyzing the Collective Psyche of Musta'arabim and Refugees

The discussion that follows explains the background for why and how the Palestinians conducted a huge fraudulent operation beginning in 1948. The need to go into detail of the false figures reported and the 'doctoring' that took place is not designed to present anyone as a cheat or a liar. Rather it is because it is imperative to ascertain what the real numbers are and to prevent the issue from continuing to be driven by erroneous data. The true numbers enable us to formulate a just solution to the conflict in Eretz-Israel and put it into action, while a solution based on the erroneous and inflated data is unacceptable to the Jews due to the demographic risk entailed. The main reason this must be settled is that inaccurate record-taking in 1948 in the granting of refugee status was 'carried forward' for decades, left to impact even on the statistics that both sides officially accept today.

The deception was not the work of a small group of individuals 'doctoring the data' behind the scenes; countless individual Palestinians participated in it and therefore one cannot discuss this aspect of the conflict without examining the psychological dimension and the circumstances that led so many Palestinians to take this path – elements that, in fact, put the need to take such a deceptive step in a *positive* light – one that any student of the conflict needs to take into consideration.

This analysis is not designed to make generalizations about the majority of the Palestinian public, and certainly does not purport to suggest that similar behavior might be a 'pattern' in other domains. The objective is to explain why certain Palestinians have behaved in a certain way under certain circumstances.

The phenomenon of readiness to lie began some one thousand years earlier with the appearance of the first *Musta'arabim* and the duality it required – a very complex process unfamiliar to most people. An entire public, a large public relatively speaking, had to live dual lives, to act as if they belonged to one identity (Muslim) outwardly, while ascribing to another identity (in most cases, Jewish) inwardly. This kind of double existence exists among spies, theater actors and IDF *Mista'arbim* today.

The double lives of spies and members of special *Mista'arabim* units is temporary and enjoys state support. Among actors, roles change from time to time and the number of hours on the stage 'as another person' is limited, liberating the actor to 'be himself' most of the time. Moreover, most of the individuals who engage in such dual roles choose to do so and receive special training.

188

By contrast, the *Musta'arbim* were forced by circumstance to adopt dual lives without end or relief, without any external support apparatus, without any guidance or training. They did not willingly or freely choose this situation. In fact, they passed on this fate from generation-to-generation, a fact that added to the difficulty, while at the same time gaining some 'training' and 'sophistication' in the art of subterfuge. Thus, over generations, special behavioral patterns became engrained among *Musta'arbim*, which are hard for outsiders to pinpoint or comprehend.

Games of 'let's pretend' (*ya'ani* or 'as if' in Arabic) – sophisticated fabrications and lie-telling – became the daily bread and life elixir for *Musta'arbim* and their offspring. This schizoid-type behavior – laying out one scenario outwardly in the presence of strangers, and playing out another conflicting scenario inwardly – became insignificant in importance, almost second nature over the generations. Repeated use of false promises and pretensions, assuming in the long-term eventually bad times would pass, became rooted in the culture. Inventing fancy excuses when caught in the act became commonplace, part of the personality makeup that hardly required any effort at all.

As fate would have it, the price that *Musta'arabim* paid, and pay to this day, is a mindset of behavioral codes that Palestinian *Musta'arabim* take for granted as legitimate, since most of the public behaves this way, and outward duplicity is hardly unique or out of place. A large percent of the Palestinian public hasn't a clue that there is something wrong in this unique behavioral system.

When one confronts this phenomenon, it may sound like an accusation; however, one must recognize and appreciate the fact that **the source of this odd behavior of *Musta'arabim* and their offspring is an undying devotion to the Religion of Israel and even more so to the People of Israel and the Land of Israel**. Such behavior emanates from the ability to stubbornly survive.

The above insights are important to grasp, first of all by those Jews who feel disgusted and 'turned off' by the behavior of the

189

Musta'arbim and by other Jews who hope these descendants of their own people will simply disappear from the scene.

Jews who loath Palestinians due to the lack of truthfulness some exhibit should keep in mind that it was evil foreigners who caused this type of behavior. And for the sake of balance, one should also recall that there were other evil-doers who created a negative stereotype of the crafty unreliable two-faced Jew over the generations regarding a large portion of European Jews, 'as *they* juggled private and public faces' in order to survive.

European regimes that discriminated against Jews, forbidding them for lengthy periods to own land or till the soil, forced Jews to engage in commerce, middlemanship, money lending and banking. Hard-pressed European peasants, taken advantage of by feudal masters, despised the Jews whom they perceived as both greedy exploiters and parasitic deadbeats.

European elites channeled part of the hatred of the masses into hatred of the Jews – a canard that fell on the fertile ground of Christianity's portrayal of Jews as 'Christ killers.' Thus, conditions for which repressive European regimes were responsible (together with the Church) forged the negative image of the Jew – which was further fueled by the existential necessity any persecuted group has to use subterfuges just in order to survive – behavior that when it took root, hardly endeared Diaspora Jews to their neighbors.

Use of subterfuge as a way of life by Palestinians can only be judged against the 'impossible' conditions Jews and *Musta'arabim* share, and the truly miserable state of Palestinian refugees, regardless of who is responsible for their state. The misery of the refugees is not a matter to be taken lightly and it would not be fair to present their behavior, the unique coping mechanisms they developed, without taking into account what they endured – suffering that is hard for ordinary people to even imagine,

190

conditions that can cause people to do things out of desperation that ordinarily they would never consider doing.

Before discussing the backdrop to falsification of the number of refugees in Judea, Samaria and Gaza – data that has inflated the numbers greatly – it is imperative to keep in mind that most of the population, both refugee and other inhabitants of these areas, were relatively needy prior to becoming refugees. Most of the refugees lost the little assets they had and were left without anything. The more affluent among the refugees lost everything, and experienced a tremendous drop in their standard of living. Many were left with no more than the clothes on their backs – perhaps a change of clothes, a few animals, a push cart, at best.

Many lost family members who were killed in battle or succumbed under the harsh conditions on the roads and in the places in which they took refuge. Some fell ill and became a burden for others whose lives were already precarious and harsh. All breadwinners lost their livelihoods, their lands or their businesses. Some lost their health or their very lives. Most of the refugees were left without any means of eking out even a minimal existence. Most, prior to their flight, had their own houses, and in the course of their flight became homeless. They slept in the open, and later were housed in crowded conditions in tent cities. Suffering from hunger, UNRWA was created by the United Nations, providing modest food supplies.

This humanitarian crisis was not the result of a natural disaster. Rather, it was the work of human beings, regardless of who or which side bears the blame. The desperate refugees, who for the most part lacked any source of livelihood, understood they were the victims of their own actions or the blunders of others or the brutality of the Jews. Many lost their faith in humanity and considered themselves entitled to substantial compensation for their losses and undeserved suffering. Under prevailing conditions of administrative chaos in 1948, many refugees were unable to withstand the temptation to improve their lot by obtaining for

191

themselves and their families extra food rations – particularly after the trauma of hunger and uncertainty they had so recently undergone in the course of the war. So, they sought ways to stockpile some reserves for a rainy day, to stave off the prospect of famine that had already claimed lives in the course of and in the aftermath of the war.

Deception was not planned in advance, but rather was a spontaneous albeit widespread response appearing when UNRWA officials created a loophole that enabled the Palestinians, through cunning and fabrications, to 'enhance' their entitlements to assistance. Taking advantage of the windfall that had fallen in their laps also entailed sympathetic UNRWA officials who were merely trying to alleviate the refugees' plight, but created a major stumbling block to a solution of the refugee problem.

Events in the Wake of the Flight and How Doctoring of the Facts Began

After the signing of the Armistice Agreement in 1949 there were 138,000 non-Jews living within the Green Line. Among them 17 percent were Arabs, most of whom were returned from Jordan (which changed its name to Jordan from Trans-Jordan after it annexed Judea and Samaria). Prior to their return, almost all the Arabs who resided in this area (i.e., Israel proper) had taken flight.

Judea, Samaria and Gaza received some 89,000 refugees from inside the Green Line in the course of their flight. Twenty-five thousand refugees joined the 149,000 permanent village and town residents of Judea and Samaria. The number of refugees in Judea and Samaria reported by the Palestinians (200,000) was greater than the number of residents reported there after the war and **inflated the number of refugees in Judea and Samaria by 700 percent!**

The number of refugees in Judea and Samaria was inflated by 175,000 persons – based on 175,000 residents including

refugees and a small natural increase, that is the number of the **overall population** was inflated by 100 percent! This was possible by counting refugees twice: In order to receive increased funding, each of the refugees identified himself under two different identities before UNRWA officials to receive more than one ID card. In addition, inhabitants who weren't refugee at all claimed to be refugees (along with the bogus refugee's genuine identity) in order to be eligible for material assistance of UNRWA, as well.

Some 44,000 longtime residents in the Gaza Strip (i.e., native Gazans) were joined by 64,000 refugees from within the Green Line. As a result there were 109,000 inhabitants (refugees, Gazans and natural population growth) at the close of the war. This figure is a little bit more than half the total number of refugees reported by the Palestinians as residing there (200,000).

Inflation of the number of refugees in the Gaza Strip was 'only' by 136,000 persons or 212% (compared to 700 percent in Judea and Samaria), **but it was a 125% increase** in the **overall population** of Gaza (compared to 100% inflation in Judea and Samaria). Twin identities operated here as in Judea and Samaria. What led to a higher level of fictitious identities relative to Judea and Samaria was the use of the names of the same people who had fled from Gaza (primarily relatives) in order to ensure their status as refugees if they would be repatriated, while in the meantime enjoying their kin's entitlements as refugees. And there were some cases of individuals who succeeded in obtained three UNRWA identity cards. Widespread fraud was set in motion by UNRWA officials' decision to take into account (rightly so) registration of refugees who had not taken with them any documentation, solely on the strength of their declaration that they were refugees, without proof of residency, not to mention *legal* residency. Like many others, such undocumented refugees had nothing but the clothes on their backs, and it would have been unreasonable to bar them from receipt of humanitarian assistance for lack of documentation. Thus,

193

UNRWA provided them with the only status document they would subsequently carry – that of a refugee.

Palestinians who prior to their flight had sojourned illegally within the Green Line, and had no Mandatory identity card to prove their residency within the Green Line, took advantage of this loophole. In intake interviews with UNRWA staff, they claimed that their documents had been left behind when they took flight, thus gaining official refugee status fraudulently from a formal-legal standpoint, but rightfully from a humanitarian standpoint.

A portion of the longtime residents of Judea and Samaria and Gaza, who were poor, were jealous of their refugee brethren. The latter received food allocations and other assistance from UNRWA. When such Gazans learned that they could 'work the system' by signing up at UNRWA offices as refugee camp dwellers based solely on a 'declaration,' countless Gaza families registered as refugees and were issued refugee cards under their genuine names or bogus ones, but with a slight change of address, to a nearby refugee camp. As this phenomenon spread, more and more permanent residents came to carry two identity cards – one, a refugee ID card from UNRWA bearing the address of a refugee camp, and another ID card with their actual identity and address.

As the rumors of the 'option' spread, even the honest and the timid, who had failed to join in, jumped on the bandwagon when they saw the ease with which UNRWA handed out ID cards without question, without danger of exposure. The few who failed to take advantage of this 'giveaway' were viewed as naïve, stupid or plain cowards. Few stood up to the temptation to freeload a livelihood or 'subsidize' their standard of living at international expense, thus almost every family head ultimately obtained refugee status from UNRWA for himself and his family – at times holding multiple cards that doubled and tripled the windfall.

194

Summary of the Overall Figures after the 1948 War

From an ethnic standpoint, compared to the situation in western Eretz-Israel on the eve of the 1948 War, the flight of the refugees reversed the decline in the portion of the overall population that was a Descendent of Israel in the Narrow Sense, a trend that took place due to immigration between 1840 and 1948 of ethnic Arabs; the percentage of Descendants of Israel in the Narrow Sense rose as a product of the war.

1949 – After the Refugees' Flight and Return of Some						
Ethnic Group	Inhabitants in the West		Inhabitants in the East		Inhabitants in the Entire Country	
	Number	Percentage	Number	Percentage	Number	Percentage
Descendants of Israel	175,000	41%	200,000	27%	375,000	32%
Brethren of Israel	50,500	12%	40,000	5%	90,500	8%
Descendants of Israel in the Broader Sense	225,500	53%	240,000	32%	465,500	40%
Roman Army	32,000	8%	6,000	1%	38,000	3%
Arabs	109,000	26%	485,000	65%	594,000	51%
Distant Foreigners	24,000	6%	12,000	2%	36,000	3%
Druze	32,500	8%	2,000	0%	34,500	3%
Total	423,000	100%	745,000	100%	1,168,000	100%

Table 27: Population of Eretz-Israel at the end of the Flight of the Refugees and the Return of a Minority.

Among those who left the region west of the Jordan and those who perished in the 1948 War, approximately half were Brethren of Israel and only an estimated 17 percent were Arab immigrants. The refugees who were repatriated from east of the Jordan to areas

195

now within the State of Israel were Arab immigrants and their offspring who returned to their pre-war homes. This gesture reduced by 8 percent the magnitude of Arab immigrants and their descendants among the Palestinians who had left the region west of the Jordan. The composition of the non-Jewish population in the aftermath of the war is displayed above in Table 27.

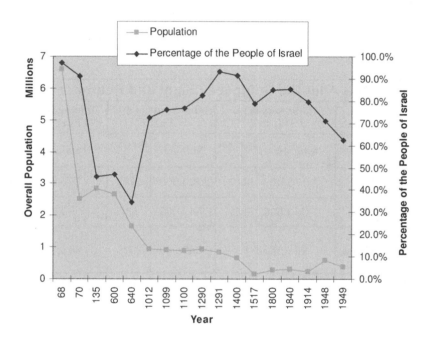

Graph 4: A Decline in the Percentage of Descendants of Israel in the Broader Sense among Palestinians between 1840 and 1949 (from 1914, western Eretz-Israel only).

Once Distant Foreigners and Druze (who are not Palestinians by self-ascription or history) are removed from the data base of the composition of Palestinians, one finds that the post-war Palestinian population was 374,000. In other words, **the percentage of Descendants of Israel in the Broader Sense dropped from 70 percent before the war to 61 percent in its aftermath.**

196

Descendants of Israel in the Narrow Sense constituted 48 percent of the Palestinians west of the Jordan in 1949 – an increase from 40.5 percent prior to the war. On the other hand, the percentage of Brethren of Israel declined from 29.5 percent to 14 percent, the most significant change of all wrought by the war. Among the Arabs, one witnesses a significant change as well – an increase from 22 percent to 30 percent of the Palestinian population west of the Jordan, although their numbers within the Green Line diminished.

Emigration and Transit of Inhabitants of Western Eretz-Israel after 1949

The period between 1949 (the aftermath of the 1948 War) and 1967 (prior to the Six Day War) was marked by emigration of Palestinians out of Judea and Samaria (which at the time had been annexed to Trans-Jordan, which named Judea and Samaria the West Bank, after changing its name to Jordan) and out of the Gaza Strip (which was governed by Egypt). Most of the emigrants were refugees who had fled in the 1948 War to these areas. Most residents of the refugee camps were not given the opportunity to settle in regular dwellings and get on with their lives since Arab leaders and the Palestinians themselves wanted to perpetuate the refugee problem. But due to a high birth rate, the crowding in the camps became unbearable, leading some to emigrate.

Another decisive factor at the time was lack of employment opportunities or agricultural land that would have allowed the refugee public – whose numbers simply grew through natural increase fueled by forced idleness and the UNRWA dole – the source of a livelihood. The lack of employment also helped Palestinian leaders mobilize a small percentage of the population to engage in terrorist activity against Israel. The attacks led to Israeli retaliatory raids that further undermined the morale of the refugees. Emigration was viewed as the only out, primarily to the

Persian Gulf States where oil production created a burgeoning labor market eager to employ them.

The situation in the Gaza Strip was much worse: a semi-arid climate and high population density, crowding exacerbated by a high birth rate in a limited space and the lack of employment opportunities. Moreover, the economic situation in Egypt was inferior to that in Jordan at the time. As a result, many migrated from the Gaza Strip and even from south of Rafiah and the vicinity to the dwelling places and holdings (and even to the mud huts) in Judea and Samaria, abandoned by inhabitants who had fled east of the Jordan.

During this period, most of the refugees who were Descendants of the Roman Army who found themselves dwelling as refugees in the Gaza Strip and in south Rafiah migrated to Judea and Samaria. They numbered some 55,000. Prior to their flight from areas left inside the Green Line, this sub-sector of the Palestinian population was the wealthiest within Palestinian society. They were quickly fed up with conditions within the refugee camps, the idleness and the arid climatic conditions. Consequently, they migrated to areas in Judea and Samaria that were more suitable to their temperament, where most of the inhabitants were Descendants of Israel with whom the Descendants of the Roman Army had much in common.

A significant portion of the Arab immigrants among the refugees followed suit. They were primarily interested in employment and standard of living – the factors that had drawn them to Eretz-Israel in the first place. There was no opportunity for employment or improvement of their standard of living in the Gaza camps.

Among the Brethren of Israel in the Gaza Strip, only a small portion – several thousand – migrated to Judea and Samaria. This population was tired of wandering. The climatic conditions, the scarce rainfall, were familiar elements in their family narratives and origins. In essence, historically this grouping had never migrated on its own initiative, only in response to external pressures that transformed realities. During this period, some 20,000 refugees who were Brethren of Israel who had sojourned in Saudi Arabia under harsh conditions migrated to Judea and Samaria. A similar number of this group returned from Saudi Arabia to their ancestral lands east of the Jordan.

A small number of Bedouin Brethren of Israel, who had migrated in 1957 from the State of Israel to the Gaza Strip, moved in the opposite direction. These Bedouin were Israeli citizens who were hostile to the Jewish state. They took advantage of the short period after the Sinai Campaign (1956), when Israel controlled the Gaza Strip, to leave Israel, since it was clear Israeli forces would withdraw from Sinai and the Gaza Strip. Most settled down in permanent dwellings that others who had left for Judea and Samaria left behind, primarily in the refugee camps, and ceased to be pastoral Bedouin.

The shifts in population, from the Gaza Strip, the emigration from the Strip and from Judea and Samaria out of western Eretz-Israel entirely, the migration to Judea and Samaria and natural population increase, all contributed to demographic change in these areas. The number of inhabitants of Judea and Samaria prior to the 1967 Six Day War was more than 600,000, while in the Gaza Strip there were only 154,000 persons. This data includes residents of east Jerusalem.

The Egyptians carried out an annual population appraisal in the Gaza Strip. The estimate for 1966 (including southern Rafiah) was 455,000. According to a May 31, 1967, UNRWA report (a week before the outbreak of the Six Day War) the refugee population of the Gaza Strip was 317,000, including 202,000 in refugee camps. In fact, in 1967 there were more than 400,000 'identities' in the Strip, including over 250,000 bogus identities. The magnitude of 'non-existent' persons stood at 170 percent of the actual population.

199

The portion of bogus persons in the Strip had grown from 125 percent in 1949 to 170 percent in 1967. This increase was assisted by some 100,000 who migrated from the Gaza Strip to Judea and Samaria, and others who went to the Gulf States during the corresponding period. Through various maneuvers, others still in the Strip managed to receive the food rations of those who had left. Others left behind with kin one of the two refugee documents each refugee possessed, so they could use them in their absence, or use the document left to request a new original for a worn document where the picture was 'lost.'

Renewal of the second document included updating the picture ID and address of the new recipient. There was no danger that UNRWA personnel would notice, since the original 'lost' card in the Gulf States card was not being used to draw rations. The old worn and faded pictures were of little value when the person 'borrowing' the original card holder's identity was of similar age and appearance, all the more so when the bearers were two veiled women...

The population in Judea and Samaria was monitored in an entirely different manner due to the difference in governance. The Jordanians conducted a population census in the year 1961, but there were no follow-ups. The 1961 census was carried out prior to the shifts in population described above. The population was 730,000 inhabitants, without east Jerusalem. This statistic included, of course, a very large number of 'double identities.'

The 1967 Refugees

During and immediately following the Six Day War, some 290,000 inhabitants of Judea and Samaria fled across the Jordan. Most of the new refugees left for no concrete reasons other than their historic fear of the Israelis. A small minority were city dwellers who lived in proximity to the Mediterranean coast who fled after the Israeli army began to demolish their houses to broaden the section in the center of the country where the Green Line ran a mere 12 miles from the shoreline.[39]

Among those who fled were 65,000 Descendants of Israel and some 39,000 Brethren of Israel. Another 119,000 were Arab immigrants and their descendants, and 67,000 were Descendants of the Roman Army who all – like most of the Arabs who fled – were new in the area and did not feel at home. For all of the latter, their 1967 flight was the third time they had fled since 1948.

In essence, as was the case in 1948, one could argue that the Arab immigrants and their offspring who fled in 1967 took flight from a land that was not their own. Prior to the 1967 war, the 1948 refugees constituted a significant portion of the population of Judea and Samaria. All the Arabs in Judea and Samaria, except for east Jerusalem and a minority in Hebron, were refugees and a large percentage lived in refugee camps, and harbored a deep-seated hatred and fear of Israelis and were easily 'spooked' into take flight, whether justified or not. Thus, almost all the Arabs who fled in 1967 were 1948 refugees. Descendants of the People of Israel who fled, returned to their nomadic 'pendulum-like' patterns of movement between the two parts of Eretz-Israel, and were part of the immigrants (and their offspring) who previously had migrated westward from the east up until 1948.

As for the Brethren of Israel, in their flight from Judea and Samaria they returned to their ancestral lands. Furthermore, since in 1949 no Brethren of Israel remained in Judea and Samaria, all the refugees of this origin in 1967 were already refugees in 1948 who arrived in Judea and Samaria in 1949 from the Gaza Strip and from Saudi Arabia. Almost all of the members of this group who had fled to Jordan were, in any case, repatriated later on.

Only 67,000 Descendants of the Roman Army, 23 percent of all those who fled in 1967, and some 1,000 Kurds (3 percent) were

---

[39] Primarily the Arab villages of Tul Karem and Kalkilia, in the area often labeled due to the shape of pre-1967 borders – "Israel's narrow hips."

201

permanent residents and had left lands they had lived on for a very long time, although the former were not permanent residents of the areas they fled from in 1967. The Descendants of the Roman Army who fled in 1967 were all 1948 refugees and their offspring who were forced to flee a second time. Prior to 1948, the Descendants of the Roman Army had not resided in Judea and Samaria at all.

In short, the 1967 war did not add any refugees to speak of to those already claiming the Right of Return from 1948 – excluding 22 percent (65,000) that consisted of Descendants of Israel and Kurds. Theoretically, the Descendants of Israel have the Right of Return to Judea and Samaria and the Kurds to east Jerusalem. The only significant change in the rights of refugees wrought by the 1967 war regards 8% of the 1948 refugees, Descendants of the Roman Army. Even prior to the war, they had the Right of Return, on an individual basis and theoretically, from the Gaza Strip (the majority) or from places beyond the borders of western Eretz-Israel, to within the Green Line.

In 1967 most the refugees who were Descendants of the Roman Army went to Jordan (that is, eastern Eretz-Israel) and only a minority stayed in Judea, Samaria and the Gaza Strip (which had been taken over by Israel). Due to the war, these 8 percent of the refugees have the Right of Return, on a personal basis and theoretically, to within the Green Line, primarily from Jordan and less from Judea, Samaria and the Gaza Strip. In addition, the number of Descendants of Israel theoretically holding the Right of Return to Judea and Samaria rose by 65,000.

If one adds Descendants of Israel who fled in 1967 (the only ones who were not refugees prior to the war) to the 1948 refugees who survived and were not returned (292,000), the total number of refugees who fled during the two wars amounts to less than 360,000. In that most of those who fled in 1967 were not Descendants of Israel, the portion of Descendants of Israel in Judea and Samaria since then has become very high, as demonstrated in Table 28:

202

1967 - After the War						
Ethnic Group	Within the Green Line Boundary		Judea & Samaria inc. Jerusalem		Gaza Strip	
	number	Percentage	number	Percentage	number	Percentage
Descendants of Israel	80,000	36%	190,000	61%	72,000	49%
Brethren of Israel	30,000	13%	40,000	13%	29,000	20%
Descendants of Israel in the Broader Sense	110,000	49%	230,000	74%	101,000	69%
Roman Army	17,000	8%	30,000	10%	23,000	16%
Arabs	60,000	27%	21,000	7%	20,000	14%
Druze	30,000	13%			2,000	1%
Distant Foreigners	6,000	3%	29,000	9%		0%
Total	223,000	100%	310,000	100%	146,000	100%

Table 28: The Non-Jewish Population in Parts of Western Eretz-Israel after the 1967 War.

1967 - After the War		
Ethnic Group	Western Eretz-Israel	
	Number	Percentage
Descendants of Israel	342,000	56%
Brethren of Israel	99,000	16%
Descendants of Israel in the Broader Sense	441,000	72%
Roman Army	70,000	11%
Arabs	101,000	17%
Total	612,000	100%

Table 29: The Palestinian Population West of the Jordan after the 1967 War.

The Census after the 1967 Six Day War

After the war, aware that the Palestinians had deceived UNRWA regarding the genuine number of Palestinian refugees, the IDF conducted a census in Judea, Samaria and Gaza to determine the true number of inhabitants. Despite Israeli attempts to prevent fraud, most Palestinians succeeded in deceiving the Israelis who were still unfamiliar with the various subterfuges used by the refugees, and UNRWA made no attempt to inform the Israelis of what they knew.[40]

The success in falsifying the census was the result of the fact that the Palestinian public-at-large had a vested interest in inflating the numbers, not just the leadership who urged them to do so and told them how to go about it. Unlike 1949, when the underlying motivation was to enjoy greater food rations and other UNRWA support, after the 1967 war the Palestinian public hoped they would receive Israeli National Insurance allowances (assuming Israel would annex them) and wanted to enhance and double this windfall with false identities and maximize benefits by utilizing the rights of those who were out of the country, as well. Moreover, Palestinian leadership feared that should the genuine number of Palestinians become known, and the real number of refugees in particular, UNRWA support would be curtailed accordingly.

But the inflated results of the survey deflated any thoughts of annexing Judea, Samaria or the Gaza Strip in the minds of most Israelis. Thus, the Palestinians dream of receiving Israel National Insurance allowances became a moot issue, save for residents of east Jerusalem (who received Israeli residency), and inhabitants of Judea, Samaria or Gaza who managed to marry Israeli Arabs and gain Israeli citizenship under family unification plans.

---

[40] Only later, in the course of the Oslo process and the second *Intifada*, did the Israeli leadership grasp the high level of soystication that typified Palestinians and their leadership. During the 1967 census, the Israeli organizers – the IDF – lacked the professional skills and technology necessary to carry out an accurate census.

204

The Israeli Government was not particularly concerned about the data, and had no serious reason to try and arrive at the truth. At the time, Moshe Dayan was waiting for Arab leaders to agree to recognize and make peace with Israel in return for withdrawal from the Territories occupied by Israel in the course of the war. Annexing the Territories was far from the hearts or minds of Israeli leadership of the time.

The census carried out by the Military Government failed to prevent forgery, primarily due to four tactics:

1.   **Passage between Census Areas**: The census was carried out over a number of days – each day in a different sector. A curfew was imposed only in the area being surveyed at the time, with a break of a day or more between regions. This allowed residents to move about and be counted more than once. Even if roadblocks prevented road traffic, few Palestinians owned vehicles of any kind at the time and for most the only form of transportation was still by foot or at most beasts of burden on dirt paths and lanes, which were not blocked.

2.   **Moving about within a Census Region**:   Even within a given region, the terms of the curfew were such that it was fairly easy to move about without being caught particularly within crowded refugee camps and small villages by cutting through backyards and courtyards undetected, while changing clothes in order not to be recognized by the census takers. This was assisted by the fact that most picture IDs were at best out-of-date and poor quality and often consisted of worn black and white photos.

Moreover, the curfew was not total and those exempted – doctors, nurses, police – had freedom of movement. Under such conditions, it was difficult for Israeli soldiers to enforce the curfew effectively particularly within densely built-up areas where persons could easily dart about, then present a second identity at a neighbor's house (or if an address failed to match, fall back on the excuse that the document had not been updated by Egyptian or Jordanian authorities).

Imposters could partially hide their faces behind a traditional *kafiyyah* headdress (men) or a veil (women). In any case most of the census takers' energies and attention focused on filling in questionnaires, not providing positive identification of the respondent. Census-takers could not be expected to remember the faces of every respondent they had queried on any given day, all the more so the day before.

3. Erasing Census-taker Markings: Domiciles of those already covered were marked by the census-takers in chalk at the entrance to avoid visiting houses twice – particularly in the labyrinth of narrow passages and alleyways that typified the refugee camps. It was hardly a challenge for Palestinians to erase the mark at the entrance to their abode in the midst of the taking of the census in order to bring a different census-taker to their door where the head of the family duly presented a *second* set of refugee documents after moving the furniture, changing clothes and headgear, and even adding some neighbors to the 'family.'

4. Counting Absent and Dead Persons: The heads of families added to the census all family members who were not physically present or had died, claiming the person was temporarily abroad or in the hospital.

Documents of a 'missing person,' alive or deceased, were presented, claiming the individual had forgotten his documents at home and would be back soon – if they were not apprehended for their absentmindedness (a convenient alibi). In other cases, copies were presented, claiming the individual had taken the original with them abroad, while the person was actually at a neighbor's or another village using the original for census purposes.

For instance, those who left for Jordan (i.e., eastern Eretz-Israel) took two documents or one document and a photocopy of the other in order to receive double assistance of UNRWA. Thus, the number of double identities reached more than 100 percent.

In many cases a family member of a neighbor who looked similar to the missing person or had a veil similar to the one on the ID was mobilized to serve as a 'double.'

Some 20 percent of the census-takers were members of the Israeli Arab or Druze minority hired due to their language skills and knowledge of Arab culture who sympathized with their kin particularly under the harsh economic circumstances they encountered, and tended to 'look the other way' assuming no harm was done. The census-takers and organizers were unaware of the widespread use of multiple identities and assumed any inaccuracies from 'bending the rules' recognizing document copies and so forth would be mild.

The census found there were 600,000 inhabitants of Judea and Samaria, not counting east Jerusalem – in contrast with the real number: 240,000. The magnitude of double identities counted was 150 percent. Such widespread 'hoodwinking' of authorities was eased by the fact that so many refugees from the 1967 war were not in their domicile at the time of the census, and every such abandoned home or mud hovel served as a reasonable 'stage' for others to use their 'second' or 'third identity' when census-takers arrived. Although the organizers of the census were aware of the role of fraud in UNRWA's figures, they were not aware of the sophistication of subterfuge vis-à-vis their own work and believed they had prevented most attempts to inflate figures.

In the Gaza Strip, however, the census showed 356,000 inhabitants compared to the real number: 156,000 (both including the Egyptian side of Rafiah). That is, the census was marred by 128 percent falsification. This figure translates into a reduction of approximately 100,000 'phantom refugees' compared to the Egyptian estimate from 1966 (170 percent falsification), which

Israeli census-takers viewed as a significant achievement in rooting out fraud.

The Israeli census curtailed inflated numbers of refugees on UNRWA's records, while exposing the magnitude of falsifications of refugee status among those UNRWA enrolled up to 1949. On the other hand, the Israeli Government thought its own census had been crowned with success, when in fact it too had fallen victim to deception on a massive scale, almost of the magnitude in the past, while providing more fictitious Palestinians without refugee status, compared with the situation before the census.

In general, the rise in the rate of 'phantom Palestinians' in comparison with 1949 was the product of the large number of deceased Palestinians and Palestinians who had left the country whose documents remained in the hands of their kin.

Another reason for a decrease in the number of 'phantom refugees' was that many inhabitants of permanent settlements who held refugee cards gained under false pretenses, presented the census-takers the 'second time around' with only their 'extra' residency cards (which they had received from previous authorities, Egyptian or Jordanian), not using their false refugee documents. The address on the two documents had already been transferred by the previous authorities and UNRWA from residence in a refugee camp to residence in a permanent settlement – based on permanent residents' claims that they had succeeded in moving their family into permanent housing.

Permanent residents holding false documents adopted this method since they believed that refugee status would be immaterial in eligibility for Israeli National Insurance – if Israel annexed them. At the same time, the permanent residents feared that the Israelis would distrust inhabitants of permanent settlements who identified themselves as refugees and were likely to interrogate them for details as to their homes inside the Green Line prior to fleeing in 1948. Because most longtime residents of Judea, Samaria and

Gaza were not familiar with the abandoned settlements within the Green Line, claiming to be refugees before Israeli authorities was liable to expose them as imposters, and result in confiscation of their refugee cards and loss of all the perks this entailed.

An unfortunate consequence of the high level of duplicity in the 1967 census was abolition of any thoughts of annexing Judea, Samaria and Gaza to the State of Israel. The true number of Palestinian residents (without Druze and Distant Foreigners) was 430,000. Together with some 190,000 Palestinians residing inside the Green Line (i.e., Israeli Arab citizens) the total number of Palestinians west of the Jordan was no more than 620,000. The number of Jews at the time was 2,400,000, and 60,000 of other origins. That is, only 20 percent of the overall population west of the Jordan (3,080,000) was Palestinian, the *same* proportion of Palestinian citizens of Israel in 2007.

Had Israeli leaders at the time known the genuine number of Palestinians in Eretz-Israel, Israel could have annexed Judea, Samaria and Gaza to the State of Israel without putting its Jewish majority in jeopardy – given all inhabitants Israeli citizenship and solved the problem of the Palestinian People residing in Eretz-Israel then and there. The figures of the census of residents of east Jerusalem raised the number of Palestinians to 1,026,000. The addition of 190,000 Palestinians within the Green Line to the number of Palestinians west of the Jordan (1,200,000) constituted a full third of the 3,650,000 inhabitants erroneously tallied as residing west of the Jordan. This number that was more than half the total number of Jews, created a serious but bogus 'demographic peril' that prompted Israeli leaders to jettison any thought of annexation.

The direct damage of the demographic bluff of the number of Palestinians in Judea, Samaria and Gaza and the grossly slanted 1967 census had far-reaching ramifications: The Israel Central Bureau of Statistics subsequent extrapolations of the Palestinian population to this day are based on updating inflated 1967 census

209

figures using input from birth rates, border control records of traffic in and out of the country and so forth. Thus, the census continues to skew decisions of Israeli leadership based on exaggerated demographics embedded in Central Bureau of Statistic statistics.

Continued Migrations after 1967

After 1967, Israeli administration led to an improvement in the standard of living of the inhabitants of Judea, Samaria and Gaza that impacted on the economy, on employment, on health and sanitation, which in turn impacted on natural population growth among Palestinians.

In addition, Israel initiated projects to evacuate refugee camps and move the residents into permanent housing under less crowded conditions. Palestinian leadership preferred, however, to perpetuate the refugee problem and opposed rehabilitation which they viewed as an attempt to undermine the Right of Return. Palestinian leadership galvanized the bitterness of the refugees and their aspirations of a Return to their former villages and towns inside Israel to torpedo the plan. In addition, despite Israeli administration, Palestinian terrorism at the street level kept rank-and-file residents 'in line'; in any case, most identified with their leaders' hard line on the Right of Return and perpetuated the refugee problem.

Yet the rise in the standard of living brought by job opportunities in Israel as a result of the 'open borders' policy between Israel and Judea, Samaria and Gaza initiated by Minister of Defense Moshe Dayan spurred a very high birth rate, particularly in the Gaza Strip. This exacerbated already crowded conditions in permanent settlements and in the camps. This process continued over a lengthy period – from 1967 to 2000 (in stark contrast with the years between 1949 and 1967). When the Second Intifada broke out in 2000, a drop in the standard of living and birth rates set in.

210

This process was paralleled by greater traffic out of western Eretz-Israel. Good relations between King Hussein and Israel and the problem of 1967 refugees in Jordan led Israel to respond positively to the King's request that they be repatriated, and by the end of 1967 (after the census), a portion of the 1967 refugees were, indeed, allowed to return to their homes in Judea and Samaria. The returnees were 37,000 Brethren of Israel – almost all of the Brethren of Israel who had fled, who previously were 1948 refugees – went to the Gaza Strip, Judea and Samaria before 1967, then fled a second time in 1967 (these and their other wanderings are almost unprecedented). Thus, with their return, the number of 1967 refugees dropped to 254,000.

Due to the tremendous increase in the number of Palestinians west of the Jordan over the years, beginning at the end of the 1948 war, one witnesses a voluntary migration of hundreds of thousands of Palestinians from Judea and Samaria and the Gaza Strip to places beyond the borders of Eretz-Israel. No small portion of the emigrants after 1967 immigrated to areas within the Green Line. In contrast with the flight in 1967 that was the product of the lack of deep ties with the land among most of the escapees, in the course of migration in times of tranquility that began in 1967 after the war, those who left **Judea and Samaria** spanned all sectors of the population equally (but not proportionally by their relative weight in the overall population). Only the Descendants of the Roman Army left in greater numbers than others, preferring to join kin already in Jordan.

All told, migration out of western Eretz-Israel, in addition to those who took flight in 1967 among whom various recent immigrants into western Eretz-Israel and their offspring constituted more than half of the escapees, 'thinned out' the component of Arab immigrants west of the Jordan. They now constituted only 17 percent of all Palestinians west of the Jordan and 7 percent of the inhabitants of Judea and Samaria, compared to 30 percent of all Palestinians after 1948 war and prior to the 1967 one, and 25 percent of the inhabitants of Judea and Samaria prior to the 1967 war.

Parallel to this shift, among Palestinians **within the Green Line** as well, there was a perceptible shift since 1949, including after 1967: Here most of those who left were <u>Brethren of Israel</u>, who preferred to join their kin in Jordan or the Palestinian Diaspora elsewhere.

In a similar manner, after 1967 <u>a portion of the Druze and most of the Arabs</u> (when the latter constituted 27 percent of the non-Jewish population <u>within the Green Line</u>) emigrated. The Arabs left because they had lost all hope that the Arab states would defeat Israel. The Arab émigrés initially came to improve their standard of living in a country they considered 'Arab.' Up until 1967 there were many who believed that the Arab states would succeed in destroying the State of Israel and transform the former Jewish state into an Arab one. But after the horrific Arab defeat in the Six Day War, then the failure to defeat Israel in 1973 under 'ideal conditions' of surprise, their dreams were crushed, all hope dashed completely by the signing of the Egyptian peace treaty with Israel.

<u>All the Arabs left the Gaza Strip,</u> both immigrants and refugees, due to the primitive living conditions. The refugees awaited a Return to their homes within the Green Line once the Jews were defeated, as they had been promised by Arab leaders, and they viewed the refugee camps where they lived as a temporary affair. The 1967 war and events that followed led them to give up hope of a Return. Because they were not native sons of Eretz-Israel, the Arabs sought more permanent housing in places with better prospects of a future. <u>Most of the Druze</u> as well left the area.

Overall, as a result of those who left <u>after</u> the year 1949, one witnesses a very significant drop in the number of Arab immigrants and their offspring, and their place within the demographic composition of the population as a whole. The percentage of Druze also narrowed to a certain degree compared to

212

their numbers after 1949, in part due to their modest birth rates compared to Palestinians.

In the year 1949 the Descendants of Israel in the Broader Sense, including the Brethren of Israel, constituted 61 percent of all Palestinians west of the Jordan, not including Druze and Distant Foreigners. All emigration henceforth led to a rise in the percentage of Descendants of Israel in the Broader Sense to 72 percent after the 1967 war. By the end of the year 2004 Descendants of Israel in the Broader Sense among Palestinians in western Eretz-Israel came to constitute a full 86 percent of all Palestinians (as shall be detailed) – identical to their place in the demographic composition in the year 1800 on both sides of the Jordan.

The flight of refugees and emigration out of western Eretz-Israel beginning in 1948 transformed the demography west of the Jordan. In fact, it reversed to a large extent the demographic trends of non-Jewish immigration into western Eretz-Israel during the preceding one hundred years.

The Numbers Today

Palestinians continue to exaggerate the number of refugees to this very day. The primary reasons are on one hand to intensify the magnitude of the problem and to 'bash Israel harder' as the guilty party and paint Israel as a perpetrator of 'ethnic cleansing,' and on the other hand pressure Israel to admit a larger number of Palestinian refugees in any compromise on the Right of Return. Moreover, the more refugees, the larger the material assistance Palestinians receive from UNRWA and other parties.

UNRWA has transferred over the years, and continues to transfer, huge quantities of food to 'phantom refugees' who never existed, are dead or have emigrated elsewhere, and to local 'social welfare cases' masquerading as Palestinian refugees including persons who have moved into refugee camps (in Lebanon) to live off international assistance. For the most part, gross inflation in the number of refugees has been the work of the Palestinians (from 1949). The original numbers submitted by the Arab states on arrivals were much more modest and accurate.

The total number of Palestinians at the close of 2004 residing in western Eretz-Israel was 2,906,000 (including those who are Israeli citizens). This includes 848,000 in the Gaza Strip and 764,000 in Judea and Samaria, without Jerusalem, 1,155,000 citizens of Israel and 139,000 east Jerusalemites who are not Israeli citizens but hold permanent Israeli residency. The large increase since 1967 in the number of Palestinians who are Israeli citizens is the product of an extremely high birth rate and genuine and fictitious marriages between Israeli-Palestinian citizens and residents of Judea, Samaria and Gaza. Most of the runaway birth rate is among Brethren of Israel who viewed this as a vehicle to 'even the score' with the Jews.

These figures do not include Druze and Distant Foreigners residing within the Green Line and Jerusalem. Also, the numbers in Judea and Samaria don't include Distant Foreigners living in Bethlehem, Beit Jallah and Hebron, and the handful of Druze in the Gaza Strip. In 2004, the total number of veteran non-Palestinians west of the Jordan counted as non-Jews were 234,000, all told.

The Palestinian claim that there are 4,900,000 Palestinians in western Eretz-Israel is the product of their constant inflation of the figures that today constitute close to 2 million 'phantom Palestinians.' According to the Palestinian Authority's Central Bureau of Statistics (an estimate that is not based on any census) the number of inhabitants in Judea, Samaria and Gaza at the end of 2004 and in 2005 was 3,800,000 persons. Another motivation for inflating the figures arose after Oslo: the Palestinian leaderships' desire to receive larger sums from the Europeans – funding which in turn was later used to finance terrorism against Israel.

Another factor in inflation was the desire to scare Israel by increasing the 'demographic demon' to monstrous proportions under the assumption that Israel would more readily agree to a Palestinian state (which Palestinians could then use as a base for the next step in the Stage Plan of the PLO for the destruction of Israel. From that platform of strength, Palestinians would demand the Right of Return, and use their demographic superiority, real and contrived, to gain the upper hand by democratic means and bury the Jewish state, even if this required new maneuvers to cover up past duplicities that could no longer be maintained, and create new ones to break the Jews' hegemony without arousing their suspicion...

In Israel today there are two 'readings' of Palestinian statistics. One, based on comparison with the Israel Central Bureau of Statistics' data, substantiates and accepts Palestinian claims. This approach has no foundation in current realities since it is based on the same slanted census taken in 1967. The second approach, closer to reality, is based on Palestinian Authority health authorities' data and Jordanian data. It argues that there are at most some 2,400,000 Palestinians in Judea, Samaria and Gaza. Another approach, presented by two American universities, is based on tabulation of all identity cards in existence, and comes to a conclusion close to the second Israeli method. Both of the latter approaches add to the genuine number of bogus identities that continue to operate today whose percentage has dropped definitively compared to 1967.

Details on falsification tactics in the past and present, explanation and comparison of erroneous and genuine data and additional information, including how maintenance of multiple identities operates and the complications they cause and curtailment of usage of fabricated extra identities as a result are presented in Appendix 3.

215

The Finding: Palestinians in Western Eretz-Israel Today

Most Palestinian families have passed on from generation to generation the narrative of their origins at least several generations back as part of a family legacy. These families are even proud of their origins, although a portion are forced to hid or obscure their origins. No small number of families has documented their family trees and among some they continue to preserve and update them to this day. Similar processes exist to a much more limited extent among Brethren of Israel, who due to their wanderings have forgotten their origins in the course of the years.

Among Descendants of Israel, many families know their origins, but are apprehensive to talk about them openly fearing they will be harmed, although today it is unclear whether these apprehensions are founded or not. Only a handful are willing to talk about their origins openly.

To date, no statistical data whatsoever has been published regarding this issue – just how many Palestinians living in western Eretz-Israel today are the descendants of Arab immigrants, and how many are descendants of longstanding inhabitants of Eretz-Israel, who haven't a drop of Arab blood in their veins, and how many these long-established inhabitants might be Descendants of Israel. The book at hand is the first to rise to the challenge and systematically investigate this question.

Before presenting current figures, one needs to recap events as they have been presented so far in this volume:

First of all – one must bear in mind the greater part and absolute majority of Jews in Eretz-Israel, and even more of the People of Israel (Jews, Samaritans, Edomites and Moabites) who resided in Eretz-Israel prior to the Jews' 2,000-year dispersion.

Except for the Roman Army, all the foreign armies and their ancillary forces in the course of history were ultimately expelled from Eretz-Israel or left when their conquest ended. The Arabs, who constituted the majority of the population after the Bar Kokhba Revolt, left Eretz-Israel for the most part by the end of Byzantine rule.

The Roman Army and other Christians, including mostly remaining Arabs of Christian faith who became the majority of the inhabitants of Eretz-Israel beginning with the Byzantine Period, relatively few remained in the aftermath of the edict of Caliph al-Hakem and the decline of the country into a wasteland. And only a tiny remnant of the Small Nations – the Canaanites and the Philistines – remained under the impact of the edict.

Most of the immigrants to Eretz-Israel up until the year 1840, they or their descendants, died in one of the epidemics, or fled the country in the course of various and sundry upheavals or due to economic distress wrought by this or that Arab ruler. On the other hand, there were the *Musta'arbim* in the mountain country and their offspring whose ancestral ties go back to the People of Israel and their Brethren who have been epitomized by their unflagging devotion to the Land and love of its soil.

In the course of upheavals, among the population of western Eretz-Israel during the 19th and 20th Centuries, the proportion of Descendants of Israel in the Broader Sense (although they were considered 'Arab') was 80 percent of the overall population of Eretz-Israel in the year 1840, the same proportion as in 1914 in western Eretz-Israel alone. Their numbers reached a low point of 61 percent after the 1948 war. This trend reversed itself in 1967, when the majority of the Descendants of the Roman Army fled to Jordan and their numbers rose to 72 percent. Since then, the percentage of Arabs and their descendants and the percentage of Descendants of the Roman Army have diminished greatly due to emigration.

Demographic history thus demonstrates that **among Palestinians in western Eretz-Israel there is a huge majority who are**

217

descendants of *Musta'arbim* who are sons of the People of Israel and their Brethren. **And indeed, among some 805,000 non-Jewish inhabitants of Judea and Samaria (not counting east Jerusalem), 524,000 souls – 65 percent – are the Descendants of the People of Israel in the Narrow Sense.** But if one subtracts from the total the 32,000 Christians from distant origins living in Bethlehem and its environs and 9,000 Kurds from Hebron who don't belong to any side in Eretz-Israel, the Palestinian population there includes actually 764,000 persons, **of whom 69 percent are Descendants of Israel, and if one adds the Brethren of Israel – 81 percent.**

Some 230,000 in the Gaza Strip (27% of a total Gaza population of 848,000 Palestinians) are Descendants of Israel (and it is known that there was a Jewish and a Samaritan community in Gaza up until a few hundred years ago). **Together with the Brethren of Israel**, the majority of refugees in Gaza – **92%! – are in fact Descendants of Israel in the Broader Sense.**

Out of 1,291,000 longstanding non-Jewish inhabitants of Eretz-Israel (this category does <u>not</u> include foreign laborers and non-Jewish family members who accompanied Jewish immigrants) **within the Green Line without east Jerusalem**, approximately 48 percent (721,000) were Descendants of Israel. But when one subtracts those who are not Palestinians – that is, Druze, Circassians, Bosnians, Turks, Albanians and foreign Christians – it becomes apparent that **among 1,155,000 Palestinians, 54 percent are Descendants of Israel, and together with Brethren of Israel constitute close to 86 percent of all Palestinians.**

East Jerusalem adds another 195,000[41] inhabitants who are not Jews but are <u>residents</u> of Israel (these residents are not citizens of Israel). This situation results from the fact that Israeli law applies

---

[41] The official number is larger because it includes residents of Judea and Samaria who hold Israeli residency although they do not reside any longer in Jerusalem.

218

to east Jerusalem, even though it was not annexed to the State of Israel. Together with east Jerusalemites, the number of veteran non-Jewish inhabitants of Israel is 1,486,000, and the number of Palestinians inhabitants of the State of Israel is 1,294,000.

If one includes the Descendants of Israel from Jerusalem, there are 700,000 Descendants of Israel who are residents of the State of Israel. This number constitutes 47 percent of the non-Jews who are inhabitants of the State and 54 percent of all Palestinians who are inhabitants of the State. Together with Brethren of Israel, their numbers rise to 85 percent.

End of 2004						
Ethnic Group	Within the Green Line & Jerusalem		Judea & Samaria exc. Jerusalem		Gaza Strip	
	number	Percentage	number	Percentage	number	Percentage
nts of Israel	701,000	47.2%	524,000	65.1%	230,000	27.1%
Brethren of Israel	401,000	27.0%	96,000	11.9%	548,000	64.5%
Roman Army	150,000	10.1%	45,000	5.6%	70,000	8.2%
Druze	117,000	7.9%			1,000	0.1%
Arabs	42,000	2.8%	99,000	12.3%		
Forieginers	75,000	5.0%	41,000	5.1%		
Total	1,486,000	100%	805,000	100%	849,000	100%

Table 30: Veteran Non-Jewish Population Today by Regions.

Table 30 above presents the veteran non-Jewish population according to regions of western Eretz-Israel. The geographic-demographic details by population groups in these districts are found in Appendix 4. The composition of Palestinian population in western Eretz-Israel by sub-divisions is detailed in Table 31.

219

End of 2004						
Ethnic Group	Within the Green Line & Jerusalem		Judea & Samaria exc. Jerusalem		Gaza Strip	
	number	Percentage	number	Percentage	number	Percentage
Descendants of Israel	701,000	54.2%	524,000	68.6%	230,000	27.1%
Moabites	235,000	18.2%	75,000	9.8%	343,000	40.4%
Edomites	166,000	12.8%	21,000	2.7%	205,000	24.2%
Descendants of Israel in the Broader Sense	1,102,000	85.2%	620,000	81.2%	778,000	91.7%
Roman Army	150,000	11.6%	45,000	5.9%	70,000	8.3%
Arabs	42,000	3.2%	99,000	13.0%		
Total	1,294,000	100%	764,000	100%	848,000	100%

Table 31: Composition of the Palestinian Population West of the Jordan Today.

Ethnic Descendants of Israel: At the end of 2004, out of a total Palestinian population west of the Jordan of some 2,906,000 persons, 50 percent of 1,455,000 are Descendants of Israel.

Arabs: At the end of 2004, the number of genuine Arabs including Egyptians, west of the Jordan was 141,000 – that is, it decreased since 1949 from 30 percent to 4.85 percent! All told 118,000 of them reside in east Jerusalem and Hebron and the vicinity – places of importance to Islam. In other areas there are only some 23,000 Arabs, 0.8 percent of all the Palestinians in (western) Eretz-Israel, or a mere one-fourth of a percent of all inhabitants of the country.

220

End of 2004

Ethnic Group	Western Eretz-Israel	
	Number	Percentage
Descendants of Israel	1,455,000	50.07%
Moabites	653,000	22.47%
Edomites	392,000	13.49%
Descendants of Israel in the Broader Sense	2,500,000	86.03%
Roman Army	265,000	9.12%
Arabs	141,000	4.85%
Total	2,906,000	100.00%

Table 32: Summary of the Ethnic Composition of the Palestinians West of the Jordan at the End of 2004.

Descendants of the Roman Army: Another sub-grouping that does not belong to the People of Israel is Descendants of the Roman Army, who number 265,000, and constitute 9 percent of the Palestinians west of the Jordan.

Brethren of Israel: Approximately 1,045,000 Palestinians are Brethren of Israel, whose numbers constitute 36 percent of all Palestinians west of the Jordan.

Descendants of Israel in the Broader Sense: Together with the Brethren of Israel, **descendants whose ancestry can be traced back to the People of Israel number 2,500,000 out of 2,906,000 Palestinians all told residing west of the Jordan** – that is, **86%**!

The data demonstrates that the sum total of Descendants of Israel in the Broader Sense, together with Descendants of the Roman

Army, that is to say Descendants of the *Musta'arbim*, together with the sons of the Judham tribe and Descendants of the Arab Army, all of whom have resided in Eretz-Israel for more than 1,400 years, constitute 96 percent of the Palestinians west of the Jordan. Only less than 4 percent – who are mostly Arab, in addition to most of the Druze and all the Distant Foreigners except for the Kurds – have resided in Eretz-Israel for less than 180 years.

The forefathers of the Brethren of Israel were converted to Judaism and added to the People of Israel by King David and by the Hasmoneans. One could argue that ascribing them as part of the People of Israel is unjustified, just as one should not accept the 'Arabness' of all *Musta'arbim* and their descendants due to the element of coercion involved in their Islamization. But the symmetry between the two cases of 'coercion' is partial at best: Forceful conversion to Islam was a religious matter, where the conversion of a given grouping did not necessarily transform the convert into a member of the Arab nation. Most of the Muslim world today is not Arab. Only flooding conquered territory with Arabs led them to become Arab lands and this did not happen in Eretz-Israel.

By contrast, conversion to Judaism, at least in Eretz-Israel, transformed the convert into a member of the People of Israel. Moreover, conversion under King David occurred in an early period, long before the *Musta'arbim* developed as a coping strategy. The Edomites and Moabites were considered Sons of Israel (*Bnei Israel*) for a very long time and were even converted a second time and again became part-and-parcel of the People of Israel during the Hasmonean Period.

In the course of the Great Revolt and long afterwards, including the period of the al-Hakem Edict, Brethren of Israel remained loyal and devoted to the People of Israel and the Religion of Israel even more than the 'original' Sons of Israel, and were considered an integral element within the People of Israel. Only after they went to Persia did they forget their origins and the historical linkage to

222

the People of Israel, losing the ties to their roots and began, unavoidably, to adopt an Arab identity. In essence, the Brethren of Israel were considered part-and-parcel of the People of Israel for thousands of years and were considered Arabs only for a few hundred years. Furthermore, the ethnic affinity of the Edomites to the People of Israel is irrefutable. The blood that flows in their veins is at least half Israelite. Even the rest of the Edomite bloodline is more closely affiliated with the Israelite bloodline than the Arab one, since the Edomites were the descendants of Esau, the son of the patriarch Isaac. The Moabites were kin of the People of Israel through Lot, the patriarch Abraham's nephew, despite the similarity of the link to the Arabs, via the offspring of Ishmael – Abraham's eldest son (born by his wife's handmaiden Hagar).

To complete the picture of longstanding non-Jewish inhabitants of Eretz-Israel, there is one more grouping that is not Palestinian that needs to be mentioned: the Samaritans, last but not least. They also remained devoted to the Religion of Israel through thick and thin. Their numbers rose a bit from 1800, to 170 in the year 1914. Afterwards the Samaritans succeeded in increasing their numbers which now stand at 700 souls.

Half of the Samaritans reside on their ancestral lands above Nablus on **Mount Grizim**, and the other half live among the Jews in the Tel Aviv suburb Holon. To this day they preserve paleo-Hebrew script (different from the Aramaic-based Hebrew script used by Jews) and use a Samaritan lunar calendar in which leap years are different from the Jewish lunar calendar. Thus, Samaritan holidays are sometimes a month apart from those of the Jews.

One of the interesting phenomena in regarding the Samaritans in Nablus is the fact that they hold Israeli and Palestinian citizenship and can vote in both Knesset elections and Palestinian Authority elections. Most of the Samaritans today are members of the tribe of Ephraim and only one large family – Tzadkah – is from the tribe of Menasheh. The Samaritan priests, whose dynasty has remained

223

unbroken since the Exodus from Egypt, are members of the tribe of Levi, the descendants of the High Priest Aaron.

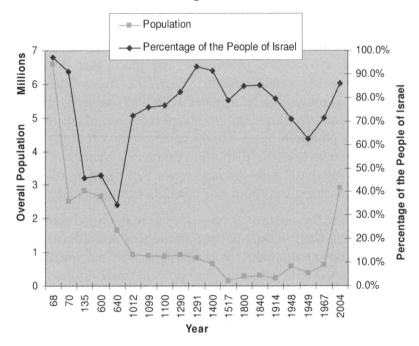

Graph 5: Growth of the Palestinian Population and the Portion of the People of Israel among them since 1949.

Parallel to the Samaritans, one must mention the Descendants of Israel in Samaria who originally were Samaritans prior to becoming *Musta'arbim*. They constitute some 30 percent of the Palestinian population of Judea and Samaria, without Jerusalem. Together with others who originally were Samaritans, the Descendants of the Samaritans number 297,000 persons, or 10 percent of all Palestinians in western Eretz-Israel. Forty percent of all Palestinians in western Eretz-Israel and 38 percent of those in Judea and Samaria are descended exclusively from original and authentic Jews.

224

Numbers East of the Jordan River Today – in the Kingdom of Jordan

After the 1948 war, the population of Jordan numbered some 750,000 persons, including 200,000 Descendants of Israel and 485,000 Arabs. The remainder was 40,000 Brethren of Israel and 6,000 Descendants of the Roman Army.

Beginning in 1948, due to the density of the population that developed east of the Jordan relative to the resources of the area, the Descendants of Israel in the Kingdom of Jordan began gradually to leave. Most of them immigrated to Western Europe. As a result, their weight within the population of the Kingdom of Jordan declined. Today, they number a few thousand; hundreds live in the vicinity of **Wadi Mussa**. The exodus was spurred by the first wave of Palestinian refugees in the 1948 war. In 1949, most Descendants of Israel, originally from east of the Jordan, who fled to Lebanon from Haifa and Akko, went to Europe. The refugees from the east who 'discovered' Europe led more of their kin still in Jordan to join them.

Jordanian territory, with its far from abundant rainfall and limited land suitable for agricultural cultivation, could not support the influx of refugees and the Jordanians' own high birth rate. The fertility of the soil and standard of living east of the Jordan was much lower than Western Europe and the disparity led not only Descendants of Israel to depart for Europe. Greek Christians who had settled east of the Jordan in the 19th Century did so as well.

The exodus of the Descendants of Israel from Jordan to Western Europe continued steadily and even increased after 1967. The first families to emigrate from Jordan after 1949 established themselves, then convinced their extended families to join them. This uprooting process was not only unfortunate, it was a watershed event, a sharp departure from the exceptional devotion that the Descendants of Israel had exhibited to Eretz-Israel through thick and thin over thousands of years. In contrast, the Brethren of

Israel remained steadfast in their homes east of the Jordan, their genuine ancestral homeland, and did not leave – a fact that impacts on contemporary demographics.

The number of inhabitants of the Kingdom of Jordan is a very complex matter, just like Judea, Samaria and Gaza. The actual population today is approximately 3,400,000, including a small, insignificant number of Descendants of Israel who remained. Due to their small numbers, the Descendants of Israel intermarried with other ethnic groups in Jordan, but the remnants now seek ways to leave Jordan to join their kin in various other places.

The official population figures of Jordan are 5,900,000. This number, however, includes 2,500,000 fictitious Palestinians (individuals who left, died or are merely 'phantom' supplementary identities of the same individual), another facet of the great population hoax regarding Palestinians and Palestinian refugees in particular. The refugee camps in Jordan have already become permanent settlements in which 380,000 refugees and their descendants reside. There are no Descendants of the People of Israel there.

Among the current Jordanian population, close to 2,000,000 are those who came from western Eretz-Israel beginning in 1948. Yet, approximately 1,300,000 are Brethren of Israel whose ancestral home, not just their current permanent place of residence, is Jordan, and therefore logically they should not be considered 'belonging' to the west. Most of the 700,000 Descendants of the Roman Army in Jordan are refugees from the west and their offspring (mostly since 1967) whose home since ancient times has been in western Eretz-Israel. Some 5,500 residents of Jordan today are Circassians, and nearly 1,400,000 are Arabs.

The proportion of Brethren of Israel in Jordan today (40 percent) is eight times their weight after the 1948 war (5 percent). The primary reasons are their tremendous birth rate and immigration, mostly from west of the Jordan, from Saudi Arabia and from Syria.

226

The relative weight of the Descendants of the Roman Army in Jordan is much higher than one would expect from the 67,000 who fled there in 1967. Parallel to a high birth rate, most of the growth is the result of migration from western to eastern Eretz-Israel in times of tranquility. A portion of the immigrants were refugees who resided in Judea, Samaria and Gaza prior to moving eastward. But no small number went to Jordan from within the Green Line. Therefore a significant portion of the population was not refugee-generated, although most are refugees or the descendants of refugees.

In light of the above data, and primarily in the wake of the emigration elsewhere of almost all the Descendants of Israel who arrived there during various periods, the overwhelming majority of Jordanian inhabitants today cannot be considered Palestinians from eastern Eretz-Israel. Only 21 percent of the Palestinians have ancient longstanding ties west of the Jordan. Consequently, talk of Jordan as a Palestinian state is baseless from a demographic standpoint, the semantics of 'eastern Palestine-western Palestine' notwithstanding.

Only if one adds the Brethren of Israel to the equation can one say that 59 percent of Jordan's population is Palestinian. This number is significantly lower than the data quoted by various parties. Exaggeration is based on tallying some 2,500,000 fictitious Palestinians that boost the number of Palestinians to 76 percent.

The 2005 data from the Palestinian Authority's Central Bureau of Statistics inflate the number of Palestinians residing today in Jordan only by one million. According to their figures there are only 3,000,000 Palestinians in Jordan. The Palestinian Authority's data puts the number of Palestinians in Jordan's population at 51 percent.

The data cited above undermines arguments that Jordan is already a Palestinian state, thus bolstering the legitimacy of a separate

227

Palestinian state west of the Jordan. On the other hand, the data preserves the right to a Palestinian state west of the Jordan that will take over Jordan sometime in the future.

Out of 2,000,000 Palestinians of all stripes in Jordan, approximately 1,500,000 are citizens of the Hashemite Kingdom, while 500,000 are stateless residents. Thus, the percentage of Palestinians among Jordanian citizens is 52 percent. By preventing a quarter of the Palestinians from gaining citizenship, Jordan is able to artificially maintain a balance where almost half its citizens are not Palestinian. This percentage is almost identical to the percentage of Palestinians east of the Jordan according to the Palestinian Authority's figures.

This raises the question, regarding the identity of the Brethren of Israel – 'Who is a Palestinian' as an outgrowth of the question 'What or where is Palestine?' since Palestine is a translation into Arabic of the name given to Eretz-Israel by the Romans and while parts east of the Jordan were part of historic Eretz-Israel, not all the territory of the Hashemite Kingdom is Palestine.

If one examines the settlement pattern of Jordan, it is apparent that most of the relatively densely-populated areas of Jordan are part of Palestine or Eretz-Israel, thus all the inhabitants today are Palestinians – regardless of their origins. One should not speak of the percentage of Palestinians in Jordan, but rather of inhabitants who *originate* in Palestine in contrast with Arabs or their forefathers who *immigrated* to Palestine. It is evident that Jordan is not part of Palestine if only 21 percent of its inhabitants are Palestinian in origin.

The Contribution of the Palestinian Diaspora to Anti-Semitism

The emigration of the Descendants of Israel from Jordan to Europe is unfortunate, involving loss of part of the original population of Eretz-Israel. But this dispersion includes Arab refugees who, in

228

part, consider themselves (without justification) to be Palestinians. These Arab refugees, together with part of the Descendants of Israel in Europe, constitute the primary reason for the anti-Semitism and hatred of Israel one encounters in Europe today.

Palestinian exiles in Europe are in part Arabs who lack any rights to Eretz-Israel, and the majority of the others are immigrants from Jordan. Only a small portion are refugees who are Descendants of Israel from Akko and from Haifa, who came to Europe via Lebanon, and to whom Israel and the Jews did no harm whatsoever, although Israel is blamed for their flight. These immigrants identify with their Palestinian brothers from west of the Jordan and their bitter fate and therefore harbor such a deep hatred of Israel. This hatred they pass on to Europeans. Palestinian immigrants attract friends they have made in their European Diaspora into creating an anti-Semitic and anti-Israel climate, primarily in Western Europe. The most susceptible to their influence are other Muslim immigrants, as one witnesses in all its intensity in France, as well as among the extremist Left in Europe.

Palestinian immigrant activism in France has won widespread support among North African Muslim immigrants. The latter, those who have not acclimated to French culture and remain on the margins of French society, are jealous of the successful manner in which North African Jewry has integrated into French society.

Among the factors behind the failure of North African Muslim immigrants – some 6,000,000 in number – to be absorbed, are their low level of education, cultural and religious differences and high crime rate. Their frustration makes them easy marks for Palestinian propaganda and the opportunity to take out pent-up hatred through anti-Semitic violence.

The impact of Palestinian hate-mongers is very prominent in the Scandinavian countries, primarily Denmark. It is highlighted in Belgium where the largest concentration of Palestinians in the diaspora is located. It is manifested in Austria and Germany, and to

229

a lesser extent in Holland and England. It is most extreme in France, the second largest concentration of Palestinians after Belgium. In Canada, primarily in Montreal, the negative influence of Palestinians is evidenced despite their relatively small numbers. Their impact has even permeated the United States and Argentina, and to a larger extent Chile.

The Alawi Today

In closing this recap of demographic history, one should add a word about the Alawi ethnic group. Most of these Descendants of Israel reside in Syria, in the northwestern sector of the country. They preserve their traditions and live under the pressure and perils of a small minority in a sea of extremism. The Alawi constitute 10 percent of the Syrian population which numbers 7,000,000 inhabitants.

According to the small Alawi minority that remain in Israel to this day, after part of the Alawi returned from Syria to the Galilee at the end of the 17th Century, and from stories told by Moroccan Jews who immigrated to Israel, the Alawi are a very interesting case. The Alawi have traditionally sought fraternity and peace. Although outwardly they are Muslims, they continue to preserve Jewish and Christian tracings. Their mourning customs and circumcision ceremonies (to some extent) seem to rest on Jewish antecedents.

The extremism exhibited by the **Assad** family and other Alawi in the Syrian ruling class is the product of their need as Alawis to 'be holier than the Pope' so to speak in their hatred of Israel, to avoid being accused of being 'Jew-lovers.' The elder Assad, Hafez Assad, was aware of the importance of the ethnic component in the rights of each side in the Middle Eastern conflict. He often argued (erroneously) that Ashkenazi Jews were of Khazari origins and therefore had no historical rights in Palestine (see Chapter One under the discussion of **genetic research**).

230

Since Syria under the Alawi has historically been a leader of the most uncompromising positions vis-à-vis Israel among the Arab states, and today is one of the most steadfast supporters of terrorism against Israel, it would be wise for Arabs, all the more so the moderate among them, to be cognizant of a well-known fact in Jewish history: Jewish apostates, those who need the approval of their new gentile 'brothers,' have often been the worst, most unbridled anti-Semites of all.

Another place where members of the Alawi community ended up was Morocco. The royal family and members of the ruling elites in Morocco are primarily of Alawi origin. By contrast to Syrian leaders, the Moroccan branch of the Alawi has exemplified the Alawi tradition of seeking peace and harmony. The Alawi arrived in Morocco in the third decade of the 11th Century from the Byzantine Empire, from an area that today is part of Turkey. At the time, their community numbered 7,000 persons. Today the Alawi are a full quarter of the Moroccan population – 2,200,000 out of 8,700.000 Moroccans today.

This, however, is not the end of the story of Jewish descendants in Morocco. In the course of the past three hundred years, over 200 Jewish families were forced to convert to Islam, and to this day they continue to maintain Jewish practices in secret. Their numbers have grown through natural population growth, and some of the members of these crypto-Jewish families are close confidants of the Moroccan monarch. The reigning queen of Morocco hails from one of these families.

Chapter Five

Substantiation of the Finding and Its Significance

Saying to the prisoners: 'Go forth'; To them that are in darkness: 'Show yourselves'; They shall feed in the ways, and in all high mountains shall be their pasture.
(Isaiah 49:9)

The Geographic-Historical Foundations of the Finding

In his study in Hebrew *Zion will be Redeemed with Judgement* (*Tzion ba-Mishpat Tepadeh*[42]), attorney-at-law Elon Yarden arrived at a similar conclusion regarding the origins of the Palestinians to those presented in the previous chapter. His book is based on a principle that the author examined thoroughly and found to be reliable. Jarden found that over a period of thousands of years, the inhabitants of the mountain regions of Eretz-Israel – that is, the Galilee, Samaria and Judea – did not, for the most part, leave their ancestral lands. On the other hand, the various people who immigrated to Eretz-Israel went primarily to the lowlands of Eretz-Israel – the plains and the valleys, sometimes expelling those who preceded them, sometimes joining them – sojourning there for a period of time, then ultimately moving on to other countries.

According to Elon Yarden, the Palestinian inhabitants of the Triangle (the low and hilly area bordering with the Samaria Mountains from its west) were a mélange of immigrants and original residents of the mountain region who sought a livelihood in an area close to centers of new Jewish settlement. The pattern where residents of the mountain country tend to remain permanent, while the inhabitants of the low country change over and over, is a well known phenomenon in the history of other countries, as well.

---

[42] See source 8.

233

The mountain country is always less accessible for conquering armies to transverse and control than the flat plains and valleys, and it is less amenable to agricultural cultivation. Due to harsher living conditions, the inhabitants of the mountain regions are generally more hearty, more difficult to subjugate or uproot from their ancestral lands which the mountain people doggedly clung to after investing so much of their energies, generation after generation, to prevail.

Even when new conquerors or oppressors appeared in the region, their persecution of the mountain peoples was less burdensome than that experienced by inhabitants of other regions. Due to their toughness and hostility to outsiders, relative to the more pacific-natured dwellers in other areas, mountain people generally are a poor source of revenue. Dwellers in the mountain country adopt attitudes towards conquerors, even in the worst of times, based on the belief that the outsiders' presence will pass, and with geography in their favor, the best survival tactic is to 'hunker down' and let time take its course.

In Eretz-Israel, there were exceptions to this pattern particular to mountain peoples, mainly internal migration within Eretz-Israel, but also in the period during the 15th Century when the land became a wilderness, prior to the Ottoman Conquest. These phenomena were offset to a large extent by the devotion of the mountain populations to their land: Ultimately, the majority of those who left returned to their ancestral lands after conditions improved.

In the case of the internal migration of the Descendants of Israel to eastern Eretz-Israel in the 18th Century, the émigrés remained devoted to the west, and called their communities in the east by the same names, and behaved as if they were still residents of the western Sanjaks. Indeed, most returned to the west although some continued to wander farther afield.

234

The Impact of the Finding in the Israeli-Arab Realm

Based on the finding and its details, even if we ignore, for the moment, the linkage and historical affinity of the Brethren of Israel to the People of Israel, nevertheless **an absolute majority of 60 percent of Palestinians living today in western Eretz-Israel (except for the Gaza Strip) are Descendants of the People of Israel in the Narrow Sense.** If one adds the Palestinians in the Gaza Strip to the picture, **50 percent of the Palestinians in western Eretz-Israel are Descendants of Israel in the Narrow Sense.**

When one adds to the equation the Jews in Eretz-Israel, it becomes evident that the **Palestinians who can be considered Arabs (most erroneously), constitute only 16 percent of all the inhabitants of Eretz-Israel. This state of affairs clearly indicates that on the Israel-Arab plane, what should be the answer to the question – Who does Eretz-Israel belong to? And it demonstrates the total lack of logic or justification for establishing an additional Arab state on the territory of Eretz-Israel.**[43]

It is self-evident that this should be the reply to all those in the world (including the Israeli Left and the Center) who support a logical but alas superficial solution – the Two States for 'Two Peoples' formula. In any case, for their part, the Palestinians hardly see this as their dream come true. Of course other than the Israeli-Arab realm, there is also a far more important Israeli-Palestinian realm. The above finding only demonstrates that the solution to the Eretz-Israel question is not establishment of a Palestinian Arab state in western Eretz-Israel. A genuine solution that will be both just and proper can be found in the innovative solution presented in Chapter Seven.

---

[43] In addition to the 22 Arab states including Jordan, whose territory is in part land that belongs to the historic Eretz-Israel.

An even clearer picture emerges when one examines **historic rights to Eretz-Israel**. In contrast to examining the composition of the current population, historic rights take into account compounded rights of inhabitants among the various groupings, benchmarked in terms of relative 'seniority,' measured in the accumulated length of their residency throughout the course of the country's history. Addressing this 'test' is conducted here, because the Arabs needed it in the past both to diminish as much as possible the rights of the Jews returning to Eretz-Israel after their long period of Exile and to strengthen as much as possible the rights of Palestinian refugees no longer present in the country.

When the benchmark of historic rights is applied, the rights of Arabs to Eretz-Israel shrink even further than the feeble 'rights' they hold from a demographic standpoint in the composition of the present population. Historically, less than 5 percent of the Palestinians today, or about 1.5 percent of the current overall population, are genuine Arabs (including Egyptians).

The cumulative rights to Eretz-Israel of both of the majority of the tiny minority of Palestinians descended from Arab immigrants who now reside in (western) Eretz-Israel, and of genuine Arabs among Palestinian refugees, is at most 170 years (1831-2003). Out of all the genuine Arabs, only some 24,000 members of the Judham tribe and descendants of the Arab army, or less than three thousandths of the current population, have cumulative rights in Eretz-Israel (and even these rights hardly equal the cumulative rights of the other permanent residents and the Jews).

The large minority of the Brethren of Israel among the Palestinians are historically (and in regard to the descendants of the Edomites, ethnically as well) closer to the People of Israel than to the Arabs, although in terms of self-ascription they now consider themselves Arabs, but in any case, their rights in western Eretz-Israel as 'veteran inhabitants' are at best about 170 years old (1840-2007). Over an unbroken period of 1,500 years, the members of this minority group were considered sons of the Jewish People and

236

Descendants of Israel. Only for a few hundred years have they been considered Arabs, and only during the past 200 years as inhabitants of Eretz-Israel. Their limited historic rights in western Eretz-Israel apply to all the refugees from this group, those who reside today in western Eretz-Israel and those in other places.

If one must 'attach' this minority historically to one side or the other, they justifiably belong more to the Jewish side. **Hence, all of the historic rights that Brethren of Israel hold anywhere in Eretz-Israel accrue to the Jews and their historic rights, almost to the same extent that it accrues to the Brethren of Israel themselves – far more than it 'belongs' to the Arabs.**

In terms of seniority, the historic rights of these minorities to western Eretz-Israel are almost insignificant compared to the rights of the People of Israel and most of the permanent inhabitants west of the Jordan whose residency in western Eretz-Israel spans thousands of years. As for the Jews, their historic rights are no lesser than those of the permanent residents since most of the Jews did not leave Eretz-Israel of their own accord, but rather were exiled by various conquerors. This refers not only to the aftermath of the Great Revolt in Second Temple times and repressive discriminative regimes that followed, but also those from the Babylonian Exile in First Temple times.

According to the above data (and even to a larger extent) **the absolute majority of Palestinian refugees living outside the western Eretz-Israel today possess less historical rights to western Eretz-Israel** – in terms of 'seniority' – 127 years (1840-1967), and in most cases even far less than that.

Only a minority of the refugees have significant rights in western Eretz-Israel. This right belongs to the original Descendants of the People of Israel, and to the Descendants of the Roman Army (whose historic rights in Eretz-Israel are, however, lesser than those of the Descendants of Israel).

The elements within the Palestinian population whose status is less clear than others are the Brethren of Israel and the Descendants of the Roman Army. The Brethren of Israel, on one hand, are too closely affiliated to the People of Israel and historically – albeit not continuously, were part of the People of Israel in the past, for a period spanning thousands of years. On the other hand, this linkage was the product of forced conversion to Judaism, which is no 'better' than the forced conversion to Islam the Brethren of Israel encountered later on in their history.[44]

As a result of the above state of affairs, it is difficult to 'assign' this important component of the population in a clear manner. But, since their historic rights in <u>western</u> Eretz-Israel go back only 165 years, this component can't determine the future of Eretz-Israel. Most of this public, some 53 percent of those who reside today west of the Jordan, are concentrated in the Gaza Strip, and constitute two-thirds of Gaza's inhabitants. Therefore, this public can, at most, only decide the future of the Gaza Strip. Despite this, one needs to keep in mind that at least half of the Edomite bloodline emanates from the People of Israel, and their descendants among the Palestinian public are closer to the People of Israel than they are to any other group.

The Descendants of the Roman Army were also forced to convert to Islam. They are not Arabs. Most of this public resides west of the Jordan today, within the Green Line. Because their overall numbers west of the Jordan is not great, one should not assign them much clout in determining the future of Eretz-Israel, and certainly not the future of Judea, Samaria and the Gaza Strip. Judea and Samaria constitute only 6 percent of the Palestinian population, while the Gaza Strip constitutes 8 percent.

Judea and Samaria constitute the heart of the conflict, while 68 percent of the Palestinian population in Judea and Samaria are Descendants of Israel. When one adds Jewish settlers in these

---

[44] And in the case of the forced conversion of the Edomites, was far worse.

238

territories to the equation, it is clear that the Arabs have no rights here – except for the rights they possess to sites important to Islam in Jerusalem and in Hebron – rights they preserved and 'earned' among other things, through the longtime residency of genuine Arabs in these cities.

Under the circumstances prevailing in Judea and Samaria as a whole, there is no logic to Arab sovereignty in Hebron or any part of Jerusalem. The Arab inhabitants of Jerusalem are Muslims who reside there, like Christians of various origins do: due to the holiness of the city to three religions. Like the Christians, the rights of the Arabs in the city are limited primarily to issues concerning Islamic holy sites.

As for Hebron, its <u>historic</u> importance for the People of Israel is seven times greater than its importance to Arabs – for alongside their shared forefather Abraham, the Tomb of the Patriarchs in Hebron also contains the remains of two 'solely Jewish' Patriarchs and four Jewish Matriarchs.

The Simple Implications of the Finding

The finding was known, in a general sense, to a number of parties for many years – including the founders of Zionism, but knowledge of the 'Jewish origins' of the Palestinians lay like an unturned stone for reasons that will be elucidated forthwith. The research at hand, through its comprehensiveness and detail, statistics and explanations, substantiates the credibility of this finding.

In fact, even most of the Palestinians claim they are not Arab in origin. But in contrast with the finding, they claim they are the descendants of the Canaanites and other Small Nations including the Philistines who dwelled in Canaan/Eretz-Israel prior to the Israelite conquest under Joshua.

The demographic changes documented in this book void entirely this Palestinian claim. The Biblical narrative of the extinction of the Small Nations, except for a small group of Gibeonites, weakens the Palestinian claim, even if the description of the scope of Israelite conquests in the Book of Joshua is exaggerated.

According to historic research, Joshua did not conquer the majority of the coastal plain. One of the Small Nations of gentiles who remained in the coastal plain for a lengthy period and caused the Israelites countless troubles spoken of in the Biblical narrative was the Philistines. They came to the country prior to Joshua. It was King David who finally vanquished the Philistines and made them, together with other entities among the Small Nations, part of the Kingdom of Israel.

A decisive historical turn of events occurred when the sons of various Small Nations became detached from the country with their exile by the Babylonian king Nebuchadnezzar in the course of the destruction of the First Commonwealth and the Babylonian Exile. A conversion process in Eretz-Israel in the course of the Hasmonean Period left only a handful of Philistines, Canaanites and other members of the Small Nations. Since conversion was not imposed on Hellenists, this conversion passed over remnants of these Small Nations who had been Hellenized and by then worshipped Hellenistic idols.

Ironically, of all possible rulers, it was in the name of the Caliph al-Hakem that the last of the gentile Small Nations were finally expelled from Eretz-Israel, after almost all converted to Christianity during the Byzantine Period. Only a miniscule number who didn't do so remained in the country. Their descendants are a tiny number of idol worshippers who remain in Eretz-Israel today (a few score Canaanites and Philistines in Gaza and in the village of **Jisr a-Zarqa** near Caesarea). Only the lack of detailed historical-demographic documentation and genetic support brought to light in earlier chapters left this possibility so shrouded in mystery. Without authentication, the finding concerning the Jewish

240

roots of Palestinians was neglected and pushed into the shadows for so long. There are other factors that strengthen authenticity of the finding and its far-reaching implications that need to be detailed now.

Supportive Evidence in Religious and Other Customs

There is evidence of customs and religious traditions that support the research finding. Gathering of testimony began primarily at the advent of the 20th Century.

Evidence of various kinds, including those concerning the origins of the Palestinians, not their customs (as will be detailed further on in a sub-section of this work) concern a small grouping, but this does not necessarily indicate that only a very small group had Jewish origins, since the distancing process from inhabitants' Jewish origins was gradual, and the evidence relates solely to the last to abandon their Judaism.

The Samaritan author, **Ratzon Tzadka,** speaks of an elderly Arab woman from **Kfar Qufer** near Tul Karem (from the word *Kofrim* or 'unbelievers' or 'heretics,' the name that the Arabs gave to the village where Jews lived in the past). The grandmother of this elderly woman told her to secretly light candles every Friday night. The author, **Yehuda Boorla** – a Jew from Eretz-Israel – spoke in his narrative *B'Ein Kochav* (In the Eye of a Star) about his service as an officer in the Turkish Army during the First World War and his Arab servant from Eretz-Israel. The latter heard Boorla speak about the Muslim custom of cutting off Jewish women's breasts to prevent the Jews from reproducing over the generations. Thus, Boorla's own manservant learned that his mother – who suffered from this form of mutilation – was Jewish.

It is well known to many that the **Makhamara** clan (wine-makers) from the village of **Yata** (in Judea, the biblical village of Yuta) and of **Kfar Anzah** (near **Sanur** in Samaria) continues to this day to

241

light candles on Hanukah and the villagers who do so are labeled 'Jews' by their neighbors. One of dignitaries of the largest clan in Yata (that encompasses half the village's inhabitants) possess a silver Hanukah menorah that had been passed on from father to son over the generations, that originated from Khaybar (North Yemen).

Up until almost the middle of the 19th Century, the village, which was still called Yuta, was the only village in Eretz-Israel where all the inhabitants were Jews. Later, as Brethren of Israel joined the village, preservation of Jewish customs faded. Nevertheless, as Yitzhak Ben-Zvi noted in his research from the 1920s, the elderly villagers would meet every Friday night near a tree that grew out of a rock on the southern environs of the village to light Sabbath candles. This tradition was halted only in 1989 under pressure of the younger generation following the First Intifada.

The remains of the village's synagogue add further credibility to the village's historic legacy: On the site of the biblical Yuta are the remains of a large synagogue. The **Abu-Aram** branch of the Makhamara clan lived near the synagogue in the past. The community has grown tremendously and has become a large town – Yata – where most of the new construction has been north-east of Yata.

Three members of the Makhamara clan who reside in nearby Samoa (Eshtamoa in biblical texts) have already converted to Judaism or begun the conversion process, despite threats from terrorists and the use of torture to dissuade them. One of the old women, who continues to light Sabbath candles and to fast in commemoration of the destruction of the Second Temple, speaks of an unbroken matriarchal lineage within her family that testifies to the *halachic* Jewishness of their offspring. In Samoa one can find the remains of a large synagogue that has been preserved and still stands that also testifies to the origins of at least part of the inhabitants of the village. Up until the mid-20th Century all the houses in the village were marked by niches in the stone mantels

242

where mezuzahs marking a Jewish house had once been attached. As these houses deteriorated and were replaced by newer dwellings, the number of houses bearing the telltale signs of past Jewish occupants gradually disappeared.

Forty percent of the villagers belong to the **al-Macharik** tribe ('the burners'), who had preserved the traditions of Israel up until a hundred years ago. Later on, they continued to light Hanukah candles and Sabbath candles and spoke of their origins in Judaism. They preserved their uniqueness by marrying only within the tribe. One member of the tribe recently reaffirmed his faith by becoming a practicing Jew (baal-tshuvah). The sons and daughters of the residents bear typically Jewish names translated into Arabic (rather than purely Arabic names) – such as Sara, Ka'ukab (Kochav or 'star'), Iyish (Haim or 'life'). Due to Israeli authorities' disregard of their Israelite identity over the course of the years, they no longer speak of this identity today, and when pressed, they reply 'now we are Muslims.'

Many of the villagers from the southern section of the Hebron Mountains who belong to the Makhamara clan live in caves in their villages up until 1983. Since then they have completely moved to regular housing in Yata, but they have not given up their ancestral lands and continue to work the soil in the vicinity of their former cave dwellings to this day.

When Yitzhak Ben-Zvi visited the biblical site of **Carmel** in 1927 he found signs of a synagogue among the ruins. The site is located adjacent to the village of **al-Karmel** at the southern end of the Hebron Mountains, where the Makhamara clan resided at the time. Yitzhak Ben-Zvi saw mezzuzot on the doorposts of houses and heard about 'candle lighting' from villagers. The sheik of the village **Abu-Aram** told Ben-Zvi 'we are the offspring of Jews.'

At the biblical **Tel Ma'on**, near the Jewish settlement **Ma'on,** there is a small synagogue and mikvah (ritual bath). In **Beit Aziz** there was an ancient and dilapidated synagogue at the center of the village that gradually fell into ruins, and after the signing of the Oslo Accords (under the Palestinian Authority control) was totally destroyed and the site plowed over.

At **Khirbat Anim al Fa'uka** ('upper Anim'), bordering the Green Line in southern Judea to the north of Ma'on, dwell descendants of Jews. During the 1948 War the IDF drove them out of **Anin al Tachta** ('lower Anim') which borders the Green Line to the south near **Shani** (Livneh). At Anim al Tachta there is a magnificent synagogue. A well-reserved synagogue exists in Susia (which unlike the other synagogues bears an inscription that testifies that the structure became a mosque in the year 787. In Susia as well, Palestinian inhabitants lived in caves up until 1983.

Throughout the entire southern sector of the Hebron Mountains, as well as the town of **Dura**, to this day Palestinian villagers bury their dead in burial caves - an ancient Jewish custom totally foreign to Islamic customs, preserve graves[45] and visit the cemeteries annually – a Jewish practice.

At the village of **Awarta** south of Nablus, according to a tradition passed down from father to son, village elders fasted one day of the year on a date in proximity to the Jewish Day of Atonement. The date seems to be tied to the Samaritan calendar (that is slightly different from the Jewish calendar). In a similar manner, in the village **Punduk** east of **Karnei Shomron** in Samaria the inhabitants light candles around the time of Hanukah.

In an Arab city in the Triangle (east of the Sharon) dwells a local dignitary, an offspring of Jews from the Maghreb, who has in his possession a Jewish holy book, and who tells of the forced conversion of his forefathers, on condition that his testimony be kept secret. It is known that a portion of the population of the Triangle carry out a ceremony to this day in the fall that resembles the *Tashlich* purification ceremony ('casting one's sins into the

---

[45] In Islam, cemetaries are only maintained for 50 years.

sea' as described in the Book of Micha) that Jews conduct on the first day of the Jewish New Year, as part of the High Holiday customs.

Among clans in the township of **Katanah** – adjacent to Abu Gosh in the Jerusalem Corridor, newborns are circumcised on the 8th day (as do many other Palestinians elsewhere in Eretz-Israel), in contrast with the custom in Islam of circumcising males at a much later age. Up until 300 years ago, Jewish members of the priestly class (Cohens) dwelled in the abandoned community **Kfar Anan** (Kfar Hananya in the Galilee).

The last local Jew left Shfar'am in 1920, and left the keys to the synagogue with his Muslim neighbor. The synagogue has been well cared for to this day. The synagogue that remains standing to this day in **Sakhnin**, and the Jewish cemetery in **Kfar Yasif,** all in the Galilee, are also mute evidence of the past Jewish ties of at least some of the local inhabitants.

All these signs are accepted in Jewish religious circles as signs of Jewish heritage that justifies a return to Judaism. Yitzhak Ben-Zvi wrote on this issue in his book *Uchlusei Artzeinu* (The Populations of Our Country) published in 1932.[46] He invested considerable time and energies at the time, traveling throughout the country on both sides of the Jordan to study the Palestinian-Jewish linkage. The evidence he uncovered at the time is crucial, because not all the customs he found at the time are preserved today:

"Thirdly – the religion. Officially it is Muslim, but in practice the *Falakhim* (peasantry) know very little of the Koran and the fundamentals of Islam religion, except for the common mantras (*formulas*) they mouth. Even their mosques, for prayer purposes, were only built in recent years, and primarily by the Turkish government. To this day there are areas where mosques are very few and far between.

---

[46] See Sources 2 and 3.

Moreover, it is well known that the *Falakhim* are not very meticulous in [following] the commandments [of Muslim] – whether the lightest or the most cardinal of precepts. The Moslem faith prohibits, for instance, women from going out with their faces uncovered, but the *Falakhim* go out with uncovered faces, and not only to work the fields, but also when they go to town to work, on business, or for prayer, although this is in contrast to everything customary of Islam. (In Turkey before the war,[47] for example, the Turkish *Falakhim* did not go with uncovered faces in the city). It is clear that here, in Eretz-Israel, the Islamic faith did not catch on as deeply.

Or take for example the matter of oath-taking: One should not take the word of the *Falach* who swears on the name of the Prophet Mohammed seriously. But if he goes to "Holy" – the grave where the village's or the region's personal holy man is buried – and takes an oath there, one can indeed take him at his word. Thus I know of a case of a blood vendetta, when the sides decided to make amends and the side where the guilt resided had to swear that [their side] was innocent and clean of all suspicion. The guilty parties had no scruples over swearing in the name of the Prophet [Mohammed], but when they were asked to swear on the grave of that same holy man [Noah the Righteous] they flinched. The *Falakhim*'s veneration of local holy men and their fear of them are greater than their veneration of the Founder of their Faith [Mohammed].

The religious celebrations and the '*musamim*' (the set times when they go to pay respect to a venerated holy man) are indicative of the force of local tradition, from pre-Islamic times. Take for example '*Nabi Musa*' [the place where Muslims believe Moses was buried, between Jericho and Jerusalem but east of the Jordan] with tens of thousands of pilgrims. Among we Jews, the Nebi Musa Celebration has become associated in our minds with

---

[47] WWI.

246

demonstrations against Zionism that began in 1920 with the attacks on 'Musa's' people. Yet, we should not forget that Musa was our forefather Moses, the Jewish lawgiver, and this ritual is an ancient echo of the religious regime of the patriarch Moshe in Eretz-Israel, which the *Falakhim* inherited from the Jewish inhabitants of Eretz-Israel. The same is the case for Nebi Rubin, Nebi Sh'ab and other celebrations of this sort. These *musamim*, which attract tens of thousands of Muslim, are a continuation of popular festivals that were common among peasants in Jewish times, and even perhaps in Canaanite times.

The memory of all the Jewish prophets, all the forefathers of the nation, and tribal heads (Judea, Benjamin, Yosef, Zebulon, etc.) are alive and well among the *Falakhim*. While the Jews themselves have ceased to visit these graves, the Muslim peasantry continues to prostate themselves on these spots. This is not Islam; it is a continuation of the religion that was dominant here earlier, before Islam, that became integrated in the new religion. Moreover, these holidays are not customary in all of Islam, and they are practices particularly here in our Land.

The ritual applied not only to heroes from the Holy Book alone. Anyone who has attended the religious celebration [in honor] of Rabbi Shimon Bar-Yochai [at Meron], or Rabbi Meir *Baal HaNes* in Tiberias, has noted the presence of *Falakhim* and Bedouin who come to dance together with the Jews at these celebrations, and who take oaths in the names of Rabbi Shimon and Rabbi Meir. In Pek'in, the Druze and the Muslim venerate together with the Jews the 'Jewish righteous men' Rabbi Ushiyah of Tiriyah and Rabbi Yossi Daman Pek'in. It is clear from this that what we observe here is a continuation of a Jewish ritual among *Falakhim* even after they converted to Islam."

It is important to note in substantiating Yitzhak Ben-Zvi's claims, that beyond the mosques on the Temple Mount, it was King **Hussein** of Jordan who initiated the building of the first mosques in Judea and Samaria. Within the Green Line prior to the establishment of the State of Israel the number of mosques was also very limited. Ironically, it was the National Religious Party that for decades controlled the Ministry of Interior and Ministry of Religious Affairs and used these ministries to initiate the building of most of the mosques one finds throughout Israel today...

Israel Belkind preceded Yitzhak Ben-Zvi as a scholar of the origins of longtime inhabitants of Eretz-Israel. Belkind was the first to preach recognition of the Israelite identity of Palestinians and to call for establishment of close ties with them. Belkind, who was an agronomist, was sent by the Turks on missions east of the Jordan. He reported what he found there, in Wadi Sirchan: an isolated Jewish tribe that had preserved Jewish customs. In his general article *HaAravim asher be'Eretz-Israel.* (The Arabs in Eretz-Israel), written prior to the close of the 19th Century, Belkind reported:

"Throughout the Land holy burial sites are found (*vali* in Arabic) that the Arabs go to prostate themselves on and carry out oath-taking. Among these holy men, many of which are holy to the People of Israel as well. Thus near Nes Tziona one can find the well-known grave called Nebi Rubin, believed to be Reuben the Prophet, who is Reuben, the eldest son of the Patriarch Jacob. And the Arabs from the entire vicinity consider it a duty to come and spend some time there during a set month at the end of the summer. Near Kfar Saba is found the grave of Nebi Benyamin [Benjamin] , and not far from it Nevi Shim'on [Simon]."

Traces of Jewish Origins in the Language and the Names

Another source of substantiation of the finding can be found in the accent of spoken Hebrew and use of aphorisms of Hebrew origin one can find in the vernacular of Palestinian 'Arab' villagers in the Galilee such as Sakhnin and **Arebe**. In addition, the level of usage and expression in Hebrew and the richness of the command of the language among many Palestinians, particularly those within the Green Line, are noteworthy: Such fluency in Hebrew is at times greater than that among many Jews, even native *sabra* speakers. Hebrew language usage by Palestinians is but one of additional factors that already ties many Palestinian citizens of Israel to the Jews.

The names of their communities are another element that hints of the Israelite roots of the inhabitants. An outstanding example is the Hebrew word Kfar (village, pronounced **Kafar** or **Kufur** in the Palestinian Arabic dialect). This word appears in the place names of many communities – Kafar Yasif, Kafar Kana, Kafar Yata, Kafar Manda, and Kafar Samia – while this word (which is not Arabic) is not employed in Arab countries. The names of other villages have names such as **Jaba** (from Geva or Giv'ah, 'hillock,' 'hill' in Hebrew) or **Tira** that have meaning solely in Hebrew.

Yitzhak Ben-Zvi found that the names of 34.5 percent of Palestinian villages in 1932 remained in their ancient Hebrew form. In western-Eretz-Israel alone he found that two-thirds of the Palestinian village names were Hebrew-Aramaic, including 277 names that can be identified as Hebrew settlements from the Second Commonwealth Period. Another study from the 19th Century found that within communities in the mountain country the ancient names are more similar and the intonation closer to the Hebrew language than one can find in points of settlement in the lower lying areas. Yitzhak Ben-Zvi claimed in his study:

"…And behold, had the Jewish settlement indeed been replaced by another settlement, they would not have preserved the Hebrew names (what is known to be the case in those places where the settlement changed, such as eastern Transjordan). This is not so in western Eretz-Israel – Here the ancient names have been preserved, **which proves the continuity of settlement in this locale** [emphasis, the author's]." [In North America when Indian names were preserved by the settlers, they were preserved as is by intention, and were not distorted, like they were in Eretz Israel.]

249

The matter of preservation of names is not limited to villages. Most of the cities have also kept their original names, except for small changes in spelling and/or pronunciation: Tzfad (**Tzfat** or Safed), **T'veria**, Jaffa (**Yafo**), Acca (**Akko**), Ah-Natzra (**Natzrat**), **Beit Lechem**, Halil (Chever in Arabic – **Hebron**) and el-Kuds or the Holy city – Jerusalem). Here the similarity carries less weight, of course, since cities by their nature, due to their size, rarely disappear or need to be reestablished.

Besides place names, the family names of inhabitants also reveal Palestinian-Jewish linkages. The English researcher **Condor** was the first to note biblical names among the Palestinian peasantry. Many of these names have no similar roots in the Arab dictionary. Large important families (clans) in the Gaza Strip, in Jaffa and in Nablus bear Jewish or Samaritan family names, for example the following families:

Abu Chatzeira: The Abu Chatzeira clan encompasses some 3,000 persons and controls fishing in the Gaza Strip. They not only bear the name of this important Jewish family, they also maintain the mosque where the family prays that boasts a picture of the forefather of the family, the Rabbi Yaakov Abuchatzeira – with a caption in Arabic.

K'chil: The roots of this family (which made 'a name for itself' due to the violence of some of its sons), goes back to Jews from Yemen who came to Eretz-Israel in the 11th Century. In Bnei-Brak, one can find rabbis who bear this family name.

Elbaz: The Elbaz clan encompasses thousands of members whose roots are Jews from Morocco who came to Eretz-Israel, most probably with the aliyah of the Maghrebi.

Abulafia: This family's roots go back to the Kabbalist (Jewish mysticism) Rabbi Avraham Abulafia who lived in Spain in the 13th Century.

250

Elrazi: Is a name found in Gaza that is identical to the Jewish sage from Turkey, Rabbi Yaakov Israel Yom-Tov Elgazi, who became the Chief Sfardi Rabbi in Eretz-Israel (the *Rishon le-Tzion*) in the 12th Century.

Ya'ish: This Nablus family includes the current mayor of Nablus, **Adali Ya'ish**, whose roots go back to the Samaritan **Metukhia** family, who trace their lineage to the Tribe of Ephraim.

In the town of **Arrabe** in the Galilee near Sakhnin there are families with Jewish last names, such as **Ibri** (from Ivri or 'Hebrew') and **Kana'ana** (from the Hebrew K'na'ani from 'Canaan'). Among the residents of Midia, near Mevo Modi'in one can find families bearing the names **Tzadok** and **Solomon**.

Yitzhak Ben-Zvi relates to traces of Aramaic found in the Palestinian vernacular:

"...Secondly – the language. The Hebrew language was replaced very early in the mouths of the people by Aramaic. In Talmudic times, Aramaic already was more dominant than Hebrew... Over the first generations after the [Arab] Conquest, the inhabitants used Aramaic, and traces of Aramaic remain among the *Falakhim* to this day, and according to experts in the [Palestinian] *Falakhim's* dialect spoke in Eretz-Israel there are many words in Aramaic that are not used among Arabs in the Hejaz, as well as among Arabs in other places, where they never needed Aramaic."

Israel Belkind wrote of similar findings in his article *HaAravim asher beEretz Israel* (The Arabs that are in Eretz-Israel[48]):

"Linguists show that the Arabic vernacular spoken today among inhabitants of the country have many foundations in the Hebrew tongue or in Aramaic that inhabitants of Eretz-Israel spoke when they were conquered by the Arabs, foundations that are not found in written Arabic, or spoken Arabic in other countries. And Major

---

[48] See Source 5.

Condor, one of the scholars of Eretz-Israel, already has established, that **the 'Arabs' even in the days of the Crusades spoke Aramaic** [emphasis, the author's] – the language that the Jews spoke until the Arab Conquest."

Aramaic didn't disappear so fast – even after the period studied by Condor. In 1974, when the Jewish settlement **Ofra** was founded in the heart of Samaria, members of the group found that the language of the biblical Ofra [Ephron], the village of **Taibiyah**, was Aramaic!

Another aspect of the language question which further strengthens claims that there was no Arab settlement in Eretz-Israel is the fact that the Palestinian dialect of spoken Arabic is considerably closer to literary Arabic than other vernaculars (with the exception of Saudi Arabian dialects which are the course of literary Arabic). This shows that Arabic did not become rooted in Eretz-Israel through discourse between local inhabitants and Arab settlers, rather mainly through the reading of Arab texts and documents.

Oral Testimony

Additional significant support for the finding emerges from the testimony of Palestinians and Bedouin whose family history has been passed on from generation to generation, and whose legacies note their Jewish roots. One can find many who claim Jewish or Samaritan origins – particularly among various Bedouin tribes and Palestinians in Samaria, Judea and the Galilee.

Most of the Palestinians who tell of Jewish or Israeli origins do so only on condition of confidentiality. Most keep this as a family secret fearing to speak of such publicly. But one can encounter individuals who openly speak of their Jewish roots – including cave dwellers south of Hebron, some Christians from **Kefar M'ar**, and some Bedouin from **Rahat**. The Bedouin' Jewish roots are what motivate them to serve in the IDF, collaboration that began even during the pre-State period when the al-Heib tribe established

252

a military unit which was attached to the Haganah's elite fighting force – the **PALMACH** (PLugot MACHatz or 'strike force') – called **PALHEIB**.

Avraham Ya'ari relates in his book *Zichronot Eretz-Israel* (Eretz-Israel Memoirs) that in 1903, **Zalman David Levontin** wrote about the chiefs of the Bedouin tribes – tribes that migrated between the Sinai and the Negev – noting that they had gone all the way to Jerusalem in order to propose they join forces with the People of Israel and make a covenant with the 'King of Israel' – Theodore Herzl. They also spoke of tribes that relate themselves to the People of Israel and call themselves *Bnei Israel*. The Jewish origin of the **Amsulam** Emir that dwells on the border between Egypt and Eretz-Israel was also mentioned by them.

On April 29, 1929, the Hebrew newspaper *Davar* carried an article in which the author (R.B.) reported that in 1925 he had spoken with the Christian *mukhtar* (village head) of **Ein Aroch (Ein Arik)** near Ramallah. The *mukhtar*, who appeared to the reporter to be a credible source, said according to his family's tradition he and his kin originated in the Tribe of Benjamin. The village head said the forefathers of his village inhabitants and six other villagers in the vicinity were descendants of the Tribe of Benjamin who had settled in their villages after leaving Jerusalem prior to the destruction of the Second Temple by the Romans. The *mukhtar* said that the place name of their village derived from **Hushai the Archite** (the advisor to King David, mentioned in the Bible in Second Samuel 15:32).

In the village **Chizmah** (there are those who claim the name is derived from *Az-Mavet* – 'Fierce as Death' in Hebrew) the number of testimonies among inhabitants claiming Jewish roots was so widespread that an anthropological study was conducted. The examination indicated a similarity between the contour of the skulls of local inhabitants and that of Jews.

253

Inhabitants of the large cluster of villages, **Beit Sourik, Beit E'an'an, Bidu** and Katanah, on the outskirts of Jerusalem claim that 99 percent of their forefathers were Jews-Samaritans ('Israelis' according to their tradition), and that all of the inhabitants are the descendants of four brothers, each of whom founded his own separate village that ultimately became a community with thousands of inhabitants. The fact that a particularly dangerous terrorist cell emerged from among the young people of Beit Sourik indicates that many of the younger generation in the village apparently have not heard from their elders about their real origins.

The name K'ata'nah in literary Arabic means 'we lived here' or 'we dwelled here.' The name was given to the village after Descendants of Israel returned from east of the Jordan to western Eretz-Israel and settled in the same spot where they had dwelled prior to migrating eastward. The original name of the settlement prior to its inhabitants moving eastward was Beit Sourik. Since prior to their migration east of the Jordan, the entire family resided in one place and upon their return the four brothers took up residence a distance from one another to gain control over a larger section of land, they needed to adopt new names.

The villagers of Tibiya near Ofra in Samaria were Christian by faith that spoke Aramaic and trace their ancestry back to members of the Jewish People who were Christians. Jews lived in the village of **Ain-Siniya** near **Shiloh** up until the beginning of the 20th Century, and this is the reason that the family of **Moshe Sharett** (Israel's first Minister of Foreign Affairs) originally settled there after immigrating to Israel from Russia in 1906. The village's native Jews testified that all the other residents of the village were originally Jewish.

Claims of Jewish origins void of residual Jewish practices have been found in the village of **La'kef** near the Jewish settlement Karnei Shomron in Samaria, and the village **Kha'res**, near the Jewish town of Ariel in Samaria, in Sakhnin and among the **Al-**

254

Alliyan clan – one of the three largest *khamulot* in the village of **Beit Tzafafah** on the outskirts of Jerusalem.

The village **Beit Awah** on the southern edge of the Hebron mountains is the center of the Maslamah *khamula*, whose members claim they originate from Jews who came from Yemen. Unlike others who make the same claim, members of the Maslamah clan are not known to practise any Jewish customs. Yitzhak Ben-Zvi, who traveled around the southerly parts of the Hebron mountains in Judea, cited the Jewish background of villagers in **Beit Awah** who told him members of their *khamula* could be found among the following villages: **el-Borej, al-Majid, a-Siqa, Beit a-Rus al-Tachta ('Lower Beit a-Rus'), Beit a-Rus al-Fa'uka ('Upper Beit a-Rush'), Dir al-Asal Tachta ('Lower Dir al-Asal')** and **Dir al-Asal Fa'uka ('Upper Dir al-Asal)**.

The Abu-Aram branch of the Maslamah *khamula* reside in the village **Taw'ani**, and also say that they are descendants of Jews. The southern sector of the Hebron Mountains is peppered with cave-dwellers from the same branch who voice similar claims, for example: The inhabitants of **Khirbet a-Taban** and **Khirbet al-Fchot**, in **Bir al-Iyid, Khirbet Sirat, Awad Ibrahim, Khirbet al-Mufqara** and the former residents of **Khirbet Bani Dar** adjacent to **Nebi Yakin** who left their caves to live in **Bani Na'im**.

Another branch of the Maslamah *khamula* – the **Salamin** family – resides in **Khirbet Salameh** on whose name the Salamin family takes its name, as well as **Khirbet De'rat** and **Khirbet Bruq**.

In Hebron, primarily close to the southern exit, there dwells a huge family called **Du'ek,** a family name known to be of Jewish origin. One member of the Du'ek *khamula*, **Aziz Du'ek**, was taken into custody by Israel in 2006 while serving as chairperson of the Palestinian Legislative Council. The **Muslemani** (meaning 'convert to Islam') was the last Jewish family to convert to Islam in Hebron. Family elders of the **al-Muchtasabin** ('the clever ones') family from Hebron also claim they are descended from

Jews. Two other families whose Jewish origins are known are the **Kaysi** and **Tamimi** families ('complete' in Islam, from the word *tamim* - honest – stoping outwardly to pretend to be Muslim, while continuing Jewish customs in the home).

The 'headquarters' of the ruling clans in the city is also called **Tamimi** because it originally was comprised of families of *Musta'arbim* whose final separation from Judaism marked completion of their full conversion. In the town of **Khalkhul**, north of Hebron, dwells a *khamula* of some 5,000 souls known to descend from Jewish-Maghrebi origins. In the village **Sa'ir**, also north of Hebron, and in East Jerusalem, lives a *khamula* of few thousand members called **Aramin**. Some members the *khamula* claim for the Jewish origin of the clan.

One of the local leaders in Rahat claims that most of the Bedouin in Eretz-Israel are Descendants of Israel and the Brethren of Israel among them are descendants of the various tribes that dwelled in Judea. Other Bedouin from **Rahat**, including members of the **el-Huza'iel** tribe,[49] claim that 99 percent of the Bedouin in Eretz-Israel have Jewish ancestors. Among the el-Huza'iel tribe kosher Jewish butchering of animals is used till this day.

Inhabitants of **el-Arish** are called by the Arabs *Yahud-Sina* or the 'the Jews of Sinai.' The residents of el-Arish make the same claim. In essence, their forefathers left Eretz-Israel for Sinai during the period that Eretz-Israel became a wasteland at the end of the 15th Century, and they and their offspring never went back to Eretz-Israel.

The offspring of the **Saliman** family from the village of **Bo'eenah/Bugidat** in the Galilee, also testify to Jewish origins. According to a genealogy record book in the village, 700 offspring of the **Fukara** family are all descendants of a forefather who was still Jewish four generations ago.

---

[49] There are those who claim the name of the tribe is actually Uziel.

256

King Feisal went even further, when in the year 1917 he wrote **Frank Port: "We are the sons of the same race and blood and cooperation will bring prosperity to the country."** The mother of Feisal's grandfather, **On,** hailed from a family who were Descendants of Israel that dwelled east of the Jordan and later returned to their village in the west. Unlike the situation today, at the time that Feisal was growing up, the Israelite origins of his grandfather's mother was well known, and there was no attempt to hide this fact.

Anton Atallah (a leading Christian Palestinian Jordanian political figure from East Jerusalem) told **Natan Yellin Mor** after the 1967 war: **"We are basically one people.** I am a resident of Jerusalem for generations who surely converted to Christianity after the destruction [of the Second Commonwealth] when the Christians were persecuted. In any case, we the Jews and the Muslims fought to defend Jerusalem at the time of the Crusades."

The chairperson of the Jordanian Parliament was quoted in the newspapers as saying: "If one would dig deeply in the soil, they would find the bones of our common grandfathers." **Yasser Arafat** was quoted as saying to journalist **Smadar Peri** in the Hebrew daily *Yediot Aharonot* after the outbreak of the Second Intifada – sending up a trial balloon which due to the limits of Arafat's knowledge of history did not gain much attention: **"We Palestinians and Jews, all of us are the sons of the Prophet Samuel."**

The above candidness is on the whole a limited phenomenon among Palestinians living today within the Palestinian Authority. This seems to be a carryover from fears of the past when foreigners took over the country. But, the more terrorism and extremism gain a foothold in Palestinian affairs, the greater the reluctance of most Palestinians to talk about the matter, even on condition of anonymity, and even within the Green Line In the past, awareness of Jewish origins was reflected in a few special cases when a number of Palestinians, including well known figures, stood up

257

and decided to convert to Judaism. But opposition – whether the Israeli security forces' suspicion of their motives or of the Israeli rabbinate's reluctance to accept such candidates, or fear of retribution by terrorists for thinking of abandoning Islam – has dampened enthusiasm to take such a step.

The Palestinian claims that Jesus was a Palestinian and that the first Christians were Palestinians greatly bolsters the finding, as well. Arafat went even further, calling Jesus "the first Palestinian" (thus contradicting his ridiculous claim that the Palestinians were the descendants of the Canaanites). Palestinian Christian leader **Hanan Ashrawi** insists adamantly that the Palestinians are the descendants of the first Christians.

Since Jesus and the first Christians were all members of the People of Israel, and since Jesus and since the concept and the name Palestine were created several hundred years after the death of Jesus, one could easily argue that this Palestinian claim is a lie for propaganda purposes.

But, at most the Palestinians are 'guilty' of lack of accuracy. The original Palestinians who were longtime inhabitants of Eretz-Israel, including the Christians among them, are Descendants of Israel. They can view part of them, particularly the small Christian minority among them, as descendants of the first Christians, although their ancestors were not called Palestinians at the time.

Despite all the evidence above, one should note that there are Bedouin in the Negev who only know that their ancestors hailed from the Arabian Peninsula, but they are unaware of the huge number of Jews who lived in the Arabian Peninsula in the past, and therefore don't even consider they might be Jewish. Others from the Galilee, and not just the Bedouin, know that their forefathers came to Eretz-Israel from Syria and from Lebanon in the first half of the 20th Century, but they are unaware of the movement of Descendants of Israel from the Galilee to these countries in the 19th Century, and their return to Eretz-Israel in the course of time. Due

258

to ignorance of this fact, they also don't even consider they might have Jewish origins.

In the coastal plane, in the Galilee and in a number of other places, there are Israelis of Egyptian origin who know of the Egyptian origins of their forefathers who came to Eretz-Israel primarily in the 19th Century, and sometimes their family names reveal their origins. Most are positive (and rightly so) that they have no Jewish origins.

The Problem Itself Substantiates the Finding

Another facet that supports the finding – raised by attorney-at-law Elon Yarden – is the essence of the conflict itself: There is no precedent of two separate nationalities believing that the same exact country is their homeland. There are or were many local conflicts over territorial rights in the world: Kashmir, Northern Ireland, the former Yugoslavia, Kurdistan, Armenia and many other places. These conflicts are on religious, not national grounds (Kashmir and Northern Ireland), or between national entities in adjacent territories at odds where the border should be between them or over the independence of one nation from a neighboring other nation (former Yugoslavia, Armenia and Kurdistan) without any intention of dispossessing the neighboring national entity from all of its territory.

While in the case of South Africa there was a conflict between two different communities over control of the same country, white South Africans never claimed that they originated in South Africa. And the majority of the black community is not originally from South Africa, which until white settlers arrived was largely empty, relative to its population today.

In light of the unique nature of the Eretz-Israel case, one could argue (together with all the other evidence presented above) that if two national entities demand the same country, each claiming it is their historic homeland, it is reasonable that the two are not greatly different from one another. This phenomenon and the common emotional attachment to Eretz-Israel should be enough to forge a sense of solidarity between the sides. Unfortunately, other differences between the two contenders have led to protracted suffering on both sides. It's high time the joint suffering begin to forge a sense of solidarity between the two.

Those who would like to create an analogy between Eretz-Israel, and Yugoslavia and similar cases, forget that talks between the sides in 2000 at Camp David broke down over the Right of Return, a cardinal issue, among other things, in the eyes of the Palestinian leadership, designed to preserve the dream of ultimately gaining control of the part of Eretz-Israel left to the State of Israel through the power of demographics. The uniqueness of the Eretz-Israel conflict is that both sides believe the same land in its entirety is their land, and any attempt to agree on partition of any sort is doomed to failure.

How the Finding was Pushed to the Sidelines in the Past

The fact that the finding presented here has remained hidden from the eyes of many people resulted from two facts: Jews returning to Eretz-Israel at the advent of Zionism pushed it into the shadows. At the same time, one witnesses erosion of collective memory over the generations among Palestinians where the fact that so many of the Palestinians' forefathers had been *Musta'arbim* led a portion of the Palestinians to forget their origins and led most to hide it. The impact of the Arab occupation upon them, further fueled by the influx of Arab immigrants and their Arabic mother tongue, did not exactly contributed to any sense of affinity with the Jews returning to Eretz-Israel. Members of the First Aliyah had a very different Eastern European mentality, totally different from the *Musta'arbim* and Arab mentality that the Palestinians had become rooted in.

260

Another factor behind the gap between Palestinians and Jews was lack of communication. At the beginning of the second Return to Zion (in modern times), only a small minority of Jews from Yemen and a handful of others, spoke Arabic. The Palestinians had no command of Eastern European languages or Hebrew or Yiddish. Most of the Jews from Arab countries arrived in Israel only after the 1948 War when animosity between the sides already ran high, and any positive impact that Middle Eastern and North African Jews that might have bridged the gap was limited to areas within the Green Line. Moreover, many Jews came to Israel from Arab countries harboring a deep hatred of Arabs for the oppression and persecution they had endured at their hands – feelings that hardly contributed to creating a sense of affinity between the two Arab-speaking publics.

Traumatic movement of Brethren of Israel to western Eretz-Israel, a migration that came for the most part prior to the Jewish and Arab immigration to western Eretz-Israel, was a key factor in creating the milieu of estrangement between Palestinians and Jews. By this time the Brethren of Israel had already entirely forgotten that they once belonged to the People of Israel. This population suffered from a low threshold of tolerance of any threat to their continued presence in the places where they had settled, and therefore the Brethren of Israel were 'easy marks' for vested interests who sought to incite them against the Jews.

But there was one decisive factor above all others: The Jews settled initially in the valleys and in the coastal plain (except for Jerusalem, Safed and Hebron). The Descendants of Israel resided at the beginning only in the mountain country. Therefore the meeting of the two peoples took place primarily between Jews and those who were not unmistakably Descendants of the People of Israel; rather, they took place vis-à-vis other permanent inhabitants and various and sundry immigrant populations – initially Descendants of the Roman Army and Brethren of Israel.

The first encounter of these populations led to friction and even alienation and hostility and unwillingness to believe in any form of kinship. This situation in turn sharpened or 'artificially elevated' the 'borrowed' secondary identity among many Palestinians at the expense of any residual kinship with their Jewish origins and led to a growing sense of kinship with Arab immigrants, and Arabs in general. Palestinians who knew about their forefathers were forced to hide this knowledge. When they spoke of it openly, they were repudiated by both the Jews and other Palestinians. Unfortunately, such attitudes became deeply rooted in the thinking of Israelis and some of the Palestinians – including the leadership of both sides – and has played an important role in nurturing hatred between the sides.

Despite this, historians at the beginning of the modern Return to Zion indeed examined local folklore that was common among (non-Jewish) longstanding inhabitants – narratives that support the finding. The first to raise the possibility that the lineage of local inhabitants might be tied to the Jews from ancient times were German scholars in the 1860s. Colonel Condor from the **Palestine Exploration Fund** discovered traces of Aramaic and Hebrew in the speech of Palestinian peasants. But the first to raise this possibility in a cogent and coherent manner was Israel Belkind; in 1894, based on testimony he had gathered, Belkind began publishing articles that held that **"the 'Arabs' in Eretz-Israel are blood brothers of the Jews."**[50] One of the key ideological architects of Socialist Zionism, **Ber Borochov,** claimed as early as 1905 that **"The *Falakhin* in Eretz-Israel are the descendants of remnants of the Hebrew agricultural community."**

The Jewish religious and Zionist Establishment did not, however, adopt or endorse these ideas because Jewish settlement was still in its infancy, at the time, a small minority of Jewish settlers facing a large Palestinian majority. But the animosity that developed

---

[50] See Sources 5 and 7.

between the sides due to the initial estrangement led to any further curiosity being cast aside and the finding being ignored. The issue was problematic even from a cultural standpoint: Who would 'swallow' whom in light of the demographic disparity? The Zionists' – who had aspirations of building a new 'progressive society' – were unwilling to assimilate into Arab culture. This led to a milieu of arrogance where those who came from European culture disparaged the local culture and living standard within the ailing Ottoman Empire and its neglect.

David Ben-Gurion and Yitzhak Ben-Zvi, however, adopted the finding. They raised it in a book they co-authored: *Eretz-Israel Ba'Avara oobaHoveh* (Eretz-Israel in the Past and the Present), published in 1918. Raising the possibility that the local population was descended from Jews was used to justify the Zionist endeavor, but also out of hope that Jewish immigration to Eretz-Israel would change the situation and the Palestinians would become a minority that could then be absorbed within the People of Israel. **David Ben-Gurion assigned the issue great importance and believed that it was the key to the future!** He closed an article entitled *Birur Motza haFalakhim* (**Investigation of the *Falakhim*'s Origins**) published in 1917, saying:

"In the vicinity of the Carmel and the Sharon Valley one encounters many *Falakhim* villagers with blond hair and blue eyes, whose facial features testify that their forefathers came here hundreds of years ago from Northern Europe [descendants of the Roman Army that Ben-Gurion erroneously thought were remnants of the Crusaders].... But despite the profusion of intermixing, **most of them and most of the offspring of the Muslim *Falach* in western Eretz-Israel impart, after all, a different racial type and an entire ethnic division, and there is no doubt that in their veins runs a lot of Jewish blood – the blood of the Jewish farmers, the simple folk (*am-haaretz*), who chose under pressure of the times to deny their faith so long as they would not be uprooted from their soil** [emphasis, the author's]."

Several years later, Ben-Gurion sought to forge cooperation between Palestinians and Jews on the basis of class – seeking to unite Jewish laborers and Palestinian laborers. Ben-Zvi invested much energy in researching this subject, seeking evidence throughout Eretz-Israel on both sides of the Jordan. After publishing his volume *Uchlusei Artzeinu* (The Populations of Our Country) in 1932, Ben-Zvi continued to investigate.

Massive Arab immigration into Eretz-Israel which took place parallel to Jewish immigration, and the periodic assaults on Jews by the Palestinians, intensified hatred between the two parties. This milieu of animosity most probably led Ben-Zvi to abandon his research of the origins of the Palestinians relatively early on. Events in Eretz-Israel, compounded by the outbreak of the Second World War, with news of the Holocaust of European Jewry, in conjunction with intensive activity to bring about the establishment of a Jewish state, followed by a war for survival in 1948, all forced Ben-Zvi to focus his energies on more burning issues.

The War of Independence led to a partition of Eretz-Israel. The number of Palestinians remaining in the State of Israel was small, and in any case far less than the growing flood of Jewish immigrants entering the country, temporarily dwarfing the importance of Palestinian origins. Unfortunately, the issue did not attract much attention while Israelis were grappling with more pressing issues of building a new country, absorbing countless immigrants with little more than the clothes on their backs, forging a common denominator from scores of Diaspora communities, and keeping Israel's hostile neighbors at bay.

The wars and countless clashes between Jews and Arabs that took place over the course of the formative years of state-building only increased mutual hostility, sharpened differences and distanced any thoughts of kinship between Jews and those who were viewed as an integral part of the Arab world (although the wars were fought against external forces and the Palestinians in Israel did not collaborate with any foreign-enemy forces).

To this one must add the fact that at this point in time such a revolutionary notion could not be substantiated by genetic evidence that bolsters the reliability of the finding with objective scientific evidence, and the finding lacked the demographic detail in this book and the sources that assisted in collecting this data.

In any case, Ben-Gurion did not forget the finding, and in fact tried to realize it first among the Bedouin who were friendly to Israel and had volunteered for service in the IDF, thus throwing their lot in with the Jews. The plan for the Bedouin was labeled **Yeehud,** or Judaization, a concept that in contrast with conversion does not put emphasis on religious issues among a population that is not for the most part very religious. But the stumbling blocks presented above, as well as fears among GSS security personnel that enemy elements and spies would infiltrate the ranks of Bedouin joining the People of Israel, and particularly the opposition of religious circles under the leadership of Rabbi Maimon (Fishman), the National Religious Party Minister of Religious Affairs, weakened David Ben-Gurion's determination.

In 1956, Ben-Gurion appointed a team headed by Moshe Dayan and **Haim Levakov**, to try and 'Judaize the Bedouin.' The team brought religious Jews to the Bedouin to teach them Jewish customs. But the instructors were unable to withstand the harsh living conditions in the Bedouin encampments and quickly pulled up stakes. Ben-Gurion's initiative and the very idea of Judaization was abandoned entirely after Moshe Dayan warned that attempts to Judaize the Bedouin might enflame the entire Muslim world against Israel.

Another reason the finding concerning the origins of the Palestinians failed to have any effect was the shame *Musta'arbim* felt about their desertion of the Jewish religion, as well as the low educational level of these peasants prevented the creation and preservation of written documentation of the religious conversion process.

Even today, many Palestinians who know about their Israelite origins rarely speak about this, and their vast majority does nothing to change their status. Those living under a Palestinian terror regime are deterred from even talking about this subject openly, fearing they will be harmed. More than once, members of families suspected of having Jewish origins have been forced to prove their loyalty as Arabs by aiding terrorist operations, to one degree or another. Some were able to avoid suspicion and keep out of harm's way by giving their children 'patriotic names' names like **Jihad**.

Such behavior deterred Jews who tried to establish ties with such families. Even among many Palestinians who are Israeli citizens there is fear of discussing this touchy subject, primarily due to conventions on both sides and particularly the disbelief they encounter among Jews. Palestinian-Israeli citizens who know of their Israelite roots, encounter ignorance among Israelis on this topic. They fear that if they try and promote their claim, the Jews will think they are trying to improve their inferior status under false pretenses.

Moreover, **the issue of the Israelite origins of many Palestinians is not raised by Palestinians because they fear they will be caught 'between a rock and a hard place.' The minute they claim they have Jewish origins, there is a genuine danger that the Arabs and the Iranians will stop supporting them, while the Jews will spurn them.** It is natural that they fear they will then be forgotten along with the Palestinian problem for without the ongoing support of the Arabs and other Muslims, the Palestinians will continue to remain in an inferior state.

Under current circumstances, dissemination of information on the origins of the Palestinians **becomes a Jewish duty, to serve as a voice for the Palestinians and to use their auspices to spread the word in Israel and the world of the finding, to liberate the Palestinians – prevent them from being lost forever to the Jewish people and free them from their long years of**

266

subjection and suffering, without waiting for the Palestinians to request this.

Many Palestinian parents know about their Israelite origins but don't tell their young sons and nephews, although they know that these youngsters endanger their own lives by committing suicide in the struggle against Israel. It is time for these parents to expose the truth, despite the dangers this carries.

Another no less important reason for the lack of evidence is that the loss of these sons of the Jewish people was not a single event in time, but a slow, lengthy, gradual process over hundreds of years. Except for the al-Hakem Edict, there is no dramatic event of importance that can be retold and handed down from generation to generation.

Parallel to this, the Arabs were not particularly proud of the forced conversions they instituted and were not interested in leaving evidence behind – not of their deeds and not the fact that the inhabitants of Eretz-Israel were not Arab in origin. On the other hand, preparation of incriminating evidence by the inhabitants of Eretz-Israel might have increased the jeopardy they faced as a downtrodden captive population that was persecuted in any case by the Muslims.

With regards to testimony surrounding this issue, the Samaritans are a positive exception to the rule: They left evidence in writing of the Islamization process they underwent during the Abbasid Period.

Ignorance – the Only 'Occupying Force' Left in Eretz-Israel

One of the factors behind the disregard of the finding is the result of the manner in which history is taught in the Israeli educational system, specifically, the absence of material on the history of

Eretz-Israel and the area as a whole beginning with the period prior to the Arab Conquest up until the beginning of the modern Return to Zion. The reason: Concentration on Jewish life in the Diaspora and the sparse known Jewish population in Eretz-Israel during this period, and the tiny numbers of Jewish inhabitants (or so it appeared). Another factor behind the disregard and rejection of the finding was the product of the Palestinian educational system and the Arab system that preceded it: They hid and continue to hide the truth known to many Palestinians, while spreading lies based on pure speculation as to the origins of the Palestinians. In both cases – the primary reason is lack of knowledge and lack of precise data.

Indicative of this are the words of Yasser Arafat about the kinship between Palestinians and Jews through the Prophet Samuel. Despite its good will and good intensions, the 'facts' are indicative of the level of ignorance among Palestinian leadership on this issue. Most of the Israeli leadership is partner in this neglect for having led David Ben-Gurion to abandon the issue.

This is hardly a laughing matter, considering the fact that this ignorance has triggered countless wars, Intifadas and terrorist acts by Palestinians, and the suppression of countless innocent citizens by Israel as an act of defense. Moreover, it has reverberated around the world due to a problem that refuses to be solved and has dragged the entire world into a terror maelstrom. Beyond the direct damage, these events have become a plague and an economic burden on the inhabitants of Eretz-Israel, and of late many other peoples in the world.

In order to put things on a practical track, considering the importance of knowing the history of Eretz-Israel in order to understand the serious problem faced today, it is imperative that a drastic change be undertaken in the educational systems of both sides of the conflict.

The key question that paves the destiny of the region – 'Who are the Palestinians?' – suffers from the lack of detailed data that is supported by the prevailing realities among Palestinians. Although today most of the Palestinians in Eretz-Israel are Descendants of Israel, as a result of the Muslim Conquest of Eretz-Israel and other phenomenon discussed in this book, this fact has been hidden from world cognition.

Since the reality of foreign occupations has ended, and Eretz-Israel today is in the hands of the Jews and the Palestinians, it is imperative to change the rules of the game in the deadlock that has developed. Israel and those Palestinians who know the truth about their origins must challenge the distortion of history and present the facts as they are: **Most Palestinians in western Eretz-Israel are Descendants of Israel**. They (and others) have the duty to **finish the expulsion of past conquerors who remain among them and continue to subjugate them on the cognitive level. This 'occupation' of perceptions, whose foot soldiers are ignorance, continue to control and enslave conventional thinking about the past, conventions that were created by physical domination and coercion.**

Validation of the Finding

As presented in this book, the finding rests on seven major pillars:

1.   **Historio-Demographic,** set forth in the preceding chapters;

2.   **Historio-Geographic**, as set forth in the work by Alon Yarden;

3.   **National-Territorial**, as Alon Yarden argues in regard to the uniqueness of the conflict;

4.   **Genetic**, as scientific research surveyed in preceding chapters demonstrates;

5.   **Behavioral-Religious**, in Palestinian customs related to religious practice reveals;

6. **Nomenclature and Linguistics,** as reflected in geographic place names and family names, traces of Hebrew and Aramaic in spoken Arabic, and other signs;

7. **Palestinian Tradition**, as preserved as an oral tradition in testimony and narratives of Palestinians about their family legacies.

Some of these perspectives lack the quantitative data presented in the historio-demographic sphere, yet the historio-geographic input and some of the genetic substantiation serve as supportive evidence to the precise historic-demographic data presented in this work.

The Significance of the Finding

According to the finding, the People of Israel are divided into two major groupings: one that left Eretz-Israel and remained faithful to its religion and as a result also kept its nationality, and the second that left its religion but remained faithful to Eretz-Israel whose original national identity faded as a result of leaving the Jewish faith. Of course, one needs to mention a third very small element: several thousand Jews, the majority of whom at the end of this process are labeled *Musta'arbim*, and less than 200 Samaritans (in the 19th Century), that together remained part of the People of Israel and faithful *both* to the religion of Israel and Eretz-Israel.

Another part is all the Descendants of Israel whose identity was partially or fully lost, who assimilated and intermixed with the gentiles around the world. But this 'lost' portion of the People of Israel is immaterial to this book because any title to Eretz-Israel among these people who left Eretz-Israel, the Religion of Israel and the Jewish nation pales in comparison with the title held by the former two groupings. Just as the first group (e.g., 'world Jewry') that left Eretz-Israel contains 'appendages' of converts to Judaism, the second group that left the Religion of Israel has 'appendages' from various immigrations. Most of these immigrants (the

270

Brethren of Israel) were a very loyal component of the People of Israel in the past, and even today should be viewed as an inseparable part of the People of Israel. The other immigrants in the second group constitute only 16 percent of this group that dwells within western Eretz-Israel.

The difference between the two typologies of partial detachment from the continuity of national religion and national homeland and between the patterns of living that each side took does not require either group to see the other as a rival enemy. Such hostility is very tragic, and only adds to hundreds of years of terrible tragedies that befell both groups, each in its own way, over the course of the past 1,900 years.

Parallel to the suffering of the People of Israel during its two-thousand year exile, well known to many, one needs to cite the suffering that was the portion of the inhabitants who remained in Eretz-Israel, beginning with the destruction of the Second Commonwealth and through numerous conquests and wars. Such suffering, relative to the size of the population, does not fall much in magnitude to the suffering of the Jews in the Diaspora – with the exception of the Holocaust and the pogroms of 1648-1649.

The only difference in the equation of the distant past and today is that in the past 100 years, each of the two groups has been responsible for the tragedy of the other. Neighboring countries that were conquered in the past by the Arabs have been dragged into this awful muddle and suffered the consequences (and of late many others have been drawn into the conflict). **From prevailing realities it is clear today that the redemption of the People of Israel, the redemption that began with the founding of modern Zionism, cannot be completed without redeeming those brethren who constitute the majority of Palestinians in western Eretz-Israel! Ignoring this fact will lead the Zionist movement to lose its way.**

Assistance to Israeli Hasbarah (PR)

The importance of the finding is first and foremost an asset in presenting Israel's case in the court of public opinion (*hasbarah*), although such advocacy is only the means to a far more important goal – reducing the hatred and solving the conflict. If Israel will base its case on the finding, the State of Israel can explain to the world, and first and foremost to its own citizens, to the Palestinians and to the Arabs as a whole, that **most of the Palestinians in western Eretz-Israel are Descendants of Israel, 'the unsung *marranos* of Eretz-Israel' so to speak, and there is no basis for the hatred between them and the Jews.** On the contrary: If one needs to hate someone, the Palestinians should hate their oppressors who are long since gone…and the terror regime and terror strategy that prospers today in Eretz-Israel as a 'legacy' of those past oppressors, who continue to subjugate and torture the inhabitants of Eretz-Israel.

Most of the Palestinians west of the Jordan constitute, in essence, a sizable 'Eretz-Israel ethnic community' within the People of Israel. In contrast with today's *sabras,* native-born Jews, who for the most part no longer define themselves by their disparate ethnic origins in this or that Diaspora community of their parents/grandparents, but consider themselves simply 'Israelis,' the Palestinians remain in a Diaspora-like mentality cognitively in terms of self-ascription. Thus, although they are native-born sons of Eretz-Israel, like all those born abroad, they constitute a separate ethnic community.

Moreover, although there is no longer any Arab rule in Eretz-Israel, most of the **Palestinians remain captive to their 'Arabness.' Ignorance about the true identity of the Palestinians or attempts to hide it, together with terrorism, is what prevents their liberation and is what preserves their enslavement within an 'occupation' by a false identity.**

Ignorance of Palestinians' true identity causes anguish among the People of Israel. In May 2003, even Ariel Sharon declared, painfully, that Israeli control of Palestinians' lives (as distinguished from control of all the territory of Eretz-Israel) was **'an occupation.' Unfortunately**, what brought Ariel Sharon to make this declaration was in error: **The 1967 War only liberated the territories (Judea, Samaria and Gaza); it did not liberate the Palestinians themselves** from the chain of conquests that they have endured in the past that have left them 'captives in their own land.' If they are occupied, they are solely 'occupied' by a false identity forced upon them, although their captives had long disappeared. <u>It is high time to end this captivity, not by giving up parts of the homeland – but by not 'giving up' brethren in the homeland!</u>

Throwing around the word 'occupation' has little utility. And if one nevertheless wants to shout slogans such as 'End the Occupation' they should not be directed towards the Jews; they should be directed at the Iranian and Arab despots and their partners within the Palestinian people who continue to embrace terrorism as a vehicle and 'occupy' Palestinians in hating and killing Jews. In general, it would be better to drop the slogans altogether, and master the realities and the complexities of the issues – then implement the solution that becomes self-evident when one possesses the facts.

Those who brand Israel 'imperialistic' and an 'occupying power' are the only empire that remains today on the face of the globe – the 'Arab Empire.' This empire embraces today a host of countries that other than the Arabian Peninsula were all conquered by the Arabs and 'Arabized by force' – an occupation and brutal form of 'cultural imperialism' or 'cognitive ethnic cleansing' if you wish. This imperialism included Eretz-Israel, and led to the estrangement that exists today between the two parts of the People of Israel. The fact that this 'cultural empire' is divided into separate states does not weaken its hegemony. On the contrary: Political division or

273

proliferation enables the 'Arab Empire,' together with other Muslim countries, to almost totally control the United Nations and other international forums by virtue of numbers, and weakens the one Jewish state far less than it does the 'Arab Empire' itself.

The Israelis are not the reason for the Palestinians' ongoing suffering. Rather, it is foreign conquerors and their heirs who are the guilty parties: on one hand, the ignorance of Palestinian identity, and the despots and their collaborators in terrorism, on the other hand. There is no justification for claims against the Jews, who were the primary victims of this terrorism-imperialism.

Now when the origins of the Palestinians are finally out in the open, those **Palestinian leaders who continue to champion terrorism become traitorous collaborators with past persecutors, and perpetuate the real occupation and violation of their own people, by their own hands.** They intensify the suffering in Eretz-Israel and the world at large. **Palestinians who employ terrorism are not freedom fighters** as they themselves and many people around the world believe. Rather, they are people whose terrible deeds against Jews…and against Palestinians (!) perpetuate the imperialistic occupation of almost a thousand years ago when their forefathers were forced to abandon their religion and subsequently to mask their true identity.

Moreover, ironically, the victims of this violation, these 'unknown' sons of the People of Israel have become the spearhead and the cannon fodder in the fight of Muslim and non-Muslim anti-Semites to kill the only chance the People of Israel have to exist as a free nation within the family of nations. **All those who brand survivors of the Holocaust who are fighting for their existence 'Nazis'** should be reminded that terrorism was a guiding principle for the Nazis. **To this one must add the role of Palestinian terror leadership in causing the Holocaust of European Jewry.**

Furthermore, if one views Jewish **Settlers** (*Mitnachalim*) in a negative light, they must first and foremost view in the same light those **Arab leaders who came to Eretz-Israel without any historical tie to the country and without any title to its land, and the Brethren of Israel, who likewise migrated into western Eretz-Israel from the east. All of them complicated and exacerbated the situation** to a magnitude that is almost impossible to grasp. There is no logic in that the majority of these immigrants and their offspring, who today constitute the majority of Palestinian refugees, should be allowed to continue to spearhead and 'drive' the continuation of the conflict.

The Palestinian refugees are for the most part settlers (*mitnachalim*) themselves, who in their flight merely returned to their countries of origin. Many of the refugees were neglected purposely and shamelessly to serve as a battering ram to bash Israel and fuel the war of terror against its citizenry.

Those who criticize Jewish settlers returning to the land of their forefathers from which they were *forcibly* expelled and view their settlement activity negatively, must – in all fairness – benchmark the settlement activity of foreigners in western Eretz-Israel at least in the same 'negative' manner.

The People of Israel tied their fate with Eretz-Israel as early as the period of the Patriarch Abraham and re-affirmed, and reclaimed its title to Eretz-Israel following the Exodus from Egypt and conquest of the land under Joshua – a period of thousands of years during which members of the People of Israel resided in the land – including the *Musta'arbim* and their descendants. During a good part of this period, the People of Israel controlled the destiny of their land.

On the other hand, the Arabs controlled Eretz-Israel for only a few hundred years, and then were replaced by other non-Arab Muslims – the Turks. Together Muslim Arabs and Muslim Turks controlled Eretz-Israel for 1,100 years. During this entire period of Muslim rule there were very few Arabs in the country – only *Musta'arbim* and their offspring who were considered, erroneously to be Arabs...and are still considered Arabs 'thanks' to forced conversion, discrimination and persecution by Arab-Muslim regimes.

The forced expulsion of Jewish settlers from Gaza in August 2005 and any future evacuations are what will create genuine refugee problems among people who have genuine title to Eretz-Israel – who again have become or will become refugees after two thousand years of homelessness as refugees from Eretz-Israel. Those who might raise an eyebrow at the relatively short time such settlers have lived in Judea, Samaria and Gaza, at most a little less than 40 years, should take into account the following rather amazing fact: According to United Nations criteria, eligibility for refugee status among Palestinians who became refugees was only two years residency in Eretz-Israel.

The Terror Leadership

Yasser Arafat, the recognized architect and leader of Palestinian terrorism, was born in 1929 in Cairo. Except for visits with his kin in Eretz-Israel, Arafat remained in Egypt until 1957 when he was expelled for terrorist activity due to his association with the Muslim Brotherhood. Egypt exiled Arafat to Kuwait. From there, he went on to Judea and Samaria, and then fled to Jordan in 1967.

Arafat was a relative of the Palestinian Husseini family on his mother's side. Palestinian blood ran in his veins, but from an ethnic standpoint, Yasser Arafat was primarily a descendent of Moabite extraction on his mother's side.

In 1948, at the age of 19, it should be noted, he visited Eretz-Israel and visited with Husseini kin in Jerusalem. At the beginning of April of that year, mere days prior to events at Dir Yassin, the young Arafat accompanied his uncle – Abdul Kader el-Husseini – in the course of a visit to the **Qastel**. Abdul Kader, who was the commander-in-chief of Palestinian forces in Eretz-Israel, did not know that the fortified village overlooking the road to Jerusalem had been taken by a small Jewish force. The Jewish soldiers spotted the group, opened fire and killed al-Husseini.

Al-Husseini's death was a blow to Palestinian morale, followed by another blow – events at Dir Yassin – and circulation of stories as a bogus massacre that further undermined Arab morale. As was the case time and again, Arafat's life was saved, and in September of the same year he returned to Cairo. Every time Arafat has been involved in warlike actions, the Palestinians have suffered disasters.

On his father's side, Arafat's family history and geography reveal that Arafat was more of a foreigner than a Palestinian, and could at best be viewed as a 'settler.' In February 2004, an Arab newspaper wrote that Arafat's father had immigrated to Egypt from Morocco from a village where most of the inhabitants were Jews, and that his father may have been Jewish.

In light of suspicions regarding his father's possible Jewish lineage, it is not surprising that Arafat preferred to parade his kinship with the illustrious al-Husseini clan. His declaration to the Mufti of Johannesburg that he was an emissary of the Almighty to complete the extermination of the Jews begun by the Nazis is closely tied to this issue. His declaration was prompted first of all to magnify his maternal pedigree as the 'heir' of Haj Amin al-Husseini's legacy – as the Arab leader who led the Nazis to choose extermination over expelling the Jews to Palestine, as a way to rid themselves of the Jews. His use of the nickname **Abu Amar,** the same nickname the Arabs gave Adolf Hitler, is another facet of this aspiration. On the other hand, such declarations were designed to act as a smoke screen to conceal his problematic origins on his father's side, through expression of extreme hatred of the Jews.

Regardless, Arafat's historic role in bringing the Palestinian issue to the center stage of world affairs must be viewed against the backdrop of these serious revelations. If a just solution is ever to be found to the problem of Eretz-Israel, Arafat's contribution to creating the need for a solution was tremendous.

In the course of countless incursions into Palestinian Authority territory by the IDF, again and again it became evident that the terrorists – including the most extreme ones, as well as most of the bomb-making and rocket-making factories, forbidden under the Oslo Agreements – are located in refugee camps. The pattern of flight of the refugees, their emigration and movement from the Gaza Strip to Judea and Samaria, shows that most of the residents of refugee camps west of the Jordan are, in fact, Brethren of Israel. On one hand, this population has very aggressive traits that it developed during the Brethren of Israel's sojourn in Persia. On the other hand, they have suffered more than other sectors of the Palestinian population due to numerous wanderings and neglect in the refugee camps.

In addition, at the beginning of the Second Intifada (October 2000 riots broke out within the Green Line among Palestinian Israeli citizens in the Wadi Ara area. As discussed early in Chapter Five, the inhabitants of this area are for the most part Brethren of Israel, who have kin among the residents of the refugee camps in Judea and Samaria. The Brethren of Israel public is extremist and possesses a low threshold of resistance to incitement directed towards it by terrorist leaders and their collaborators. Members of the Brethren of Israel need to keep in mind that they are mere 'guests' west of the Jordan, and it is hardly in their best interests to allow themselves to be sucked into engaging in terrorism.

The Palestinian terrorist organizations were established, funded and nurtured and continue to be supported by Arab and Iranian despots. In addition to the Palestinian 'rejectionist' organizations, supported for years by the Arab rejectionist 'anti-peace front' and Iran, it is well known that the Saudi Arabian regime finances Hamas. It is no secret that in the 1950s Egypt under the leadership of Abdel Nasser established FATAH. The Palestinians who collaborated with Arab despots were primarily

278

Palestinians in the Palestinian 'Diasporas.' This included the PLO leadership who returned to western Eretz-Israel only after the Oslo Accords, and the leadership of the rejectionist camp, who for the most part remain abroad. Parallel to them, a local leadership has developed, primarily in the Gaza Strip.

The refugees who were foreign immigrants to Eretz-Israel, such as the Arabs who came to the country for economic reasons, were not interested in entering into a lengthy conflict with the State of Israel. The refugees who were Descendants of Israel immigrated to Europe. Those who remained to collaborate with Arab despots – that is, **the terrorist leadership, came primarily from among the Brethren of Israel, the overwhelming majority of the 1948 refugees, whose flight took them to Arab countries – including the Gaza Strip which after the war ended up under Egyptian control.**

As was already discussed regarding their sojourn in Persia, the Brethren of Israel, and all the more so their leaders, are the brightest, most sophisticated and experienced sub-grouping among the Palestinians, attributes that have paved their way to a leadership position among Palestinians as a whole.

The Brethren of Israel leadership, together with their blood brothers, have suffered more than any other Palestinian. Due to this problem, for more than 50 years, they have perpetuated the problem in order to gain camp followers both among those of their brethren who continue to suffer and among the Arabs and others who feel sorry for them. Their objective is not a practical compromise-based solution of the refugee problem; it is their demand of the Right of Return to the places from which they took flight, in order to take over control of these areas and regain their property from before the 1948 War. These areas are practically all the land within the Green Line.

Other immigrants who sojourned in areas that were later delineated inside the Green Line remained in these areas only for a relatively brief period, and a large portion of them even dwelled there in temporary living quarters, illegally or as nomads. By contrast, the majority of Brethren of Israel, who arrived a long time before all the other immigrants were able to acquire property of substance in the places they settled, primarily houses and land, a lot in places that are highly prized real estate today.

Despite their suffering, western Eretz-Israel, and certainly the area within the Green Line, is not the homeland of the Brethren of Israel. Rather, it is part of the homeland of the Jews who returned and settled there. The position of the terrorist leadership regarding the Right of Return has no legitimate basis compared to Jewish title. They should relinquish this demand without anyone having to compensate them, except for fair compensation for assets they abandoned – compensation that would enable this population at least reasonable permanent substitute dwellings to their refugee camps.

The only Palestinian refugees who morally have the Right of Return to their former homes inside the Green Line are the Descendants of the Roman Army, who constitute a very small portion of the inhabitants of Judea, Samaria and the Gaza Strip, and whose involvement in terrorism is very limited. This Right extends to the moral right of Descendants of the Roman Army situated in Jordan to resettle inside the Green Line, as well. The moral rights of the Descendants of the Roman Army exists only if one ignores that their forefathers all were part of an imperialist army, a foreign occupation, which caused countless trials and tribulations – the original 'first cause' of all the complications that exist today.

In that, today, most of this group are not the same adults who fled in 1948, but rather their descendants only, one can view the entire past history from a different perspective, and there is no impelling reasons to pity the majority of this group which resides in Jordan and whose situation is relatively good there. The right of these offspring in Jordan to return to western Eretz-Israel only carries weight if it is based on reciprocity – that is, provided it is linked to the rights of the Brethren of Israel who remained west of the Jordan to return to eastern Eretz-Israel. There is a more detailed discussion of the refugee issue in Chapter Six.

What can one learn from all of the above? Terror and the continuation of the conflict in Eretz-Israel are driven by despots from abroad and are led by Palestinians who have no historic rights west of the Jordan. The terrorist leadership together with the Arab leaders who support them and rank-and-file Palestinians they have succeeded in inciting, have transformed all the other inhabitants of western Eretz-Israel – some 8 million Jews and Palestinians – into victims of terrorism and all its ramifications.

Terrorist leadership is supported internally primarily by those Palestinians, slightly over a million persons, who are Brethren of Israel (1,045,000) and Hebronite Arabs (91,000), who all reside west of the Jordan without any historical rights there. This support imposes terrorism and misfortune on all the inhabitants of Eretz-Israel, or at least on the rest of the inhabitants of Eretz-Israel. Therefore, **the victims of terrorism are the People of Israel, the Descendants of Israel and a small number of others. For the most part, this public is not interested in terrorism; on the other hand, they hold no true title to western Eretz-Israel.**

Of course, those who support terrorism have long ago become victims of their own devices, but the fact remains: **Most of the Palestinians who together with the Jews hold true title to western Eretz-Israel have become hostages of foreigners in their own homeland who control their lives, force terrorism upon them and control the monies designated for Palestinians.**

Another factor that needs to be mentioned here is **the kinship between the Brethren of Israel and the Shi'ites of Iran from an historical standpoint and in terms of mindset,** an affinity that is

281

the product of the sojourn of the Brethren of Israel in Persia. **A shared history has forged an ideological 'confederation' between the two in terms of outlook or world view, based on self-sacrifice on behalf of Islam. It serves as a seedbed for the dangerous collaboration we witness today between the Iranian Muslim dictatorship and the Palestinian terror leadership.**

The long road that the Brethren of Israel have traveled, from their beginnings as converted Edomites and Moabites who were the most devoted group within the People of Israel, to being the Israelis' worst and most bitter enemies seems to epitomize the age-old Jewish adage: "Converts are as taxing for Israel as Psoriasis" (*Kashim gerim leYisrael ke-Sapachat*).

The Big Lie in the Term "Palestinian People"

To sum up the contribution of the finding to Israel advocacy (*hasbarah*) – one must address the essence of the term "Palestinian People." These "people" are for the most part part-and-parcel of the People of Israel. **There is no other party, certainly not an Arab one, which possesses the right to 'compete' with the rights of the People of Israel over western Eretz-Israel and with their linkage to most Palestinians.**

The error in identity that occurred in Eretz-Israel was the product of the detachment of the descendants of Jewish forced converts to Islam from the rest of the People of Israel. Originally, this breakdown was the result of imperialistic deeds of Roman conquerors that forcibly severed the tie between the People of Israel and its homeland in Eretz-Israel, and the Arab-Muslim conquerors that followed who severed Jewish forced converts to Islam and their offspring from their religious faith. This detachment was exacerbated by settlers and immigrants of various sorts who settled in western Eretz-Israel, although they were foreigners.

The natural solution to the problem of Eretz-Israel is for the descendants of Jews who were forced to convert to Islam to return to living among their kind -- the sons of the People of Israel – and for Arab settlers (who have already left Eretz-Israel) to settle down gracefully among their Arab brethren in their original countries or other countries where they have settled. There is no room for talk of 'legitimate rights of the Palestinian People' because Palestinians do not constitute a separate entity! They are, in fact, the artificial product of the forced conversion of part of the People of Israel who remained in their homeland through thick and thin. There is no Palestinians collective with natural or legitimate rights *per se*.

Moreover, separate rights of Palestinians as a collective or 'People,' if there was such a thing, is in conflict with the Jewish People's right to exist in its own homeland. In essence, within a number of generations, **demographically they would negate the right of the Jewish People to exist altogether.** In light of this, one must ask: **Does the 'right to exist' of the People of Israel, a nation that has contributed so much to mankind, not override the right to a separate existence of a Palestinian People, separation that its main contribution to mankind is terror?**

In conclusion, the maliciousness (of the ministers of Caliph al-Hakem) that in the last analysis gave birth to a separate 'Palestinian People' is the same malevolence that paved the way for the Crusades that led to such widespread killing and countless injustices in the past. The results of such sins continue in all their force to this day. The separate existence of a Palestinian 'People' hasn't brought anything to the world except the abomination of terrorism. Of late, this terrorism has escalated to levels that now threaten the global population as a whole. **The problem of Eretz-Israel will not be solved by perpetuating it through establishment of a Palestinian state! The problem of terror will not be solved by broadening the platform from which terrorism can operate freely!**

283

The tremendous divisions among Palestinians, and more than that, the lack of their ability to overcome the terrorism that has spread within their midst, brings one to the harsh conclusion: That first of all, the Palestinians are, at best, a mélange of clans and tribes. Secondly, only a serious 'outside' party such as the State of Israel that has rights to Eretz-Israel has the power and the right to extricate the Palestinians (and Israelis themselves) from the terrible situation that has developed as a result of the malevolence outsiders have wrought in the past.

When one speaks of malevolence, one cannot ignore the worst type of all: **The 'Big Lie.'** Hitler and his propaganda minister Joseph Goebbels argued that the bigger the lie, the greater its effectiveness and more it will be believed. **There is no greater Big Lie on the face of the earth,** unprecedented in the scope of its appeal and its audacious-evil intent, **than claims of Palestinian 'Arabness' and its corollary, the contrived 'estrangement' of Palestinians from the People of Israel.** One can only hope and strive to limit the number of potential victims that this Big Lie will cause, that it should not get near the magnitude of victimhood that the Nazi leaders imposed on the Jews.

Unlike the Nazi propaganda machine, the Big Lie regarding Palestinian identity is not the result of conscious fraud. Those who champion it do not view it as a lie. They promote it without malicious intent but as an innocent error, the product of complex circumstances. Because the power behind the lie is not something that someone consciously seeks to 'stoke,' because it is a widely held convention forged by a falsehood, there is no vested interest in spreading this falsehood that one can pinpoint, confront and combat. This makes it all the harder to expose the Big Lie for what it is.

On the other hand, the above facts have not lessened the unprecedented power of confusion and the scope of adherents that the falsehood has gained. There is no shortage of illusions (and delusions) this error is capable of generating almost a thousand

284

years (1012 CE) after the first seeds of this artificial identity were planted. The dangers and 'cost' that accepting the finding will prevent make it **imperative to uproot the Big Lie from the hearts of all those who embrace it, if one is to uproot the hatred that fuels the conflict.**

Uprooting the Hatred

The crowning contribution of the finding is this: Only this revelation has the potential for lowering the antipathy between most Palestinians and most of the Jews in Eretz-Israel. One of the possible 'side effects' is the possibility that a sense of kinship and shared fate between Jews and Palestinians might emerge from this. As a result, world Jewry and the world community most surely will go out of their way to assist the Palestinians. As a result, the Palestinians' circumstances will improve, squelching the motivation to hate. But it is clear that there is little chance of such a situation unfolding without vigorously uprooting terrorism from Eretz-Israel in a manner that can have a calming effect.

Moreover, the Palestinians are not very popular in the Arab states. They were hated even in Jordan, which absorbed more Palestinian refugees than any other Arab state. Up until 1967, residents of Judea, Samaria and Gaza were not allowed to enroll in institutions of higher learning in Jordan. The Palestinians in turn view the inhabitants of the Arab countries as inferior to themselves. They perceive themselves as the smartest grouping among Arab populations. It is not coincidental that the Palestinians were dubbed 'the Jews of the Arabs.' Knowledge of these facts can bring even more of a rapprochement between Palestinians and Jews when the hatred between them will no longer be the greatest in the region – a region in which hatred seems to be intrinsic to its existence.

As soon as the Arabs will no longer view the Palestinian problem as 'their problem,' as an issue they are duty-bound as Arabs to solve, the minute that every change in the status quo is no longer tied to their own sense of honor, the hatred among the overwhelming majority of Arabs will lessen. They will understand that they have no rights to western Eretz-Israel and will come to realize the magnitude of the tragedy that has taken place in Eretz-Israel – a tragedy that their own leaders were confederates in worsening.

It is no secret among most inhabitants in the majority of Arab countries that their own forefathers were subjugated and forced by the Arabs to change their faith and even to blur their own unique heritage. To this day the ramifications of this ancient conquest continue to have an effect, preventing the region (and of late the world as a whole) from enjoying some semblance of peace and stability. Weakening the support of the Arabs and their leaders in the Palestinian hatred will also weaken this hatred.

Even if the Palestinians – and first and foremost those who lead them down the path of terrorism – will reject the finding presented here and fight against it, surely it will raise doubts among countless rank-and-file Palestinians, primarily because so many of them or at least their elder generation know the truth about their origins. Moreover, the less self-doubting about the justification of Zionism erodes Israeli society, or conversely the more steadfast and unified Israelis will be, the more Palestinians will begin to question their own hatred of Israel and the more such antipathy is likely to wane.

Beyond any gradual lessening of hatred, the finding has relevance as to the solution to the problem. This situation can bring, at its climax, a full resolution of hatred that in the end will bring an end to century-long built-up hatreds. The solution that arises from the finding is presented in the chapters that follow.

Uprooting the Schism

Zionism's primary 'sin' – if such exists – is suppression of the historic truth about Eretz-Israel, and ignoring the finding and its ramification (although this was done, in fact, for objective

286

reasons). In light of the finding, it is clear that the Zionist movement was not seriously mistaken in any other part of its doing. All those who seek to undermine the legitimacy of the Zionist movement and the State of Israel are in grievous error themselves. Thus, there is no justification for the continued schism within the People of Israel over Eretz-Israel.

The schism within the People of Israel is responsible for most of the trouble this people faced during its entire history. The rift began during the First Commonwealth Period at the hands of Rehoboam (the Son of King Solomon) whose mishandling of power upon his ascent to the throne led to a split in the Commonwealth and a civil war between the Kingdom of Judea and the Kingdom of Israel that caused half a million casualties. This bent for divisiveness continued with the refusal of builders of the Second Temple to allow the Samaritans to participate, and the estrangement towards them in later periods.

The schism in the Second Commonwealth period between Jewry in Eretz-Israel and those Jews in Babylonia who chose not to return to the homeland weakened the People of Israel in its struggle for freedom against the Roman Empire. Even then, this struggle could have ended on a far less catastrophic note had it not been for the civil war that brought about the destruction of the Second Commonwealth. Further divisiveness and schism marked the response to Jesus and his followers, which the Jewish leadership of the time chose to push beyond the fold rather than co-opt them or seek the common ground. This led the first Christians to part ways with Judaism, leading to unfathomable hatred of the Jews among foreign Christians and untold suffering among the Jews over a 1,600 year period at the hands of Christianity.

Later there was the rift between the rabbis and the Karaites over the propriety of interpretation of the biblical text (Oral Law), between *Hasidism* and its opponents – the *Mitnagdim* – over different emphases in Jewish observance and the propriety of mysticism, then between Zionists and *haredim* over the propriety

287

of a Return to Zion before the coming of the Messiah (that sealed the fate of many who perished in the Holocaust, when *haredi* rabbis prohibited their followers from going to Eretz-Israel in time), and between the leadership of the Haganah, and the revisionist ETZEL (NMO) and the LECHI over Zionist ideology, political policy and military tactics.

Today the schism is between Right and Left over foreign and domestic policy (particularly the peace process), and between religious and secular over Israel's character as a 'Jewish state' (as well as between Orthodox and Reform in Israel), but this is not all. Besides the Reform movement that constitutes a very small public, each of these components is plagued by sub-fissures within its own camp – reflected in the plurality of political parties in the Knesset.

Yet, the worst schism of all is the Israeli-Palestinian schism. Continuation of this rift after exposure of the finding is parallel to two divisions in the same army – after a prolonged period of battles, due to breakdown in communications – mistakenly identifying the other as an enemy force, and opening friendly fire on one another. Due to the growth in casualties on both sides, hatred becomes so great between the two divisions that even after they recognize the mistaken identification and reestablish communication, they continue their friendly war, refusing to accept that all this was merely the result of a tragic error.

Bridging the Israeli-Palestinian schism will save countless lives and suffering, and automatically rectify the most dangerous schism within the People of Israel today, the division between political Right and Left. If the Israeli-Palestinian division can be mended, it will neutralize the power of political extremists, factionists, and political extortionists of all sorts, and limit the damage they do. Therefore, the most important issue at hand is to mend the Israeli-Palestinian schism.

The People of Israel and the Spirit of Freedom

There is not another People on the face of the earth that has fought for so many freedoms over the course of history as the People of Israel has. These struggles have become a symbol for countless enslaved populations who seek freedom and independence. Suffice it to cite iconic events such as the Exodus from Egypt, the first Return to Zion after the Babylonian Captivity, the revolt against the Greeks and the Romans, the collective suicide at Massada, the Jewish People's survival in the Diaspora, the second Return to Zion and the 1948 War of Independence and Israel's survival and prosperity surrounded by hostile Arab nations. The People of Israel have become a symbol of aspirations for freedom.

Add to this the Jewish People's institution of a day of rest, the liberation of slaves every seven years, and tolerance towards foreigners within its midst (foreign residents). All these landmark events have become principles of freedom that the People of Israel gave to the world – precepts that were adopted thousands of years before other Peoples adopted them from Judaism, at times improving on them.

Despite this, the Palestinian problem badly tarnishes Israel's image. Due to this problem, many freedom fighters in the world and even some people of good intentions among the People of Israel perceived the People of Israel as the antithesis of the symbol of freedom Jews have presented throughout history. Attempts by Ehud Barak's Government to bring an end to the problem in the summer of 2000 at Camp David, and give Palestinians independence failed (though from no fault of Israel). The summit only laid bare the Palestinian terrorist leadership's plot, using the Right of Return to turn Palestinian demographics into a weapon for re-subjugating the People of Israel in its own homeland.

In light of these realities, the People of Israel must find a way to re-assert itself as the beacon of freedom it has epitomized throughout its long existence, even when dealing with the

289

Palestinians. This should be done in the spirit of freedom that the Zionist movement brought to the People of Israel when it 'seized the moment' to establish the State of Israel, against all odds and prevailed. Now the time has come to consider, after the dismal failure of the simple logic of Oslo, whether **the time has not come to 'seize the moment' and use the spirit of freedom inherent in Zionism vis-à-vis the Palestinians.**

The People of Israel must consider whether it is willing to continue to accept a situation where members of the People of Israel **remain forced Muslim-Arab converts in their own homeland,** manipulated by terrorists to bash Israel and tarnish its image as a longstanding beacon of freedom and justice in the world. Far worse, the People of Israel must decide whether they are willing to let this phenomenon ruin its own independence and very existence!

When Palestinian origins become an issue on the world agenda, the Palestinians themselves will finally be free to discuss what they know about their genuine identity and 'fill in the blanks' about their own family legacy. As a result, they will be able to understand who they have been fighting for and who they have been fighting against all these years, and reach some new self-evident insights – including the reality that they cannot achieve their own liberation at the expense of the freedom of their original kin.

Chapter Six

Possible Solutions

The ramifications of the finding about Palestinian origins on a solution to the conflict can be far-reaching. This work only addresses the main options for a solution that arise directly from the finding about Palestinian origins. Among the Existing options (even ignoring the finding...) will be discussed briefly only if they have a high probability of implementation – that is, the partition of western Eretz-Israel into two states. The impact of the finding on this solution can be positive, if it will enhance the likelihood of success.

The multiplicity of solutions suggested today by various factions on both sides of the conflict are reminiscent of Krylov's famous parable about the six blind men and the elephant, how each described the elephant as an entirely different entity based on objective but partial personal experience of each of them, based on the part of the elephant each happened to touch. In the case of Eretz-Israel, the People of Israel, its various and sundry sub-groupings are both the elephant and the blind men operating on partial information. To date, 'solutions' have been based on partial, fragmented experience and subjective perceptive of the 'elephant' in the eyes of this or that party that were totally beyond the experience of the other parties; thus, the 'solutions' were infeasible to implement and therefore all failed. A real solution must be based on a correct self-ascription that will end the blindness that lies at the heart of the problem.

Unfortunately, a conflict that arises from 2,000 years of history can't be fully solved overnight. The Oslo process's goal was to reach a final and comprehensive solution in a relatively short period of time of five years. The attempt was correct and timely, but misplaced and set at the wrong tempo.

To achieve full implementation of a suitable solution to such a complex problem will require at least one to three percent of the time it took to create the problem – that is, a period of several decades. It is advisable that the solution advance slowly, rather than building illusions and false expectations that again will lead to disappointment, despair and countless victims, as in the past. In other words, the world community and the inhabitants of the region need to be patient. They must understand there are no shortcuts and a solution will take time.

Beyond a long-term solution to the problem of relations between the People of Israel and the Palestinians, one cannot ignore the issue of Palestinian citizens of Israel within the Green Line, and Palestinian residents in Jerusalem. A portion of this public label themselves 'Israeli Arabs' in order to avoid being accidentally 'lumped together' with hostile Palestinians in Judea, Samaria and Gaza, but these 'Israeli Arabs,' for the most part, are not Arab at all. They are caught between their loyalty to their country and their loyalty to their Palestinian kin, and their loyalty as Arabs.

The Israeli-Palestinian conflict intensified and sharpened this problem. The events of October 2000 – violent demonstrations by Israeli Arabs within the Green Line following the outbreak of the Second Intifada that climaxed in a lethal clash with police in Wadi Ara that left nine dead – only underscores the danger of neglecting this issue. In addition, the demographic threat to Israeli Jews' hegemony that the high birth rate of Israeli Arabs presents cannot be met with indifference or swept under the rug. Parallel to this, there are many Palestinians who are Israeli citizens who, despite their loyalty to their country, feel like second-class citizens. A fitting solution needs to solve these issues as well, or they will become another time bomb in Jewish-Arab relations.

Option One – An Imposed Settlement

The probability that the two sides in western Eretz-Israel can reach a compromise solution freely and willingly is extremely small. In broad terms an imposed settlement implies a total end to terrorism and the signing of a peace treaty that will end the conflict and any future demands by either side, without solving the underlying problem.

This kind of settlement has a better chance of materializing and of 'holding water' if it will take place in a milieu of reduced animosity and openings for improvements (by peaceful means) in the imposed *status quo* – as presented in Option Two. Even if the possibility of a full and just solution in the future remains a distant dream, leaving this option open can serve as a pressure valve for letting off steam and preventing the build-up of frustrations on both sides due to unrealized aspirations that are beyond the terms of an imposed settlement.

Option One in short means: **The only way to reach a settlement on the basis of present conventions of agreement is by imposing the terms on both sides.** The Road Map is the leading framework for an imposed solution. Israel's dependence on the United States is so great that it cannot reject an imposed solution if this will be the will of the US Administration, and the only leeway that remains is to hammer out the details with the United States and the Palestinians.

The period of negotiations or bargaining between the sides vis-à-vis the United States will be very heated. It will include a Palestinian-Arab public opinion offensive designed to strengthen as much as possible the proposed Palestinian state while weakening as much as possible the State of Israel. There will be plenty of opportunities to divide the Israeli public... The finding and its implication presented in previous chapters can help bolster the Israeli position and garner support for Israel.

The most dangerous mistake that can be made regarding peace in the region is to establish a Palestinian state in the foreseeable future. President Bush has declared time and again his commitment to support establishment of a Palestinian state. The United States needs the cooperation of the Arabs behind the American presence in Iraq and regarding oil prices. In addition the Americans hope that through the Road Map they can neutralize the primary hub of global terrorism. Thus, the US Administration will not backtrack on their commitment to a Palestinian state. As for the future of a Palestinian state and what shape and form it is likely to take – such a state is likely to drag the entire Middle East into one of two possible scenarios:

Scenario 1A: Deterioration and Escalation of the Conflict

According to this scenario, an imposed settlement and a Palestinian state will only signal a new phase in the conflict that will require a new more far-reaching solution.

Scenario 1B: Success of a Settlement

According to this scenario (whose prospects under prevailing realities are not great) the imposed settlement will hold together. If the finding presented in Chapters Three and Four of this work will fall on fertile soil and bring about a reduction in the hatred, this factor could enhance the likelihood of success. But in the last analysis, a Palestinian state will not fulfill the aspirations of both sides, particularly if such a settlement will be based on a long-term *hudna*, or temporary Islamic cease-fire. Ultimately, a new stage, based on renewed negotiations, will be required during which the two sides will need to move forward to fulfill more of their aspirations.

The Second Stage of a Settlement

The two scenarios presented above have a very high probability that they will require an additional phase in the peace process to reach a solution to the problem of Eretz-Israel. Such a second stage can take place only after a period in which the milieu among Palestinians will be radically transformed (and the atmosphere among Israelis to a lesser extent). Of course, such a change in the political climate can come about through a new war in which the two sides will suffer even more than in the past.

Yet, even if somehow a miracle will occur and the optimistic scenario will be realized, the milieu can be changed, among other things, by changes in *hasbarah* and the educational system. These systems must be founded on genuine data concerning the history of Eretz-Israel, and first and foremost intensifying the study of Arabic (mainly spoken Arabic) by making Arabic a third language unit in high school curriculums (alongside Hebrew and English) and establishing adult education courses throughout the country that will teach Arabic to Jews, as well. Similar courses in Hebrew among Palestinians would be a positive move.

The finding presented in Chapters Three and Four suggests another route, an alternative, in the long run, to a Palestinian state, once such a polity has been established. This alternative is the primary contribution of the finding at the heart of this work regarding the origins of the Palestinians.

Unfortunately, due to lack of sufficient time, it is hard to believe that this alternative can take root fast enough to prevent the catastrophe that establishment of a Palestinian state in the current stage almost surely will bring. But in the second phase, after such a polity arises (and probably only after this Palestinian state causes untold unnecessary damage) will the alternative come to the fore as a realistic option.

The alternative is Option Two. But Option Two requires considerable openness of mind if this complex proposal is to be allowed to be considered in all seriousness. Examining the proposal with an open mind is imperative, because the alternatives are either to acquiesce to a Palestinian state with all the troubles it will bring, or adopt the idea of a transfer of Palestinians out of the country, that in light of the finding would be wrong, even vis-à-vis the most extremist Jewish settlers.

Chapter Seven

Option Two – One State for One Nation: The Re-Engagement Scheme

And say unto them: Thus saith the Lord GOD: Behold, I will take the children of Israel from among the nations, whither they are gone, and will gather them on every side, and bring them into their own land; <u>And I will make them one nation in the land, upon the mountains of Israel [!]</u>, and one king shall be king to them all; <u>and they shall be no more two nations</u> [!], <u>neither shall they be divided into two kingdoms any more at all</u>;...Moreover <u>I will make a covenant of peace with them – it shall be an everlasting covenant with them</u> [!]. (Ezekiel 37:21-22, 26)

Although Ezekiel's prophecy sounded fitting for the first Return to Zion, the fate of the Second Commonwealth can hardly be considered a peaceful covenant that would be an everlasting covenant. Ben-Gurion once commented that 'to live in Israel without believing in miracles is impractical.'

The renowned physicist David Bohm said in his work *Wholeness and the Implicate Order*[51] [emphasis, the authors]:

"<u>The notion that all these fragments are separately existent is evidently an illusion, and this illusion</u> cannot do other than lead to <u>endless conflict and confusion</u>. Indeed, the attempt to live according to the notion that the fragments are really separate is, in essence, what has led to the <u>growing series of extremely urgent crises that is confronting us today</u>."

David Bohm's observations regard humankind as a whole, but his words are truly 'on target' when one considers the inhabitants of Eretz-Israel and they can serve as a beacon for Israelis and

---

[51] See Source 16.

Palestinians against the backdrop of all the wars, the terrorist acts and counter measures and reprisals, all the innocent victims, and the great confusion that seems to have enveloped Israeli leadership and the total chaos that has enveloped the Palestinian Authority! Confusion and crisis have spread to other countries as well, whose citizens have, in turn, been subjected to the impact of the rising terrorist tide.

This complex state of affairs that grips the region demands that one approach the problem in a new and broader light than has been the case in the past. Tremendous negative energies have been poured into the Israeli-Arab conflict. These negative energies need to be reversed by a positive orientation. This will not only provide the People of Israel with the peace and security they seek, but also take the People of Israel a quantum leap forward in terms of its sheer size and power.

Mark Twain envisioned the tremendous potential inherent in the advent of the Zionist Movement and the vision of a Jewish state (as he wrote in his essay "On the Jews"):

Dr. Herzl... wishes to gather the Jews of the world together in Palestine, with a government of their own...I am not objecting; but if that concentration of the cunningest brains in the world were going to be made in a free country (bar Scotland), I think it would be politic to stop it. It will not be well to let the race find out its strength. If the horses knew theirs, we should not ride any more.

Like Herzl's vision, Mark Twain's vision also was only partly realized. In light of the finding presented in Chapters Three and Four, and against the backdrop of the schism between Left and Right in Israel discussed in Chapter One, the primary reason that Mark Twain's vision regarding the potential strength of the People of Israel has not been fully realized becomes self-evident: There is no question that the reason is the schism that still exists between Jews and Palestinians that has raged parallel to realization of Herzl's vision.

298

The communications and information revolution make it a relatively easy task for terrorist groups around the world to stay in contact and share information on how to prepare deadly weapons. But this new era also opens new horizons, and provides new information that can allow the People of Israel to base its future in a way that is fitting to its past. Thus, the inhabitants of Eretz-Israel can avoid difficulties that are the product of pursuing artificial, dictated directions that prevent these inhabitants from moving naturally along the original path from which they came.

Option Two for solving the conflict is based on the input of new information; it is innovative and far-reaching, but at the same time it constitutes a natural self-evident solution. Due to its revolutionary character, Option Two can be relevant, only after the finding regarding Palestinian origins has time to trickle down and become the dominant way of thinking among both sides of the conflict.

The author is liable to be met with disbelief, even downright derision for raising such a notion that many will perceive as utopian or pure fantasy or worse – a dire peril. Nevertheless it is imperative to do so, because Option Two constitutes the only just solution, a solution that in the end can bring peace, security and prosperity to all the inhabitants of Eretz-Israel.

This Option can become a practical and successful solution in the future once the present mindset will pass and certain fissures within the People of Israel will be allowed to heal in the wake of events. It doesn't matter whether these events will be positive (peace – whose probability is very small) or negative (continuation of the conflict and war – whose probability is high); in either case, the hope is that what has transpired up until now is not acute enough to force people to 'think again.' Lastly, it is possible to realize this Option in a manner that will neutralize many of the apprehensions that surround it.

Option Two emerges directly from the finding, and can **rejoin or re-engage the divisions facing one another, into one single united polity in western Eretz-Israel!**

On the face of it, this outlook seems to complement the original goals of the PLO prior to the Oslo Accords, and the objectives of many Palestinians today – creation of 'one secular state' in all of western Eretz-Israel. But this course can be a lasting solution, even one acceptable to the Jews, provided that there will be one significant alteration: **that it will not create a bi-national state.**

Moreover, this approach complements the original aspirations of the Israeli Right-wing – the Greater Israel Movement. Thus, it is possible to reach **a compromise between the extremists** on both sides. Such a compromise will **enable a stable peace**, in contrast to an unstable peace based on a compromise between moderates on the two sides. The most just and practical course in order to implement Option Two is **for the majority of Palestinians to re-engage with the People of Israel freely of their own volition!**

This is an explosive, emotion-loaded proposition from all standpoints. Today, joining the People of Israel is accomplished through the institution of conversion to Judaism. Clearly this is neither relevant nor feasible. Even if many secular Palestinians would accept the finding and its ramifications, the current conversion process would make Option Two very unpopular among most Palestinians. The 're-engagement plan' this work offers is not the same as the concept of 'secular conversion' that has been proposed as a solution to the problem of the large number of non-Jewish immigrants who arrived in Israel from the former Soviet Union in the 1990s together with their Jewish spouses. The process suggested for Palestinians is different because it addresses the re-unification of veteran inhabitants of Eretz-Israel, and its terms are far more comprehensive.

300

Significance of a Solution Based on Re-engagement as Part of the People of Israel

The proposed solution requires each new member to gain mastery of the following:

1. The Hebrew language (including reading and writing)

2. The culture of the People of Israel;

3. The history of the People of Israel;

4. The history of Eretz-Israel;

5. The Bible;

6. Jewish religious tradition.

The scope of knowledge or proficiencies required would be equal to that of most secular Jews, and would ensure that the act of re-engagement would have sufficient quality and depth. The scope of knowledge would actually be far greater than that required in conventional conversion to Judaism, and would not exclusively focus on matters of faith and ritual. Why is such a broad canvas required? There is the need to provide a cognitive counterweight to the hostile education and incitement that Palestinians have been subjected to in the past in regard to Israel. Moreover, in many cases such education is needed to enhance the level of education of participants to enable them to successfully integrate into Israeli society without being marginalized or becoming second-class citizens. Such education can be accomplished in a framework similar to the Hebrew language *ulpans* (intense six month 'total immersion' crash-courses designed to inculcate basic mastery of Hebrew by new immigrants used successfully in Israel for decades).

Enrollees will be required to do the following:

7. Declare their renunciation of their association to the Arab Nation;

301

8. Take an oath of allegiance to the People of Israel and the State of Israel.

Declaration of renunciation or disassociation from membership in the Arab Nation does not mean in any way that candidates must detach themselves from Arab culture – just as many Jews who came from the former Soviet Union have not abandoned their Russian cultural baggage. The decision to enable Palestinians to re-join the People of Israel requires suitable timing, after the ground has been prepared for such a move: First and clearly, only after the majority of the People of Israel will support such a move. In addition, this Option envisions (in contrast with the other Options that will be presented) that Palestinian leadership at the time will favor such a move, and re-engagement will be accomplished under a general climate of rapport and agreement that this is the best course for both sides.

Palestinians who complete the process of re-joining the People of Israel will receive Israeli citizenship. At some point in time after most Palestinians will have successfully completed this process – a process that will not be brief in any case – there will no longer be any reason on demographic grounds to prevent the granting Israeli citizenship to other Palestinian inhabitants of Eretz-Israel who decline this Option.

Although this re-unification process can be called 'national conversion,' it would be wise not to do so. On one hand, use of such nomenclature is likely to deter religious elements in Israeli society from adopting this idea. Secondly, it will only fuel opposition among many Palestinians and others, due to the association between 'religion' and 'conversion.'

This process can also be labeled a 'national convergence' or 'national re-engagement,' underscoring the symmetry. In other words, the Palestinians need to rectify their detachment from the People of Israel, just as the Jews rectified their detachment from Eretz-Israel. The symmetry, in essence, rests on the 'reciprocity of a mending process' through parallel conscious acts of will: the abrogation of two forms of detachment akin to two sides of the same coin – one geographically, one nationally.

Parallel to the re-engagement process, in order to cement new relations and bolster understanding with neighboring Arabs as well, the Israeli educational system needs to add to the curriculum sufficient content on Christianity, Islam and Arab culture that do not exist today. These need to be presented objectively, devoid of old historical scores, in order not to leave Israelis in the dark in these areas. The same is true of education in the Arab countries regarding content on Israel and Judaism.

For many Left-wingers in Israel, and no small number of other people in Eretz-Israel and in the world as a whole, the proposed solution is not only relatively easy to accept, it also provides a valid solution irrespective of the finding about Palestinian origins. In many countries in the world, sub-groupings from disparate backgrounds have merged over the years to become one nation. But among many others in Eretz-Israel, particularly the community of religiously-oriented Jews, the very notion of waiving religious conversion according to *halacha* (Orthodox religious Law) is far harder to swallow, even if they accept the finding about Palestinians.

As for religious circles, it needs to be underscored unequivocally, again and again: There is no intention here to solve one crisis and one schism within the People of Israel by creating a second one or intensifying the first. Religious circles in Judaism should not only agree to the solution (based on explanations to be detailed in the following pages); they should, indeed, harness their energies to make it happen, for the alternatives surely are far worse from their standpoint. Certainly the religious community can't simply sit on the sidelines when such a significant transformation in the development of the People of Israel is afoot.

303

From the perspective of secular Palestinians, the Option offers an avenue to re-engage as part of the People of Israel without dealing heavily in religious issues. For many Palestinians, who have turned to religion out of despair and as an outlet for their pain, presentation of a better avenue to solve their problems will no doubt bring about religious moderation and a drop in the attraction of Islamic extremism. Religious Jews have nothing to fear from the re-engagement of such a secular population with secular Jews among the People of Israel. The more gaps between all inhabitants of Eretz-Israel that will be bridged, the better off everyone will be.

Among the religious community it is well known that a Jew who converts to another faith does not have to convert in order to return to the People of Israel. This is the law vis-à-vis those born Jews. It is not valid for the offspring of proselytes, who must re-convert, although the process is less stringent. This is relevant to Jews in the Diaspora where mixed marriages are very prevalent as well as re-conversion of the offspring of Diaspora Jews who converted under pressure to another religion – such as some of the Ethiopian Jews or Spanish and Portuguese *Marannos*.

In addition, the offspring of a Jew in the Diaspora who freely changed their religious faith, who did so in order to set themselves apart from the People of Israel and assimilate into society-at-large, are not considered Jews, and don't enjoy any special status one way or another due to their 'Jewish roots'; they are treated as gentiles in every respect.

Things have always been different in Eretz-Israel. During the First Commonwealth Period, and to a certain extent during the Second Commonwealth as well, there were many idol worshippers among the People of Israel, including progressions of generations of idol worshippers. Because they resided in Eretz-Israel among their observant brethren, these idol worshippers were considered members of the People of Israel. While Israelite prophets preached (and warned them of dire consequences) for their transgressions,

304

there were never demands that they convert to return fully to the fold.

Considering the circumstances revealed in the finding regarding the Palestinians' origins, it is clear that according to *Halakha* (Jewish Law) most Palestinians are not required to convert if they wish to return to the fold.

According to the *halachic* precept **that "a person whose mother was Jewish is also a Jew,"** an individual whose grandmother on his or her maternal side was Jewish (and therefore the person's mother was unmistakably Jewish) is also a Jew by Orthodox criteria. In general, families whose maternal bloodline leads to a Jewish mother in the past is a Jewish family (that is, if a mother far back in the family legacy was Jewish then all of her daughters and her daughters' daughters in a similar fashion 'up the family tree' are to this day also Jewish). In other words, in order to be considered Jewish such families or such individuals need to desire to re-engage as part of the People of Israel and to cease to consider themselves the sons of a foreign people, as part of the declarative process and educational program described above. This method is valid due to the following circumstances:

A.   The overwhelming majority of Palestinians west of the Jordan today, including the Brethren of Israel, are Descendants of the People of Israel.

B.   Up until the *Musta'arbim*, intermarriage of Israelites with others was not an acceptable practice.

C.   Since the period of the *Musta'arbim* in 1012 up until 1914, most of the inhabitants of Eretz-Israel were Descendants of Israel and their Brethren.

D.   Beginning in 1948, the number of gentiles among the Palestinians narrowed gradually but significantly, to a mere 15 percent today.

E.   Throughout all periods, most of the Descendants of Israel resided in the mountain country of Eretz-Israel where they were isolated from gentile populations, except for the Brethren of Israel during their sojourn in Persia and after their Return to Eretz-Israel.

Thus, it can safely be assumed that the rate of intermarriage was very low among the People of Israel both due to numerical hegemony as an undisputed majority, and the geographic disparity of the majority of this majority. The likelihood of 'foreign blood' among Palestinians – that is, the scope of Palestinians who lost the continuity of a purely Israelite-Jewish maternal bloodline beginning with the Jewish mother prior to the *Musta'arbization* process – is very, very low.

Another important theorem in Judaism says that: *Kol De'parish Merubah Parish* – in other words, when there is a question about the origins of a particular party, reasonability/high probability under a given set of circumstances in favor of a particular origin is deemed decisive in determining origin. Based on this assumption, and the very high number of Palestinians west of the Jordan with Israelite origins, Palestinians should not be required to convert to Judaism in order to return to the fold of the People of Israel.

There is no question that this maxim is applicable among Palestinian inhabitants of the Galilee and the Bedouin. As for Samaria, given that the Samaritans were for the most part members of the People of Israel, or at least for a lengthy period took upon themselves Jewish practice, and given that following the commandments of the Torah constitutes conversion, these circumstances make the same maxim applicable in Samaria. In other areas of the country there will probably be strict constructionists who would take issue with applying of this maxim, but in all fairness, one can 'go the extra mile' and give such Palestinians who wish to join the People of Israel 'the benefit of the doubt' as well.

Extenuating Circumstances

And it shall come to pass, that he that is left in Zion, and he that remaineth in Jerusalem, shall be called holy, even every one that is written unto life in Jerusalem. (Isaiah 4:3)

When there are reservations to the above 'liberal' approach, one should take into account the special circumstances Palestinians faced, including:

A.   Forced conversion, not conversion of one's free will, their tenaciously practicing Jewish commandments in secret in a manner that spanned a thousand years before most of the commandments were lost or dissipated.

The Palestinians who are descendants of Forced Converts to Islam – *Musta'arbim* – never took steps to abandon the People of Israel, rather their gradual abandonment of the Religion of Israel was the product of attrition under constant pressures and perils, and even today, for many abandonment is not complete.

B.   The Palestinians are sons of the People of Israel who doggedly remained to preserve Eretz-Israel, and hold the title of the People of Israel over Eretz-Israel. Only lack of information about their origins and the ongoing persecution they suffered led to questions about their entitlements.

C.   According to the *Mishnah* "the commandment to settle Eretz-Israel balances all the other commandments in the Torah." Palestinians who remained in Eretz-Israel, practicing Islam while maintaining some of the Jewish commandments (such as worshipping only one God, refraining from eating pork, following family purity customs during menstruation, prohibition of making graven images, honoring one's father and mother, etc.); their entitlements, anchored in steadfastly clinging to Eretz-Israel, are far greater than that of Diaspora Jews.

D.   Another law, found in the *Book of the Zohar*, says that circumcision is equal in importance to all the other commandments

307

combined. Although circumcision among Muslims is not as complete as that practised by Jews, one cannot ignore that Palestinian Muslims are circumcised and enter the Covenant of the Patriarch Abraham – and no small number carry out this commandment in a manner that is closer to Judaism than to Islam.

E.   One can end the lengthy travails of the People of Israel in Eretz-Israel and in Exile without citing new perils in the world where weapons of mass destruction are within the reach of many parties.

F.   One can bring to an end the tragedies of a huge number of Palestinian families that were forced to convert to Islam, still remember their origins and await the day when they will not be in peril if this fact will become known and their own People, the People of Israel will agree to embrace them and re-absorb them as their own flesh and blood.

G.   The great suffering that the Palestinians have undergone due to their devotion to Eretz-Israel from the breakdown of government and the ecology, economic distress and natural disasters to man-made hardships from punitive taxes to forced conversion – and their suffering from ongoing conflict with the Jews returning to Zion due to errors in their identity.

H.   Correspondence of the Rambam and his father regarding the *Musta'arbim* in which they comforted and encourage *Musta'arbim* to preserve their Jewishness in secret, and rejected any ostracism by Jews. The Rambam quoted prophecy that it would come to pass that the fate of those who abandoned the faith under pressure would be restored and Israel would rein supreme.

Under such conditions, and in light of all the extenuating circumstances cited above, there is no substance for religious parties within Judaism demanding that Palestinians convert. Requiring conversion would place an impassable stumbling block in the path of solving the conflict and achieving a just and successful solution in lieu of generations of unnecessary conflict.

308

Such circles, who view Judaism as the leading faith, should strive so that those re-engaging with the People of Israel will become closer to the Religion of Israel willingly, not by force. This will be the religious leadership's 'hour of truth' – whether they can meet the challenge of translating the merits of the Religion of Israel into practical forms that can have a profound impact in shaping the future of the People of Israel. To do so, religious circles can take advantage of the large reservoir of persons schooled in Jewish religious studies, the product of the almost automatic exemptions from military service Ultra-Orthodox yeshiva students have traditionally enjoyed.

Those among the religious community who have chosen to 'serve the State of Israel' by devoting themselves totally to Talmudic studies rather than serving in the IDF can be leaders (together with others) in bringing 'Peace upon Israel' and bringing lost Jewish brethren back into the fold. These cadres of former and current yeshiva students can play an active role in schooling Palestinians in many of the topics outlined in the re-engagement process. Likewise, they can view such endeavors as an avenue for enhancing the dialogue with both the religions that sprung from Judaism (Christianity and Islam), to lessen religious rivalry and hatred in the world.

In order to prevent Israel from being flooded with refugees and others from all sorts of places from the point where suitable legislation is enacted, the re-engagement process with the People of Israel will apply only to current inhabitants of western Eretz-Israel, and in other cases only on a very limited scale, based on humanitarian considerations such as family unification.

Righting a Historical Injustice

Option Two – of 'One State for One People' – is the only solution that is historically just. It will bring back into the fold captives who were forced to abandon their religion and were literally 'abducted' by force from their own original People. Abduction of this sort did not take place anywhere else as a result of the Arab Conquest. Other peoples in countries conquered by Arabs either all of them became Arabs or they didn't become Arabs at all. Only in Eretz-Israel did the same people end up with two disparate identities, and only because of the second Return to Zion did this problem surface with such gravity.

To a large extent, the abduction is the result of the change in name of Eretz-Israel imposed by the Roman Empire after brutally crushing the Bar Kokhba Revolt. If one examines neighboring countries such as Lebanon, Syria (or *A-syria* as it is called in Arabic, which is old *Ashur* in Hebrew or Assyria in foreign languages), and Egypt, all bear their names from antiquity, without change and their Peoples did not lose their national identity, although they became a part of the Arab world.

The exception is Jordan, which was established in eastern Eretz-Israel after the British Empire partitioned Eretz-Israel. Its present name, Jordan, is an abbreviated version of Transjordan, the name given this territory after the British partition in the early 1920s. In other words, only because of the deeds of the Roman Empire are the inhabitants who remained in Eretz-Israel called 'Palestinians' today – not Jews.

To understand the damage the Romans did in changing the name of the country, one can ask the following hypothetical question: **If the Romans had *not* changed the name of the country from Judea to Palestina, and Eretz-Israel would have continued to be called Judea, would Palestinians today be called Jews or Judeans although Muslims by faith, and would all the same hostility and wars have plagued the Middle East?** It is highly improbable. It is likely that hostility would have been far less, and some of the wars, if not all of them, might have been avoided.

Thus, the abduction of the Palestinians from the People of Israel is the primary reason for the problems of the Middle East over the

310

past six decades, and Eretz-Israel for more than a century. Historic justice (and historic justice relates to events as they unfolded in the past) requires that the captives be re-united with their own People.

Moreover, the Palestinians never 'officially' left the People of Israel. The process of changing one's faith among Jews today is considered grounds for the individual no longer being considered part of the People of Israel. This approach was adopted due to the lengthy period during which the People of Israel were in Exile. A Jew who leaves the Jewish faith in the Diaspora assimilates into the surrounding culture, including the nationality of the land in which the apostate resides. Thus, such a person loses his Jewish nationality although there isn't any official 'renunciation' of Jewish nationality *per se*.

Among the Palestinians, no one underwent any process of leaving the Israelite-Jewish nation, even after, at various stages, they abandoned their religion. Even if one ignores the coercions behind their conversion, Palestinians did not reside in the Diaspora and did not assimilate into another Nation. The degree to which Muslim (or Christian) Palestinians developed an affinity for Arab culture was no different than the Arab culture that Jews in Arab countries absorbed, without changing their religious faith.

As a result of the al-Hakem Edict sparking mass conversion among those who turned to be *Musta'arbim*, the offspring of the People of Israel became the overwhelming majority in Eretz-Israel. Naturally, not all conversions to Islam were forced conversions, yet this situation could not lead to assimilation from a national standpoint and abandonment of Israelite-Jewish nationhood. From a national identity standpoint, a person cannot assimilate into his or her own original People.

What transpired in Eretz-Israel was that the identity of an entire people – the part of the People of Israel who clung to remaining in Eretz-Israel – got mixed up due to the change of the name of the country by the Romans to 'Palestina,' due to

the abandonment of the Religion of Israel by attrition and due to lack of substantive knowledge of what happened after the Arab Conquest. Thus, the Palestinians never left the Israelite-Jewish nationhood. Relating to the majority of them as Arabs is a tragic mistake. In theory, they really don't have to undergo any process in order to re-unite with the People of Israel.

Nevertheless, objectively there is a need for a re-engagement process for individual Palestinians to officially re-join the People of Israel, in order to bridge the cultural gap and prevent misunderstanding, discrimination and conflict, and because a minority of Palestinians are not originally Jewish and their absorption requires a suitable process.

In many cases, one cannot pinpoint among the Palestinians who belongs to what group, due to intermarriage among the groups and other factors. Moreover, in the absence of a re-engagement process, discrimination is likely to remain towards some of the sub-groupings and towards all Palestinians due to the difficulty differentiating among members of the various sub-groupings. Such ambiguity, if serious, could spark instances of racism, something only a formal re-engagement framework as described above can avert.

Although such a process is far from implementation today, there is room even today, after designation of nationality was eliminated from Israeli citizen's identity cards,[52] to relate to those Israeli citizens today designated Israeli Arabs as 'Muslim Israelis' or 'Christian Israelis' and not as Arabs at all. To the same extent Palestinians in Judea, Samara and Gaza should be designated simply 'Palestinian' and not 'Palestinian Arabs.'

Righting such a historical injustice this way is not necessarily feasible in terms of immediate implementation, but every

---

[52] By a religious Minister of Interior (due to controversy between religious parties and the court system over the legal definition of 'Who is a Jew' in terms of nationhood).

312

Palestinian who has fought for 'righting a historical wrong' and has demanded the Right of Return (or Palestinian control of all of Eretz-Israel) needs to decide: If Eretz-Israel belongs to them, since their own origins are rooted in the People of Israel, Palestinians should re-engage with the People of Israel and thus all of Eretz-Israel can , indeed, be 'theirs' without a fight. If Eretz-Israel does not belong to them, then they should dwell there peacefully as residents and not engage in terrorism – or they will be transferred elsewhere.

It should be underscored: The proposed solution is not in any way a declaration that all Palestinians must prefer or agree to re-engage with the People of Israel – whether as an immediate step or an option for the future. Every Palestinian needs to decide the solution he or she prefers in light of the individual's own family legacy and the future the family prefers. The call is, first and foremost, to know the truth – not to hate, not to kill and not to sacrifice oneself on the altar of a bogus perception of historical justice.

Any Palestinian can weigh the product of the past decades and see where terrorism has gotten them. Palestinians can weigh the Option that can transform them into equal citizens with equal rights in their own country, while Jews returning to their own homeland have already demonstrated what a level of prosperity they can bring to the country, provided there will be peace. While American foreign aid has been a great boon to Israel's successes, one can only imagine what Israel and all the People of Israel can achieve if there will be peace, bringing an even greater influx of capital – whether in the form of aid or investments.

By contrast, the 'Palestinian State' Option, with limited territory and limited economic potential, will bring, at best, a second-rate polity. A good proportion of the aid such a Palestinian state will receive will end up in the hands of corrupt functionaries and be directed towards a third war against Israel. Such a country will be led primarily by leaders driven by hatred and jealousy towards the 'first-rate country' across the border.

313

Under such realities, it won't take long for Palestinian leaders to lead Palestinians into another *Nakba* (a catastrophe of the magnitude of 1948) that will take the lives of countless Palestinians and lead to a transfer. The suffering this will inflict on Israelis and neighboring Arabs will offer Palestinians little consolation. In the wake of such aggression on the part of a Palestinian state, and the destruction they will wrought, not one party in the world, including the Arabs and the Europeans, will continue to support any national rights for Palestinians.

The terrorist leadership believes they have the power to exterminate the State of Israel with the help of the Iranians, Arab extremists and weapons of mass destruction. But beginning with the Mufti Haj Amin al-Husseini who collaborated with the Nazis towards the self same goal, Palestinian leaders have believed in their ability to expel the Jews from Eretz-Israel. This aspiration has only led to perpetual hardships – primarily suffered by the Palestinians themselves, and inflicted on Jews in the Diaspora – which has only strengthened the Zionist Movement.

When one considers the proposed settlement Israel offered the Palestinians in 2000 at Camp David, all the terrorist acts committed by Palestinians in the Second *Intifada* were, in retrospect, the upshot of their insistence on the Right of Return.

Thus, the business of the present occupation, even if one ignores the question 'who is the real occupier,' is not the reason for the ongoing conflict and the terrorism. The conflict, the incitement and the terrorism serve only as a declaration of intention to achieve a sinister form of 'historic justice' – a covert intention to gain Palestinian-Arab control of all of Eretz-Israel and leave Jews stateless. Those parties who champion the Palestinian cause, consciously or unconsciously, are aligning themselves with a form of 'historic justice' they may or may not have intended, and no less serious, make themselves culpable as partners in a new form of oppression against the Jews in addition to past oppressions by many of these parties.

314

All those 'justice seekers' on the Palestinian question need to reconsider: If it is historic justice they seek, then 'righting historic wrongs' needs to be based on history in full. The soil of Eretz-Israel has witnessed great suffering among its inhabitants and been soaked in the blood of many of them. The peak of all these historic injustices is the conduct of the Romans and Caliph al-Hakem's ministers. **The Second Return to Zion – modern Zionism – rectifies the injustices committed by the Romans. Likewise, the return of the Palestinians to the People of Israel will rectify the injustice of the al-Hakem Edict.** Without this taking place, the joint homeland of Jews and Palestinians will continue to be "a Land that devours its inhabitants" (Numbers 13:32).

A thought expressed by Dr. Martin Luther King, Jr., epitomizes the change in mindset that is necessary by both sides of the conflict, a change that will allow each side to accept the other as their brothers:

"All…are caught in an inescapable network of mutuality, tied in a single garment of destiny…I can never be what I ought to be until you are what you ought to be, and you can never be what you ought to be until I am what I ought to be. This is the inter-related structure of reality."

Importance of the Time Element

The primary danger that Israelis fear regarding the proposed solution is that Yasser Arafat's heirs are liable to view the Re-engagement Plan as a way to 'pull a new rabbit out of late Arafat's *kafiyah*' so to speak: to use it to mobilize a Fifth Column within Israel. It is likely that if the Palestinian leadership, indeed, adopts the scheme, it will do so in good faith. But as was clarified previously, to insure good faith, the process of re-engagement must be gradual and relatively lengthy. The process will be carried out over a period of time that can blunt, even totally obliterate the impact of Arafat's perverse mindset on the way Palestinians think and behave.

Too rapid re-engagement can present a genuine peril that would bring about a dangerous demographic change in the People of Israel. This can be countered by slowing down the process and carrying it out over a relatively lengthy time period. This period would enable Israelis to examine the process and ascertain whether it needs to be suspended temporarily for reappraisal; to correct mistakes and address problems that develop; and to ensure the process will go in the desired direction and prevent repeating mistakes.

In the first state, so long as there has not been any official decision to create a government-supported re-engagement process, the only process that is possible for Palestinians who are not citizens of the State of Israel to rejoin the People of Israel is conventional conversion. In light of the inherent problems and controversies, conversion can be expected to bring very few candidates. Yet, at this stage, a re-engagement process on a voluntary basis can be carried out within the Green Line, among Palestinians who are Israeli citizens, with the help of funds from abroad and the assistance of Israeli Jews prepared to serve as mentors to assist those interested in re-engagement to better integrate into the State of Israel and move them culturally from the margins to mainstream Jewish society.

Those Palestinians who will opt for such a process will, for the most part, be 'Israeli Arabs' who are loyal citizens of the State of Israel and their 'official' re-engagement as part of the People of Israel will not create a demographic problem and will, in fact, even contribute to lessening the demographic problem. The reasons behind their decision to re-engage will be, first and foremost, the desire to curtail negative attitudes or reservations that some of the Jews harbor towards them, and advance economically and socially.

316

According to the proposal, each stage will begin to be implemented on a serious scale only five to ten years after the previous stage commences, and will continue as long as necessary. Only in the second stage – that will begin with official adoption of the Re-engagement Plan by the State of Israel, and by the leadership of the Palestinian state – will the machinery for implementation be expanded to allow a significant number of Palestinians, primarily residents of Judea and Samaria, to opt in. Only in the third stage, after the lessons of the second stage have been implemented, will the process be put in operation on any significant scale in the Gaza Strip, as well. Parallel to this multi-stage process, in a milieu of peace and prosperity that the finding and a long-term solution can bring, together with the cessation of terrorism and incitement, one can forecast large-scale aliyah of Jews to Israel from throughout the Diaspora.

The situation as described above will make it possible to balance the process and minimize the dangers inherent in re-engagement of the Palestinians by linking the number of 'Returnees' to the number of Jewish immigrants/émigrés and birthrates among Palestinian Returnees and longtime Palestinian Israeli citizens. This will make it possible to maintain a stable ratio that will prevent the influx from demographically endangering the core mass of the People of Israel. There will have to be a serious educational campaign to lower the birth rate and raise the educational level and standard of living of Returnees.

In this manner, it will be possible to eliminate the danger that after the majority of Palestinians will be absorbed in the People of Israel, they will become a Trojan Horse. Such issues need to be voiced, whether re-engagement is done in good faith by the Returnees or whether doing so is a plot to take over the entire country. In either case, if the flow of Returnees is not monitored and kept within manageable numbers, a large number of partially or totally unabsorbed Returnees, hostile or not, could become a peril to the State of Israel and the People of Israel.

Linkage of gradual and well monitored implementation of re-engagement over time to the number of Returnees allowed to participate in the re-engagement can motivate recent Returnees and those awaiting their turn to lower their birth rate, and contribute to prosperity, security and aliyah which will enable more and more of their own brethren to join them and improve their living standard and become equal citizens in a developed First World country. Thus, mutual interests will fuel the entire process of mending the schism that was created among the People of Israel.

Any factor that can speed up this process is desirable, for example: nurturing better relations with the Arab countries; harnessing the Jewish communities of France, the UK and part of American Jewry to rapidly increase the volume of immigration from their respective communities to Israel; and particularly, a positive and 'inclusive' attitude on the part of the People of Israel to embrace the Returnees, without malice or disbelief in their motives.

Every Palestinian citizen or resident of Israel who re-engages with the People of Israel contributes to acceleration of the process. Christian Palestinians who also opt to re-join the People of Israel (after the Muslims treated them so badly at various junctures) will contribute to maintenance of a demographic balance.

A span of five to ten years of quiet between the signing of the first agreement, and commencement of the re-engagement process of most of the residents of Judea and Samaria to the People of Israel will enable enough Diaspora Jews to also return to Eretz-Israel as immigrants. Such an influx of Jewish immigrants will serve as a counter-balance that can enable the People of Israel to absorb a significant number of Palestinians from Judea and Samaria.

Despite this possibility, one should not exaggerate the prospects of mass aliyah, and should not wait for this to occur in order to begin the re-engagement process among Palestinians in Judea and Samaria. To set the re-engagement process in motion, it is

318

important that the percentage of Palestinian citizens of the State of Israel who undergo the process will be large enough to allow the process to flow.

At the outset of the process, in the first five to ten years of official implementation in the framework of the second stage, the ratio of Israel's citizenry of Palestinian origin should not exceed 25 percent. Afterwards, depending on the success of the process, it may be possible to increase the representation of former Palestinians within the population to 30 percent, and later on even a bit more. Provided there is a drop in the birth rate among Palestinians who by this time are citizens of Israel, both Returnees and Palestinian citizens who choose not to opt for re-engagement (at the close of 2004, the percentage of Palestinians in the total population of western Eretz-Israel was 35 percent).

Without the proposed re-engagement process, it can be expected that within 40 years due to their high birth rates, Palestinian citizens of Israel, who in this case will not become sons of the People of Israel, will constitute 30-33 percent of all Israeli citizenry (as will be detailed in Chapter 8). Under the proposed re-engagement plan the same percentage (a little more than 30 percent) of these Palestinians will mostly have joined the People of Israel, and the potential perils that they could present to the security and the Jewishness of the State of Israel will be significantly reduced.

The possibilities voiced above are not intended to question the motives of any Palestinians who will opt to re-engage with the People of Israel. But unfortunately they cannot be brushed under the rug. The Jewish People, who has suffered so much and, has waited two thousand years for its own state, was only recently cynically misled by Yasser Arafat to compromise its security, and despite the tremendous potential of the re-engagement vision, Israelis cannot simply take a 'leap of faith' in welcoming Palestinians, without a safety net. For the present, any attempt to change these realities is too much of a risk to take. Only a

319

successful joint test period over a long period of time can remove residual traumas on both sides and create the necessary accommodating milieu for genuine and full integration.

In light of the factors and the data presented above, chances are good that within 20 years, and at the most 40 years, it will be possible to absorb all the Palestinians within the Green Line and Judea and Samaria who wish to re-engage with the People of Israel. On the surface, this sounds like a very long period of time, unless one takes into account that 40 years have passed since the outbreak of the 1967 Six Day War and all that was achieved since then has been more war and *Intifada* that have escalated the ferocity of the conflict. From this perspective, the wisdom and advisability of being patient, of taking the long view and abandoning the folly of partial and thus transitory 'solutions,' if two to four decades can lead to a comprehensive solution, becomes evident.

Over this relatively lengthy period, the situation of those Palestinians who have still not completed the re-engagement process and have yet to enjoy full rights as part of the State of Israel is likely to improve greatly. Those who have yet to join the People of Israel will still lack the franchise and the duty to serve in the army. But after hatred dissipates, including hatred of Jews towards Palestinians, and after hostilities cease, the economic status and all the other privileges Palestinians can enjoy, will improve, and undoubtedly will be far better than they can expect in a polity controlled by terrorist organizations and blood-thirsty armed gangs.

The problem of a solution to the Gaza Strip, where the percentage of Brethren of Israel is much higher, is far more difficult to solve. On the other hand, it is less difficult to stop the attacks against Israeli territory that emanate from the Gaza Strip. A genuine solution in the Gaza Strip will have to wait between 20 to 50 years, to consummate any re-engagement there.

Chapter Eight
Option Three – A Unilateral Solution

After presenting such a weighty topic looking far into the future, it would be fitting to get back to the nitty-gritty of present realities. Option Three, as presented here, is relevant in the event that it will be impossible to stop terrorism (whether this will be after an imposed settlement takes place or not) and assuming that there will be no serious Palestinian leadership prepared to cooperate in realizing the Re-engagement Plan set forth in Option Two.

As already presented for the case of an imposed settlement, there is a high probability that conflict will be renewed after a cease-fire of sorts. Since such an occurrence will bring the situation full circle back to the point prior to the settlement, or far worse (a distinct possibility), the Options presented here will, at this point, become pertinent to the new realities unfolding, and the sooner Israel adopts Option Three, the less damage and the fewer casualties it will endure.

The contingency presented here is the likelihood that one will witness ongoing Israeli military-intelligence operations, as in the present, with more emphasis on Judea and Samaria which is far more problematic from a geographic and security standpoint, and where the proportion of Palestinian Descendants of Israel by origin is extremely high. The initial objective of this action is to protect the Jews and the State of Israel. However, in light of the finding and the absence of a Palestinian leadership devoted to peace and willing to and capable of reining in extremists within Palestinian territory, these kinds of operations will expand to meet additional targets.

However, Option Three envisions that Israeli operations in Palestinian areas will be designed not only to ensure the safety of Israeli citizens, but also to liberate the Palestinians from the yoke of the terror leadership that controls and subjugates them and makes their lives wretched, feeds them lies, and leads them from one *Nakba* catastrophe to another, causing untold damage to the entire region and igniting terrorism around the globe. Spreading awareness of the finding regarding Palestinian origins far and wide will enable Israel to expand its operations in Palestinian territory without generating any significant opposition from outside.

According to this approach, one must neutralize or eliminate war-mongering and terrorist foundations, including the violent upper levels of the Palestinian social pyramid, until a Palestinian leadership will emerge that is fair and peace-loving, not one fueled by greed and brutality. If the finding will be integrated into this approach, the War on Terrorism will undermine the effectiveness of hostile operations against Israel, while the finding can serve as a factor that can bring people together, diminish hatred, reduce the 'justification' for hostility and present a more successful alternative to an eternal conflict.

All these will increase chances of bringing hostilities to an end. After world opinion will understand that the conflict is between two factions of the same stiff-necked people, and that imposing a settlement will not work, the State of Israel will be able to carry out plans for a unilateral re-engagement, even if Palestinian leadership rejects it and refuses to cooperate.

In order for the implementation of the solution of re-engaging the Palestinians as part of the People of Israel to have a chance (even if it will require a longer period to consummate than that required to reach an imposed 'settlement') Israel must also make contingency plans should it become evident that no Palestinian leadership with peaceful intentions is going to emerge for a very, very long time – and to prepare to enforce its authority upon all factions in the Palestinian population.

A 'solution' by which Israel would implement another Disengagement from parts of Judea and Samaria or from all territory beyond the Green Line will not prevent enduring hatred or

322

the emergence of the new dangers to Israel in the Middle East. Such a solution is paramount to burying one's head in the sand.

On one hand the Disengagement from the Gaza Strip has already created a positive atmosphere in Egypt and other Arab states towards Israel; on the other hand, the Disengagement could serve as a source of encouragement to extremist Palestinian organizations, primarily Hamas, together with Iran and Hizbollah in their aspirations to destroy the State of Israel when the time is ripe. When such factions decide to spark renewal of open hostilities, ones that the Disengagement is not able to prevent, they will drag in other Palestinians. A reversal in attitudes among the Arab nations will naturally follow, cancelling any improvement in relations towards Israel garnered by the August 2005 Gaza Disengagement.

According to the solution proposed here, after a lengthy period of struggle against terrorism and as long as there is no possibility of an accord with Palestinian leadership, a stage-by-stage transition period needs to be put into effect (mostly in Judea and Samaria) from a state of protracted war, to a stage of unilateral autonomy, followed by implementation of the 'One State for One People' formula (Option Two).

The significance of such a move is that it will achieve relative calm for eradicating the hostility. To achieve this goal there needs to be Israeli control of Palestinian territories, as needed, over a lengthy period and without any agreement, in the absence of a genuine partner with which a lasting peace can be made.

The process will gather momentum because the impact of Palestinian terror leadership on most of Palestinian inhabitants will be eliminated. Due to the overall situation and the economic state, due to the lack of any other solution, due to the reluctance of Israelis to lord over Palestinians, it is possible that **unilateral** Palestinian **autonomy** (where at the beginning Israelis will fill some key functions that later will be taken over by Palestinians) will be enforced. In the framework of such an Autonomy, among other things, educational matters (including learning the truth about the history of Eretz-Israel) preventing incitement and de-terrorizing low-echelon leadership will be addressed.

This solution means one polity in Eretz-Israel within which there will be an autonomous Palestinian 'sub-governance' system in which Palestinian inhabitants will hold the franchise to vote for Autonomy institutions only. Of course, this solution where inhabitants hold citizenship in the Autonomy only, that is Palestinian inhabitants will have no right to vote in election of the central government of the country (and are exempt from military service), is not a comprehensive solution, but rather an interim solution. Later on, there will be the need for another stage in which these **inhabitants become part of the State of Israel**. Another possibility is to wave the Autonomy stage and have all Palestinians hold permanent residency in the State of Israel without holding citizenship in any political framework whatsoever, until the second stage can be implemented.

The details that follow are part of Option Three, but have relevance and possible practical application for Option Two, as will be discussed.

Joining the State of Israel

Joining of Palestinians to the State of Israel will begin to be implemented at a later stage, gradually. Realization will be able to take one of two forms: **Residents without citizenship**, or **Re-engagement with the People of Israel**, as raised in Option Two. The process will be carried out on a family-by-family basis, and in certain instances on an individual basis. In the first stage, which will be carried out gradually among all the Palestinian population, each and every Palestinian (except those suspected of terrorist activity) will have three choices:

1. **Loyal residency**: An oath of allegiance to the State of Israel and declaration of waiver of citizenship rights for oneself and one's children (as long as the individual declines to opt for the second course of action that follows). This status is reasonable, the equivalent of Green Card status in the United States which millions of immigrants hold for years, without acting on the option to become American citizens, once they are eligible.

2. **Re-engagement with the People of Israel**: The expressed desire and willingness to rejoin the People of Israel via an oath of allegiance to the State of Israel and its people, the People of Israel, and declaration that one does not belong to the Arab nation.

3. **Emigration**: Emigration and purchase of the émigrés' house by the State at a fair price (in order not to cause injury to émigrés due to fluctuations in market prices, likely to be depressed by an exodus and surplus of real estate).

In the second stage which will continue a number of years, all Palestinians who will opt to stay in Eretz-Israel will have the option of receiving an Israeli education based, among other things, on an *ulpan*-like system that will teach the elements of the re-engagement curriculum outlined in Option Two above. The children of such Palestinians will be enrolled in the Israeli school system, compulsory education just as their Israeli counterparts. Those who choose the first path (loyal residency only) will have the option to choose an Arab Islamic (or Christian) education school track, with an abridged Israeli curriculum. The children of those who choose the second path (re-engagement) will be required to enroll in the regular Israeli school system.

Only those who complete Israel education and belong to the second option (the re-engagement path) can progress to the third step – service in the IDF, taking an oath of allegiance to the Jewish People. At the beginning, the IDF will establish special units for this population (similar to separate minority units of Bedouin, Druze and Circassians in the formative years of the IDF).

Palestinians who are above draft age will undergo abridged military service (current policy for older new Jewish immigrants) then be integrated into the IDF reserve system.

Only Palestinians who will serve in the IDF will be eligible for Israeli citizenship (except for those with serious health issues or those are too old who receive exemptions). Only the army will have the prerogative to decide which candidates for military service should do civil service in lieu of military service. This principle linking the franchise with civil service or military service will hold for all citizens of the State of Israel, Jews and non-Jews. Citizenship will carry eligibility for certain civil rights including the right to vote for the Knesset and perks such as receipt of better social benefits for veterans including higher children's allowances.

A citizen who betrays the state will lose his citizenship and be harshly punished. A Loyal Resident who will abridge his oath of allegiance will lose his or her Residency rights and be deported, in particularly serious cases, after offenders complete their sentence.

In order to challenge those who will oppose linking entitlement to full civil rights with compulsory educational re-orientation, it should be stressed: This proposal is not new. The methodology is derived (with various liberal alterations) from the scheme adopted by the Austrian emperor **Joseph II** in 1780-1790 towards his Jewish subjects. The scheme was adopted in order to lead the large Jewish community of Galicia to accept general (i.e., secular) education and not to suffice with traditional Jewish education based on Torah and Talmudic studies only. Joseph II was the first world leader to institute universal compulsory education for all his subjects, upon which the educational plan for Jews was formulated. The objective was to broaden Jewish education and allow the Jews to integrate better into the surrounding community. (It did not, however, abrogate the harsh discrimination – first and foremost economic discrimination, directed at Jews.)

326

When institution of such a scheme by the State of Israel will come as a response to constant hostilities, and in order to reach a just solution demanded by Palestinians and Arabs all the time, the Palestinians' European supporters, who built this linkage in their own countries in far more coercive forms, will have no foundations to oppose such steps by Israel.

As for the Arabs – one should remind them of their own actions – the option of 'conversion to Islam or leave the Empire on pain of death' (i.e., transfer) the ministers of Caliph al-Hakem enacted and the harsh persecution of the Jews throughout Arab-Muslim rule designed to force them to convert. Such steps by Israel will be far more justified and far more liberal than their own deeds. Moreover, these steps can bring an end to the constant spilling of blood.

Furthermore, in many countries today there are exams candidates for citizenship need to pass to receive citizenship. The Israeli requirements of those requesting to re-engage with the Jewish People are based on the same spirit. The only substantive differences are that the Israeli program, on one hand, provides broad-based education prior to standing for exams, and it reflects the uniqueness of the Israeli situation: Candidates are native sons to the country, while such populations automatically receive citizenship in other countries. These steps are justified in light of the fact that the candidates and their forefathers received education that was not based on their genuine identity, including large dosages of incitement that need to be remedied.

On a tactical level, since re-engagement will be carried out over a lengthy period of time, it is possible that at the beginning preference will be given to villages in Judea and Samaria in the vicinity of Jewish settlements in order to create 'Israeli geographic continuity' that will be expanded over the years, parallel to gradual cut backs in the territory of the Autonomy.

Chapter Nine
Solution to the Refugee Problem

One of the core issues where the finding regarding Palestinian identity has ramifications is the Israeli position in any future negotiations and its *hasbarah* efforts. The finding can greatly assist in presenting a wise and just response to Palestinian demands for the Right of Return. It can assist in removing most of this demand from the public agenda. In essence, one can demonstrate that regarding the Palestinians residing today outside the western Eretz-Israel, any Right of Return that they may have would not increase the number of Palestinians west of the Jordan.

There are many points that counter the Right of Return. The finding is also germane: It concluded that most of the Palestinian refugees were immigrants (who for the most part came to western Eretz-Israel after 1914 and in part after 1840). Although a portion were originally Descendants of Israel, they came west of the Jordan from the east and settled in places in western Eretz-Israel in contrast to the permission they received from the British Mandatory authorities. When they fled, they fled back to their countries of origin or remained in their own country either in the western part of Eretz-Israel or in its eastern part, except for those who fled to Lebanon and from there to Europe.

Those original Descendants of Israel who returned to Jordan – Arab and Druze immigrants and most of the Descendants of Israel – realized in their flight their own Right of Return to their countries of origin. The Arab immigrants among them have very limited entitlements to Eretz-Israel at all, at most 50 years of 'seniority' (1917-1967). Nevertheless, one cannot deny the rights of Descendants of Israel in Lebanon and even farther away to return to their original homes in Judea and Samaria under certain conditions. For those who have settled elsewhere such a return is probably not relevant at all.

The Brethren of Israel, who constitute most of the refugees and their offspring, now dwelling in Jordan, came from their present place of residence to western Eretz-Israel beginning in 1840, and their entitlements amount to, at most, a bit more than a hundred years of 'seniority' (1840-1948).

All those willing to suffice with fair monetary compensation for the loss of property and suffering need to demand compensation, among others, from their own leadership and from the Arab countries who were the aggressors in 1948. These leaders and countries both caused their plight, and enjoyed the ill-gained profits of Jewish property left in their countries and illegally seized (plundered) by the authorities after the 1948 war.

Another party who can assist in compensation – both to Palestinian refugees and Jewish refugees who lost most of their assets in Europe and in the Arab countries beginning in the Second World War and up until their aliyah to the State of Israel after 1948 – are the Europeans. While Germany has already paid reparation to Jews who remained alive after the Holocaust, and reparations to the State of Israel in the name of those Jews who perished, other Europeans have yet to compensate Jews for their property left behind – particularly the homes of some 6,000,000 who perished in the Holocaust and whose property was inherited by other parties in Europe.

On an overall Israeli-Arab level, the Arabs are the ones who created the Palestinian problem when they invaded western Eretz-Israel with their armies in 1948, and when Syria and Lebanon called upon the Palestinians to flee the country. Palestinian terrorism as well is responsible to an equal extent for creating this problem. Israel did not initiate the war, and certainly are not those who urged most of the refugees to leave their homes, and Israel has no culpability or responsibility vis-à-vis the refugees.

The 292,000 Palestinian who became refugees in 1948, along with the small number of new refugees from 1967, total 360,000 refugees. (One should keep in mind that most 1967 refugees were 1948 refugees plus their offspring who uprooted a second time in 1967, and that a portion of the 1967 refugees who had fled to Jordan returned to Judea and Samaria after the 1967 war.) This number – 360,000 Palestinian refugees – more than balances out with the magnitude of Jewish refugees (866,000 – more than double the number) who were uprooted and forced to leave Arab countries following the establishment of the State of Israel.

On the practical level, Palestinian refugees residing in refugee camps in Judea and Samaria must be absorbed in these areas where there is no shortage of space for the genuine number of existing refugees to settle down and rehabilitate their lives. The refugees in the Gaza Strip could be settled in the areas that were evacuated by Jewish settlers in the Gaza Strip in August 2005, and adjacent undeveloped land. This would require international funding to solve the refugee problem peacefully, with the Palestinian refugees resettling within western Eretz-Israel.

But according to the Re-engagement Plan, if Palestinian refugees residing today in western Eretz-Israel would adopt Option Two as set forth above, and re-engage as part-and-parcel of the People of Israel residing in 'Greater Israel' so to speak, with the financial compensation they will receive as part of the settlement, it will be hard to prevent them over time returning to live in the areas where they dwelled inside the Green Line prior to becoming refugees. Most of the current residents of Western Eretz-Israel (or their legal heirs) who legally possessed real estate within what became the Green Line in the 1948 Armistice Agreement, and forfeited it in the course of their flight during the 1948 War, will be able to enjoy the Right of Return with a close proximity to their original, pre-1948 locations.

Moreover, genuine refugee camps outside of western Eretz-Israel exist only in Lebanon. In Jordan, most of the refugees reside in permanent housing outside the camps. Even former refugee camps have become regular low-income neighborhoods. While they contain some 380,000 persons, they are not substantively different when one compares them to other places in the world where refugees or migrants have settled, and they do not require or justify humanitarian intervention. The reason that these areas are still called refugee camps and those Palestinians who don't even dwell in the camps (who returned in 1948 to the villages from which they set out in 1914 for western Eretz-Israel) are still registered as refugees is because they want to continue to receive the economic assistance from UNRWA.

In Cairo there is a neighborhood in which 120,000 refugees from Eretz-Israel reside, a neighborhood that is depressed even by Egyptian standards, but it is not a genuine refugee camp. The residents are former Arab immigrants to Eretz-Israel and their descendants, and they have no Right of Return.

In Syria in 1962, only a sixth of the original population of the refugee camps remained and today there is no humanitarian crisis among Palestinian refugees in Syria, which demands or deserves a solution. Prior to 1967, most of the Palestinians in Saudi Arabia left for Jordan and Judea and Samaria, when these areas were still under Jordanian control.

The refugees in camps in Lebanon are the only ones beyond the borders of western Eretz-Israel who require and deserve a humanitarian solution. The overwhelming majority of refugees in Lebanon have left the camps long ago: In 1952, it was reported that only one third of the refugees remained in the camps. In 1959, the newspaper **_al-Hyyat_** reported that only 15,000 refugees remained in the camps, and thus "despite the vociferous chorus surrounding them, the refugees tend to integrate immediately."

Today the Lebanese Palestinian refugee camps are populated by 36,000 persons. Approximately 20,000 are Descendants of the People of Israel, who fled or whose forefathers fled from Akko and Haifa after they migrated there after 1914 from east of the Jordan. Most of the remaining 13,000 (36 percent) are Brethren of Israel.

A very small minority of some 3,000 of the camp dwellers are Lebanese who preferred to live in the refugee camps in lieu of their previous homes in order to receive UNRWA subsidies (under false pretences). Except for the latter, all possess the Right of Return to Jordan, and the Descendants of Israel possess the Right of Return to Judea and Samaria, as well. Regardless of how the issue of these refugees will be solved, it would be a genuine folly to hinge or harness continuing the bloodshed and suffering of unending warfare to this issue.

According to a 2003 study published by the Palestinian Center for Political Studies, only 12.6 percent of the refugees in Judea and Samaria are interested in returning to Israel. One can assume that this small percent will shrink even farther once Israel seriously reforms its reckless policy of generous government child allowances for all citizens (that turn large families and 'baby-making' into a complete source of income in itself). Those interested in a Return from Judea and Samaria to inside the Green Line are primarily Brethren of Israel, a portion of whom reside in refugee camps, who have close kin in the lowlands of Israel whom they wish to join. According to Table 31 they constitute only 12.5 percent of the Palestinian population of Judea and Samaria.

Only 5.2 percent of the refugees in Jordan are interested in a Return to the State of Israel, in contrast with 23.2 percent among the refugees in Lebanon. The result of this opinion poll was not favorably received by extremist Palestinians who sought to quash its publication.

Another humanitarian problem is families which have been split apart: The reunification issue exists primarily between residents of Jordan and residents west of the Jordan, but also among refugees in Lebanon and their kin who are citizens of Israel. In the above survey, it was found that 37 percent of the refugees in Lebanon have blood kin in Israel, compared to 24 percent among refugees in Jordan and 21 percent of the refugees in Judea and Samaria. This data does not negate the existence of family in other geographic

332

areas, as well: The percentage of refugees in Lebanon with relatives in Israel (37 percent) is amazingly similar to the percentage of Brethren of Israel in the camps there (36 percent), who have relatives among the Brethren of Israel who remained within the Green Line after 1949.

Family reunification, should it be implemented, needs to take into consideration that most of the Brethren of Israel in the area – some 1,300,000 persons – reside today in Jordan. By comparison, there are approximately 1,045,000 of this group west of the Jordan – most in the Gaza Strip. It would be reasonable and natural that family unification first be implemented by transferring kin from west of the Jordan to the natural 'ancestral' homeland of this population east of the Jordan. Only in exceptional cases would it be logical to unify families in the opposite direction, in cases where most of the family in question already resides west of the Jordan, for the most part in the Gaza Strip. A similar situation exists vis-à-vis the small Arab minority living west of the Jordan, as compared to Arab brethren in other countries.

As for the Descendants of the Roman Army, they for the most part reside today in Jordan, as well (700,000 compared to 265,000 west of the Jordan). This population group has no historic entitlements to Eretz-Israel, as do the Descendants of Israel and Brethren of Israel (the latter, rights in eastern Eretz-Israel). Their ancestors served in an imperialist army that caused all the problems in the first place. Despite their long-standing seniority rights in western Eretz-Israel, one should keep in mind that most came to Jordan of their own free will after the 1967 War – preferring to join their brethren who had fled to Jordan during that war. The natural solution for them is to remain in Jordan, except for specific exceptional cases of family reunification. It would be logical for most family reunification to take place in eastern Eretz-Israel where most of this population group resides, although it is reasonable that there may be some movement in the opposite direction, as well.

Beyond practical issues and the 'balance sheet' between Jewish refugees and Arab refugees, if one seeks to explore a just solution to the refugee problem on the personal level, one must examine personal issues as linked to designation of origin – Descendants of Israel, Descendants of the Roman Army and Brethren of Israel.

The 'natural' dwelling place for the Brethren of Israel is east of the Jordan while the 'natural' place of the Descendants of the Roman Army is west of the Jordan. Yet, this kind of argument harbors a built-in 'natural' principle of reciprocity: If one argues that Israel should in all fairness absorb 700,000 Descendants of the Roman Army presently living east of the Jordan, then Jordan should absorb nearly 1,045,000 Brethren of Israel presently living west of the Jordan.

Jordan is the natural dwelling place of the Brethren of Israel. As only a very tiny minority of the Descendants of Israel who originally went eastward and are still there today, the original reason for the Brethren of Israel migrating westward (the presence of the Descendants of Israel in the east) no longer exists. The fact that eastern Eretz-Israel has, in the meantime, filled with Arabs (an influx largely the product of the vacuum created by the movement of the Brethren of Israel and others westward) hardly constitutes grounds for the Arabs and the Palestinians making Israel responsible and demanding that Israel 'make room' for the Brethren of Israel west of the Jordan. Moreover, Israel – including the Far Right – has accepted that more than half of the Jews' historical homeland (eastern Eretz-Israel) has become an Arab country (Jordan).

A group which deserves special consideration are those Descendants of Israel who left their homeland including even eastern Eretz-Israel – particularly those who abandomed their homeland and went to Lebanon and to Europe after they had much eralier abandoned their faith – and with it their People, though hardly by choice: Most of these refugees left Eretz-Israel willingly after most migrated to Jordan and from there to Europe. One cannot reject their rights to their original homeland, although most – except for a small number in Lebanon —are relatively well off in their present circumstances, far from Eretz-Israel.

The majority of this large grouping (a portion of whom dwell in Europe) has totally detached itself from the People of Israel, its religion and historic homeland. Moreover, there is no humanitarian issue here crying for a solution. Thus, there is no logic in relating to these people any differently than any other gentile who desires to join the People of Israel.

In other words, if they see their present circumstances as problematic and wish to return to their country of origin west of the Jordan, this option is always open. Before doing so, however, they need to convert and return to the Jewish People and Judaism. If they wish to do so, they can then make aliyah to Israel as Jews under the Law of Return, as long as this Law is on the Israeli law books and the People of Israel will have to absorb them like any Jewish immigrant – with ample perks. If they do not wish to convert to Judaism they can immigrate to Jordan, which is also part of Eretz-Israel, and the land of their forefathers for no short time. In the framework of regional peace in the Middle East – if and when that day arrives, it is entirely possible that Jordan also will become a prosperous and burgeoning country whose former residents will be attracted to return.

Arafat did not plan in advance to raise the Right of Return in an organized fashion at 'final negotiation talks' at Camp David in the summer of 2000. It was clear that Israel would not accept this demand. But the unbridled determination to end the conflict that the Israeli Government demonstrated and the concessions it was willing to make took him by surprise.

On one hand, Arafat tried to take advantage of what he perceived as weakness and a 'fire sale mentality' (e.g., suing for peace at all costs) by Israeli prime minister Ehud Barak, to seize the moment for major Israeli concessions on the Right of Return. On the other hand, Arafat needed to raise this explosive issue to bring down the talks, and launch the Second *Intifada*, which he had already planned in general terms prior to signing the Oslo Accords back in 1993. The issue of Jerusalem failed to serve as a detonator (much to his surprise) when Israel made an unprecedented compromise offer that gave Palestinians control of most of East Jerusalem. The Jewish settlement issue provided a lame excuse for walking out since Israel offered an unprecedented exchange of territory based on Israel annexing Jewish settlements in Judea and Samaria close to the Green Line and ceding some of its own sovereign territory – primarily in the Western Negev adjacent to Gaza to Palestinians in exchange. Thus, the only option Arafat had left was to raise the Right of Return issue to detonate the talks.

Despite all the Palestinians' genuine suffering and their declared desire for a solution that will bring an end to this suffering, the Right of Return issue (as separate from the refugee issue) is not a core issue in negotiations and would not have attracted much attention had these issues not been intertwined by Palestinians. Therefore, anyone interested in all the arguments against the Right of Return, including new claims based on this work's finding about Palestinian origins, parallel to old arguments gathered from various sources, should refer to Appendix 4. Discussion of this issue in an Appendix is not intended to 'hide' this issue in the shadows or assume it does not need to be addressed. It is just that the solution to the refugee problem cannot come through actualization of the Right of Return.

Summary

The inhabitants of Eretz-Israel and its neighbors face a critical existential question: What is preferable? Should one recognize the old-new truth and the new possibilities it brings, even if it is very revolutionary and requires a major readjustment in thinking of a scope that is hard for the average person to grasp or to cope with? Or, is it preferable to continue to live according to the old assumptions regarding the origins of the Palestinians – assumptions that have led to hatred, wretchedness, victimhood and lack of direction in the search for a lasting solution?

While the new approach needs to be absorbed slowly, the more rapidly it gains ground among more and more people the faster will those who jumped on the bandwagon of war and hatred have good reason to climb down and save the lives of tomorrow's victims of the lies and the cover-up of the truth, the hatred and the incitement we have suffered to this day.

There is no logic to why all inhabitants of Eretz-Israel shouldn't want the Re-engagement Plan to succeed. The Europeans and the Arabs, who received the core beliefs of their religions and their faith from the Jews and spread them to almost every corner of the world, will, one would hope, support the proposed direction. For two thousand years they have repaid the Jews for what they received with acts designed to force the People of Israel to abandon their faith, by expulsions, persecution, wars and outright genocide. It is now time – at the advent of the Third Millennium for Christians and Muslims to help build the Promised Land, to finally recognize and partake in bringing this Promise to fruition, while commemorating those who have fallen and who have perished due to needless hatred (which unfortunately still flourishes) – to help fulfill the supplication **'in our times'** of the Kaddish Prayer for the Dead: **"...He who makes peace in his high holy places, may he bring peace upon us, and upon <u>all</u> Israel."**

337

Bibliography

1.   *Eretz-Israel b-Avar ooba-Hoveh* (Eretz Israel in the Past and Present) – David Ben-Gurion and Yitzhak Ben-Zvi   (Yiddish edition) – New York 1918. The Hebrew translation published by the Ben-Zvi Research Institute is abridged, and part of this topic does not appear, apparently due to reasons discussed in the body of this work.

2.   *Uchlusiei Artzeinu* (The Populations of Our Country) – Yitzhak Ben-Zvi – published jointly by the Executive Committee of "Brit HaNoar" and the World "Hechalutz" Central Committee.

3.   *Kitvei Yitzhak Ben-Zvi* (The Writings of Yitzhak Ben-Zvi), Volume 5 – *Uchlusiat Eretz-Israel* (Eretz-Israel's Population) – Mitzpeh Publishers, Tel Aviv 1936 (identical to the content in source #2).

4.   *L'birur Motza ha-Falakhim* (Regarding the Origins of the Falakhim) – David Ben-Gurion, Hermon Publishers, Tel Aviv, 1969.

5.   *Ha-Aravim Asher be-Eretz-Israel* (The Arabs in Eretz-Israel) – Israel Belkind, Hermon Publishers, Tel Aviv 1969.

6.   *Ye'amen ki Yisupar – Ba'ayat Eretz-Israel, Shorasheha oo-Pitronah* (Hearing is Believing – The Roots and the Solution to the Eretz-Israel Problem) – Tsvi Misinai, Li'ad Publishers, Tel Aviv 2006.

7.   *Moledet Meshutefet, Lo Adamat Mirivah* (A Shared Homeland, Not Disputed Soil) – Elon Yarden, Li'ad Publishers, Tel Aviv 2006.   The volume deals with the identity problem among Palestinians.

8.   *Tzion ba-Mishpat Tepadeh– Chalufa le-Heskem Oslo* (Zion will be Redeemed through Judgement – an Alternative to the Oslo Accords) – Elon Yarden, Li'ad Publishers, Tel Aviv 2002. This work contains broad details of matters explained in the body of the text of the work at hand – geographic background. Legal substantiation, details of the proposed settlement, and a lengthy bibliography.

338

9. *The Koran* (Hebrew translation of Uri Rubin) – Tel Aviv University Press, 2005.

10. "Arei Eretz-Israel Tachat Shilton ha-Islam" (The Cities of Eretz-Israel under Islamic Rule) – Professor Moshe Sharon, *Cathedra* 40, pp. 83-121 – Ben-Zvi Research Institute, Jerusalem, 1986.

11. *Kitzur Toldot ha-Shomronim* (An Abridged History of the Samaritans) – Benyamin Tzadka – A.B. Institute for Samaritan Studies Publishers, Holon, 2001.

12. "Jewish and Middle Eastern non-Jewish populations share a common pool of Y-chromosome bi-allelic haplotypes" – M. F. Hammer et al. , *Proceedings of the National Academy of Sciences*, Volume 67, No. 12, June 6, 2000, pp. 6769-6774.
   http://www.pnas.org/cgi/content/full/97/12/6769#FN152

13. "High-resolution Y chromosome haplotypes of Israeli and Palestinian Arabs reveal geographic substructure and substantial overlap with haplotypes of Jews" – Almut Nebel et al., *Human Genetics*, Volume 107, pp 630-641, 2000
   http://www.ucl.ac.uk/tcga/tcgapdf/Nebel-HG-00-IPArabs.pdf

14. "The Y Chromosome Pool of Jews as Part of the Genetic Landscape of the Middle East" – Amut Nebel et al., *American Journal of Human Genetics*, Volume 69, pp 1095-1112, 2001.
   http://www.pubmedcentral.nih.gov/articlerender.fcgi?artid=1274378

15. "Genetics of congenital deafness in the Palestinian population: multiple connection 26 alleles with shared origins in the Middle East" – Shanin H, et al., *Human Genetics*, 110(3):284-9, Mar 2002.
   http://www.tau.ac.il/~karena/manuscriptspdf/2002/Shahin_et_al_2002.pdf

16. *Wholeness and the Implicate Order* – David Bohm, Rutledge Press, 1980.

17. *Banking on Baghdad* – Edwin Black, John Weily & Sons, Hoboken, NJ, USA, 2004

APPENDIX 1

Reasons for Erroneous Identification of the Samaritans

The error in identifying the Samaritans made by Jews returning to Zion after the Babylonian Captivity was the upshot of the following factors:

Confusion of Names: Returning Jewish leaders encountered at first the more educated gentiles in Samaria who practised the commandments of the Religion of Israel. Consequently the Jews called all the inhabitants of Samaria—Cuths (*Cutim*). The name Samaritan, that was used later with the establishment of the Second Commonwealth, was considered foreign, relative to the term *Ish Yisrael* – a 'man of Israel' used to designate the inhabitants of the Kingdom of Israel after the split of the kingdom under Jeroboam the son of Nebat (as distinguished from *Ish Yehuda* – a 'man of Judea') that was transformed into the name *Yehudi* or Jew at the beginning of the Second Commonwealth.

The Cuths called themselves *Shmayrim* (Sumarians) derived from the Sumer Kingdom, from which they were exiled to Eretz-Israel by the Assyrians. The Samaritans continued to use this name even after the majority of foreigners left, because the foreigners from Sumer (in ancient Mesopotamia) were a minority from the very beginning and due to the phonetic similarity between Sumarian (with a 'u') and Samaritan (with an 'a') they did not clearly differentiate between the two. In Jewish sources, the name *Shmayrim* became *Shamrah*. Use of this designation for these definite gentiles, and its close sounding ring to the Hebrew *Shomronim* (Samaritans) led the Jews to distance the latter and assume that the Samaritans were not part of the People of Israel.

Difference in Religious Rituals: Between the Kingdom of Judah and the Kingdom of Israel during the time of the First Commonwealth, there were differences in religious practice, in calculating leap years and the location of the spiritual hub.[53] The Samaritans' religion was based on the Five Books of Moses only, and they did not adopt the later writings – the Prophets and the Writings – written for the most part after the destruction of the First Commonwealth, during the Babylonian Exile and the years of the Second Commonwealth.

Loss of Contact: The Returnees to Zion, due to their absence from Eretz-Israel for a period of several generations, did not have ongoing ties with inhabitants in Samaria, and had no knowledge of the continuity of settlement there by the People of Israel.

The 'Lion Converts' (*Gerei Ariyot*)**:** Kings II[54] relates that towards the end of the First Commonwealth, after gentiles were brought to the Kingdom of Israel by the Assyrians, lions came out of the forests and devoured them. The gentiles saw this as a Sign from Heaven from the god of this unfamiliar land, the God of Israel, and began to worship the God of Israel and to follow the commandments of the Religion of Israel, parallel to preserving their own idol-worshipping practices. The Jews returning to Zion at the outset of the Second Commonwealth Period noted this story in Kings II from the days of the First Commonwealth. They viewed the fact 'that lions prowled in the villages that had been depopulated of their former inhabitants' as a clear sign that the entire country had been laid waste and no members of the People of Israel remained. Much to their astonishment, when they returned to Eretz-Israel, they encountered local inhabitants who were loyal to the Torah – the Five Books of Moses, and assumed these people were those spoken about in the story of the lions in Kings II, and thus they viewed all the inhabitants of the area as '[lion] converts.'[55]

---

[53] The Temple in Jerusalem for Judea, and the Temple on Mount Grizim near Nablus for Israel.

[54] In Chapter 17:24 onward.

[55] Labeled by the Jews – *Gerai Ariyot* ('Lion converts') or *Gerai Emmet* ('Converts to the Truth').

341

Another even more important aspect of the narrative was the new inhabitants' request (which was fulfilled by the King of Assyria) that they bring them an Israelite priest from the Exile to teach them the ways of the Religion of Israel. The situation – where all the leadership including the priestly class had been exiled – was again erroneously interpreted by the Returnees to Zion as a sign that none of their own native sons remained in Eretz-Israel by the time of the first Return to Zion.

Deceptive Meetings: The educated classes among the Samaritans were a minority of gentiles who had remained in Eretz-Israel, while the common folk were tillers of the soil. In the encounter in Eretz-Israel between Jewish sages (returning from Babylon) and Samaritan sages, it was the gentiles who set the tone from the Samaritan side of the dialogue and spoke of their own personal roots in Assyria, without exposing that the origins of most of the Samaritans: that they were native sons of Eretz-Israel who belonged to the People of Israel.

Resentment: Even if the returning Jews heard about the origins of the simple folk among the Samaritans, resentment among the Jews – that began during the First Commonwealth Period towards the ten tribes who withdraw and split the Kingdom – with all the ramifications that had, hardly contributed to bringing the two sides back together.

Disregard: Despite Samaritan pleas to the Jews and claims regarding the genuine identity of most of their community, the relatively low educational level of the tillers of the soil among the ten tribes who were left in the country by the Assyrians and Babylonians complicated the situation. On one hand, their low level made it hard for these Samaritans to substantiate their claims to educated Jewish elites returning from Babylon and the stark class differences between the latter and these common folk hardly contributed to bringing the highly-educated Jewish returnees and this agrarian Samaritan proletariat together.

342

Lack of Knowledge: The returning Jews were unaware that, in fact, most of the Cuths and some of the other foreigners that settled during the First Commonwealth Period in the sector of Eretz-Israel allotted to the tribe of Ephraim and the vicinity had returned to their countries of origin, because at the time the Cuths left the Jews were still in the Babylonian Exile. The fact that only 3 percent of the Samaritans were not sons of the People of Israel at the time of the first Return to Zion was unknown to the Jews. The fact that a number of monarchs cite that the gentiles in Samaria worshipped the God of Israel parallel to local idols – in contrast to the Samaritans who in Second Commonwealth times worshipped only the God of Israel was, apparently, insufficient to open the eyes of the Returnees to Zion to the fact that those they encountered – the Samaritans – were in fact their own brethren.

Religiosity: Those returning from Babylon under the leadership of Ezra and Nehemiah were very religious in their devotion to the Torah and fulfilling the commandments. Memories of idol worship that had spread in the Kingdom of Israel during the period of the First Commonwealth, and the differences between commandments practised by Samaritans and those which the Jews religiously practise led the Jews to keep distance from those they perceived as less devout. The prophets during the First Commonwealth led the Jews to believe that the Destruction and Exile were Divine punishment for past transgressions, particularly religious laxity. The returning Jews who began to rebuild a Jewish polity were purists who wanted the Second Commonwealth to be founded on uncompromising devotion to their faith and what the God of Israel expected of them, down to the very last letter. Embracing the Samaritans went against the grain of this approach. Under such circumstances, considering their rigid worldview, the Jewish leadership would have done everything in their power to keep the Samaritans at arm's length, and downplay any association with them so the Samaritans could not 'undermine the faithful' or 'spoil the ranks'…even if the leaders were cognizant of the ethnic tie.

343

APPENDIX 2

The 1948 Refugees

The Flight of the Refugees – The First Wave and its Scope

From a demographic standpoint, the flight of refugees is not a simple matter at all, and since such events are rarely orderly, it is hard to measure their scope. In western Eretz-Israel the situation is further complicated due to the tremendous ethnic diversity of the inhabitants and the helter-skelter flight pattern that took place. Palestinians took advantage of the chaos and lack of information to artificially inflate the number of refugees.

Monitoring the number of persons who took flight is essential if one needs to understand who fled and who stayed, for the distribution of refugees among various elements of the population was not uniform. Monitoring the number of refugees is also essential to understand what entitlements to Eretz-Israel refugees from different backgrounds possess.

The actions of a number of Arab states – calling upon Palestinians to leave Jewish areas in anticipation of the military invasion of neighboring Arab armies – parallel to actions by the Yishuv to repel the invasion, led to the first wave of escapees – some 309,000 refugees. Some 204,000 of them fled to Arab states beyond the borders of western Eretz-Israel, 51,000 fled to Judea and Samaria, and 53,000 to the Gaza Strip.

Approximately 79,000 of the refugees from the first wave returned after a short sojourn to their original places of residence within what became the Green Line. Most were compelled to do so to regain their livelihoods and because they realized their flight had been unjustified. Out of the returnees, 72,000 were pastoral Bedouin for whom flight was no more than an alteration in the frequency and distance in their nomadic lifestyle. As a result of their return, the number of refugees from the first wave of escapees dropped to 230,000.

Of the 79,000 returnees, most came from Arab countries – primarily the Bedouin who came back from the Sinai Peninsula. The distribution of those who remained refugees from the first wave totaled 148,000 in neighboring Arab countries, 43,000 in Judea and Samaria and 38,000 in the Gaza Strip.

This statistic of net refugees from the first wave does not include 3,000 additional refugees who left their homes, mainly in Jaffa and its vicinity, and settled among other Palestinian communities that ended up within the Green Line, such as the Triangle and the city of Lod. These 'internal' refugees are not included in the tally of refugees that follows so that the findings of this work can be compared with the number of refugees claimed by the Palestinians (who do not include 'internal' refugees in their figures, because although they were refugees they do not need the Right of Return and contact with these 'Israeli Palestinians' was difficult to maintain).

The figures above include 66,000 Arab immigrants who legally should have resided in Judea and Samaria but who lived illegally within the Green Line to make a living. A portion fled beyond the borders of western Eretz-Israel and a portion fled to Judea, Samaria and the Gaza Strip where they joined refugee camps. Since their immigration certificates from British Mandatory authorities specified they were entitled to settle in Judea and Samaria only, while in practice they resided in Jewish areas illegally, at least those who fled to Judea and Samaria (where they 'belonged' legally) should not be counted as refugees.

One can also argue that the 4,500 illegal immigrants who lived in the Gaza Strip and who fled from it should not be counted as refugees. That is, all told, the illegals who were counted as refugees numbered 70,000. Once one subtracts these persons who have no entitlement to refugee status, the number of refugees drops significantly; nevertheless, there is a degree of justice in counting these persons as refugees since they ultimately found themselves dwelling in refugee camps, and therefore they have not been off-set from the total number of refugees.

In addition, there were Palestinians who fled without any reason from Judea, Samaria and Gaza to neighboring Arab countries fueled by panic after they were told to do so by the Arab leadership. When they realized this had been a mistake, most returned to their regular places of residency in Judea and Samaria (70,000) and the Gaza Strip (30,000). The overall figures above include (in regard to refugees who fled from Judea, Samara and Gaza) only those who did not return to their original dwelling places there.

Refugees after the First Wave

Additional refugees – some 81,000 in number – fled in the course of the war, trickling out as the war front approached their homes. Some 24,000 were persons who had fled in the first wave and returned, and decided to flee again. Some 38,000 of those who 'trickled out' ended up beyond the Jordan River, some 10,000 ended up in Judea and Samaria, and some 29,000 in the Gaza Strip. The number who arrived (77,000) was lower than the number of escapees (81,000) because some of these people were caught in the middle of hostilities and approximately 4,000 were killed. The killing took place mainly because the Israelis wanted to ensure that the refugees would not stay in the Jewish areas and killed some of the refugees in order to scare the others and ensure they would flee to more distant areas.

Those who trickled out originated among countless small hamlets spread out in rural and semi-rural areas. The one area from which a large quantity of refugees fled at this stage was the cities of Ramle and Lod which prior to the flight were populated by 39,000 Palestinians. Following the Israeli takeover of these cities, Palestinian residents did not flee of their own accord. Ramle and

346

Lod were the first time that the Israeli army took over a large concentration of Palestinians who had not taken flight. The residents of these cities were longtime inhabitants of Eretz-Israel and were not easily incited to flee in the wake of Dir Yassin.

The Israeli leadership – which originally was taken by surprise by the massive flight that had occurred during the first wave – came to view the phenomenon as a 'windfall' and an opportunity to rid Jewish areas of the demographic threat of a large Palestinian minority in their midst. The leadership hoped that following the conquest of the two Palestinian cities, their inhabitants would flee as had happened in Haifa, Jaffa and Akko. When this didn't happen, the Prime Minister and Minister of Defense David Ben-Gurion ordered **Yitzhak Rabin** to carry out a massacre that would cause them to flee. To carry out the order, the Israeli army massacred some 80 Palestinians at Lod. In response, after rumors of the bloodbath at Lod reached Ramle, almost half the residents of the two cities fled (more than 17,000). The majority of the escapees were among the Descendants of the Roman Army and relatively-new immigrants among the Brethren of Israel.

Another place where there was a deliberate massacre of Palestinian inhabitants, to cause them to flee, was in **Tantura**; on July 18 1948, the Israeli army massacred some 30 Palestinians to force the others to flee for their lives. In the Galilean village of **Ein Zaitun** near Safed, after the village was overrun by the Palmakh in early May 1948, Jews from Safed murdered 16 villagers in revenge for the pogroms against Jews by Palestinian marauders.

The fact that the Israeli Government at the time chose at this stage to 'thin-out' the Arab population (a partial 'ethnic cleansing') needs to be kept in context, 'paired' with the invading Arab country's promise that in the wake of their impending victory, the Jews would be expelled and their homes given to Palestinians. This declaration reached its peak in the words of the broadcaster Achmad Sa'id from *Sout al-Arab* who announced that the Arab armies would 'throw all the Jews into the sea.' In light of the fact that these intentions were 'foiled' only by the determination and sacrifice of badly outnumbered and outgunned Jewish defending forces, there is little room to blame the Jews for responding in kind, and even then, only in part. Moreover, a portion of these Israeli atrocities came on the heels of massacres of Jews committed by Palestinians and invading Arab forces – for instance, the murder of Jewish POWs at Gush Etzion near Jerusalem by Jordanian soldiers. The Jews were fortunate that the Palestinians and the Arabs had few victories that afforded opportunities to put their intentions into practice.

Among those who trickled out, some 6,000 returned within a short time to their original places inside the Green Line. Thus, the number of refugees in this group who left and did not return stands in the vicinity of 75,000, while the number of refugees who made it alive to the places where they got shelter stood at 71,000. The number of escapees who trickled out and remained in the Gaza Strip was a mere 26,000 and in Judea and Samaria 7,000.

In addition to Palestinian dead cited above, approximately 3,000 Palestinians who did not flee were killed in battles and clashes with the Israeli army. To these one must add some 4,000 Palestinians who died of hunger in the harsh conditions that accompanied their long and arduous flight on foot. Of these, some 500 were killed in the course of their flight. Some 3,500 others died afterwards – primarily those who fled west of the Jordan. This number is partially offset by the birth of 1,700 infants during the corresponding period.

The total number of Palestinians who were killed or perished in some other way as a result of Arab-Palestinian aggression and Israeli responses was 11,000, including 7,000 who were killed by Israelis. In contrast, the number of Jews killed in the 1948 was by Palestinians and invading Arab forces was 6,000.

Throughout the entire period of the war Judea suffered from hunger due to a combination of drought and wartime conditions.

The situation in Judea worsened to such an extent that the Brethren of Israel among the refugees who ended up there mistreated the Arabs who were relatively new in the country; these fellow refugees had arrived from Jewish dominated areas where they had sought to make their living. As a consequence, the Brethren of Israel led a portion of the Arabs among the refugees, who harbored hopes of returning to their homes inside the Green Line once the fighting stopped, to flee eastward. As a result, some 34,000 Palestinians left their homes (primarily temporary shelters such as tents) and went east over the Jordan River. From there, some continued to even more far-flung locations: 25,000 of this group were persons who had initially fled areas that ended up inside the Green Line to Judea. That is, the number of *new* refugees from this group totaled only 9,000.

In the course of the 1948 War of Independence there was an Israeli initiative to clear the Jerusalem corridor of Palestinian villages whose residents had participated in attacks on Jewish convoys to Jerusalem. Beyond anger at the behavior of these villagers in the past, they constituted a threat in the event of any attempts by the Jordanian Army to cut off Jewish Jerusalem by slicing through the narrow Jewish-controlled corridor linking the coastal plain and the capital city, and to counter any steps to internationalize Jerusalem, as envisioned in the United Nations Partition Plan. In the course of this initiative, Palestinian villages in the Jerusalem corridor were razed and their inhabitants expelled, except for the village of Abu Gosh whose inhabitants (for the most part Descendants of the People of Israel and a small number of Circassians) were friendly to the Jews and remained neutral in the war.

This initiative was responsible for the last small wave of refugees that led to the expulsion of 6,700 Palestinians who left western Eretz-Israel. As a result of the expulsion and hunger, the number of escapees who remained in Judea and Samaria at the end of the war totaled 25,000, while 64,000 fled to the Gaza Strip. Some 225,000 arrived in Jordan. All told, there were 315,000 refugees in the War.

APPENDIX 3
Mistakes in the Number of Palestinians Today

The Palestinian Authority's Central Bureau of Statistics claims that there are almost 5,000,000 Palestinians west of the Jordan River (that is, in Israel, Judea, Samaria and Gaza). Three research strategies have been applied in Israel and the world to approximate the number of Palestinians in Judea, Samaria and Gaza. Each has reached quite a different conclusion (although there is no disagreement about the number of Palestinians in Israel):

1. The first is the study of Professor Sergio Della Pergola (from the Hebrew University, in his work for the Israel Central Bureau of Statistics) and of Professor Arnon Soffer (Haifa University). The two extrapolated the present population based on the erroneous Israeli 1967 Census. They hold that the number of Palestinians in <u>Judea, Samaria and Gaza</u>, taking into account the birth rate in each area and immigrants, is 3,800,000 persons.

This finding is consistent with the figures published by the Palestinian Authority's Central Bureau of Statistics. (In fact, Palestinian statisticians have adjusted their data to mesh with that of Della Pergola in order to seem reliable, with similar estimates coming from both Palestinian and Jewish sides.)

2. The second method is that of Yoram Ettinger (previously Israeli consul to the US). It is based on data gathered from the Palestinian Authority health authorities and Jordanian statistics. Ettinger claims that the number of Palestinians is lower by 1,400,000 than the above figure. His analysis concludes that there are only 2,400,000 Palestinians in Judea, Samaria and Gaza.

3. The third is the work of researchers at Yale and Harvard who in August 2003 published a forecast of Palestinian demographics. Their study puts the number of Palestinians west of the Jordan

River in 2003 at 3,500,000, (closer to Yoram Ettinger's figures, when one subtracts Palestinian Israeli citizens).

At the close of the 20th Century, the above American parties carried out a thorough examination based on the approach of counting the actual number of Palestinian identity cards in existence in practice and gathering data on Palestinians entering and exiting these areas as registered by Israeli authorities (Border Police records and so forth). The findings – based on actual current records, not extrapolations – were even lower than the second and third approach: The number of Palestinians living in western Eretz-Israel at the end of 2004 was found to be 2,906,000 (including those who are Israeli citizens). This includes 848,000 in the Gaza Strip, 764,000 in Judea and Samaria without Jerusalem (all told, 1,612,000), 1,155,000 Palestinian Israeli citizenship, and 139,000 Palestinians with permanent residency status in Israel (who do not hold Israeli citizenship) in East Jerusalem.

These figures do not include 192,000 Druze and Foreigners from Distant Places, all of them inhabitants of areas within the Green Line and Jerusalem. Moreover, the data for Judea and Samaria does not include 41,000 Foreigners from Distant Places living in Bethlehem, Beit Jallah and Hebron. The number in the Gaza Strip doesn't include approximately 1,000 Druze, who live in the Dir al-Balach refugee camp. All told, the longstanding non-Palestinians west of the Jordan who are tallied as non-Jews stood at 234,000 persons in 2004. Adding these parties the number of non-Jewish inhabitants in Judea, Samaria and Gaza, not counting Jerusalem, was 1,654,000 at the end of 2004; only 1,612,000 of them were Palestinians.

From Official Palestinian publications on the rate of emigration of Jewish immigrants to Israel, one can find Palestinian claims that the number of Palestinians in western Eretz-Israel, including inside the Green Line, was only 3,550,000 in 1999. This figure is less exaggerated than the earlier Palestinian number (5 million), and closer to the figure reached by the Yale-Harvard team (3,500,000).

In addition, there are those who claim that during the second *Intifada* (that is, after 1999) some 250,000 Palestinians emigrated due to the deteriorating infrastructure and growing security and economic problems (the validity of this claim has not been examined).

If so, however, the gap between Palestinian claims and realities are not great: When one adds the 234,000 Druze and Foreigners from Distant Places (as many tend to do although there is no logic to doing so) to the number of Palestinians (2,906,000), the real population figure becomes 3,140,000, valid for the end of 2004. If one adds errors in the Israeli Population Registry, some 49,000 persons within the Green Line and 33,000 in East Jerusalem, one arrives at 3,222,000.

In January 2003 the Palestinian Authority returned to its 'original' figures and published that in Judea, Samaria and the Gaza Strip there were 3,600,000 persons, and another million Palestinians in the State of Israel. This figure adds East Jerusalem to Judea since the Palestinian Authority does not recognize East Jerusalem as part of the State of Israel.

In January 2006, the Palestinian Authority raised its figures to 3,800,000 in Judea, Samaria and Gaza – including East Jerusalem, and 1,100,000 within the Green Line. In other words, the PA claims that there are 4,600,000 Palestinians in western Eretz-Israel at the outset of 2003, and 4,900,000 at the outset of 2006.

How did the Palestinians 'jack-up' the data? It has already been discussed how the Palestinians 'worked the system' to inflate their numbers on UNRWA tallies in 1949 and how they inflated the Israeli 1967 Census. The following maneuvers (in addition to maintaining those already at work) were employed to artificially manipulate Palestinian statistics. The figures that follow relate to the end of 2004.

1. Some 15,000 persons who passed away are presented as living. Other elderly persons similar in stature and appearance are armed

with the ID card of the deceased whose photo IDs are faded or have been 'doctored' with new photos and continue to use them to substantiate that the person is still alive. The ruse is even easier for devote Muslim women (and countless other women who feign religiosity for this purpose) who are photographed wearing veils.

2. Some 65,000 who have left the country continue to be counted as if they were still residing in western Eretz-Israel, using similar methods to those in 1 above with the duplicate ID card of the absentee.

3. Some 430,000 are fictitious persons who never existed. Real Palestinians carry multiple ID cards bearing their own photo, but under more than one name and more than one address. Under crowded conditions in the camps and cities it is hard to uncover such duplicity. Issuing of so many bogus refugee status cards took place primarily against the backdrop of crowded and chaotic post-war conditions in 1949, under the noses of naïve UNRWA officials (who required no substantiation and issued cards based solely on the applicants' declarations).

Later on, the Palestinians presented the same ID cards to Jordanian and Egyptian officials and received government-issued documentation. The Jordanian ID cards (and to a certain extent Egyptian ones) were subsequently presented by Palestinians to Israeli officials after the 1967 war, along with their matching UNRWA cards.

The 1967 Census curtailed the scope of forgeries, but in most cases, the Palestinians managed to manipulate the results of the Census using duplicate identities and other ploys.

Over the years when Palestinians married, they used multiple identities to obtain multiple marriage certificates. When the couple had children, the offspring appeared multiple sets of ID papers.

Even if a real child was born in a hospital and received a birth certificate under one of the identities of the parents, in order to

353

receive an additional birth certificate (in most cases they sufficed with two...) the parents then appeared before officials bearing another identity claiming the infant had been delivered at home and were issued a second birth certificate for the same child.

All told, these various subterfuges have created some 510,000 Palestinian inhabitants that don't exist. Either they don't exist at all, or they are dead or they have left the country. If one adds to this number the genuine number of Palestinians in Judea, Samaria and Gaza – 1,612,000 – one arrives at 2,122,000 Palestinian 'identities' (real and bogus) in Judea, Samaria and Gaza today.

If one adds to the above number 41,000 foreigners in Judea and 195,000 non-Jews in East Jerusalem, 1,000 Druze in the Gaza Strip and the 33,000 error in the Israeli Population Registry of residents of East Jerusalem living outside the city who end up being counted twice, the total number of non-Jewish 'identities' in Judea, Samaria and Gaze is 2,392,000 – a figure very close to the one that Yoram Ettinger arrived at (2,400,000) and that the Yale-Harvard team arrived at (although it is not clear if their data included East Jerusalem).

The percentage of bogus identities that are circulating, relative to the genuine total Palestinian population in Judea, Samaria and Gaza, dropped at the end of 2004 to 32 percent – compared to 100 percent in Judea and Samaria and 125 percent in Gaza in 1949, and 150 percent in Judea and Samaria and 128 percent in Gaza in 1967. This drop stems from two factors: The objective difficulty of juggling multiple identities and passing them on to offspring and the rise in the standard of living of Palestinians – which make maintenance of the 'system' to receive basic food stuffs from UNRWA far less attractive than in the past.

In the end of 2004, the genuine Palestinian population west of the Jordan was 2,906,000. This figure – if one adds the 510,000 bogus 'identities' – rises to 3,416,000 Palestinian 'identities.' This is the basis, together with Foreigners from Distant Places and Druze

354

(234,000), with errors in the Israeli Population Registry (82,000) and with an invention that lacks even a forged documentation, of another 1,170,000 Palestinians, to arrive at the totally exaggerated figures the Palestinian Establishment (and Professor Arnon Soffer) flaunt.

When Palestinians are presented with contradictions in their data, they admit (in order to continue to cling to their misleading numbers) that the statistics include many Palestinians who have left Judea, Samaria and Gaza. Some of the methods that have been used to 'doctor' the truth are presented on the website of the American-Israel Demographic Research Group, at http://www.pademographics.com. The website contains a lecture by Bennett Zimmerman on this issue. Of course, the figures presented by Zimmerman tend to be higher because the research did not go deep enough to expose document supported forgery.

The explanations above and other material in the body of this work enable readers to grasp how Palestinians succeeded in getting most Israelis (despite relative skepticism) to believe and accept their exaggerated population data. One can also understand how Palestinians pulled the wool over the eyes of UNRWA officials and got them to think there was a much larger refugee population than in reality, and to allocate them food. The inflated UNRWA statistics were and still are widely accepted in the world as accurate because UNRWA is perceived as a neutral professional international body. In any case, the Israeli figures are not greatly different.

If one seeks decisive evidence of the big hoax of Palestinian multiple identities, data from the 2006 Palestinian elections are illuminating: Because the Palestinian Authority, unlike the Israelis and UNRWA, are keenly aware of the scope of duplicity, it took steps that are unusual in elections to ensure that no person would vote more than once using a second or third ID card in their possession: Authorities stamped the voter's hand with a stamp that would not wear off for 24 hours. While there are some cases of 'the dead voting' in Israel and other countries as well, nowhere else is the level of potential fraud so great that polling stations stamp the hands of all the voters.

Anyone who still doubts the accuracy of the above picture of mass fraud should compare the number of (fictitious) births that Palestinian Authority health officials register to inflate the population, and the tremendous gap in the number of children enrolled in the school system six years later – revealed in the Zimmermann et al. study, cited above!

APPENDIX 4

Geographic-Ethnic Details of the Finding

Following is more detailed data on the various geographic areas in Eretz-Israel:

In Judea and Samaria, without East Jerusalem, additional inhabitants, beyond the 524,000 Descendants of Israel, include 99,000 Arabs, 96,000 Brethren of Israel (75,000 Descendants of the Moabites and 21,000 Descendants of the Edomites), 45,000 Descendants of the Roman Army, and 32,000 Christians of Distant Places, and 9,000 Kurds (Total – 41,000 Foreigners from Distant Places).

In terms of geographic sub-groupings, after excluding East Jerusalem and villages in the city's environs, today the population of Judea stands at 312,000. They include 99,000 Arabs, 79,000 Brethren of Israel (65,000 Descendants of the Moabites and 14,000 Descendants of the Edomites), 48,000 Descendants of Israel, 45,000 Descendants of the Roman Army and 41,000 Foreigners from Distant Places.

One of the ironies of history: In this region which bears the name of the Jewish People, the proportion of Descendants of Israel today among the non-Jewish population is 15 percent (if one adds the Brethren of Israel – 40 percent) – which is extremely low compared to the number of Descendants of Israel in other areas of Eretz-Israel...

Most of the population of Judea is concentrated in the densely-populated Hebron District which has a population of 240,000. The composition of the population is as follows: Arabs – 91,000, Brethren of Israel – 72,000 (including 60,000 Descendants of the Moabites and 12,000 Descendants of the Edomites), Descendants of the Roman Army – 40,000, Descendants of Israel – 27,000 and Kurds – 9,000.

In the Bethlehem District, out of 55,000 inhabitants – 23,000 are Palestinian and 32,000 are Christians from distant places. Among the Palestinians there, 11,400 are Descendants of Israel (6,200 Muslims and 5,200 Christians), 3,700 are Brethren of Israel (2,900 Descendants of the Moabites and 800 Descendants of the Edomites), 1,500 are Descendants of the Roman Army and 6,400 are Christian Arabs.

In the Jericho District, the population numbers 17,000. This includes 9,300 Descendants of Israel (6,000 Muslims and 3,300 Christians), 3,000 Brethren of Israel (2,000 Descendants of the Moabites and 1,000 Descendants of the Edomites), 2,700 Descendants of the Roman Army and 2,000 Arabs.

In Samaria, the population is 493,000 – almost all, Descendants of Israel. Of these 230,000 are Descendants of Samaritans and the rest – 246,000 are Descendants of Jews. Some 17,000 of the residents of refugee camps are Brethren of Israel, among them – 10,000 Descendants of the Edomites and 7,000 Descendants of the Moabites.

In the Gaza Strip, the full picture shows that, in addition to 230,000 Descendants of Israel, there are also 548,000 Brethren of Israel (approximately 343,000 Descendants of the Moabites and approximately 205,000 Descendants of the Edomites), 70,000 Descendants of the Roman Army and 1,000 Druze. The Druze live in the Dir al-Balakh refugee camp. Among the Descendants of Israel in the Gaza Strip, 58,000 are Descendants of the Samaritans – approximately 7 percent of the population in Gaza (849,000) and 172,000 are Descendants of Jews – approximately 20 percent.

The population of the Gaza Strip also includes 13,000 Bedouin. On the whole, the internal distribution of Gaza Bedouin is similar to all the Bedouin in Eretz-Israel (see data that follows). The number of Descendants of Israel and Brethren of Israel among the Bedouin in the Gaza Strip is as follows:

358

Among the residents of the State of Israel, a little more than 42 percent of the 244,000 Bedouin (104,000) are Descendants of Israel. Most of the others (133,000) are Brethren of Israel (approximately 45,000 Descendants of the Moabites and approximately 88,000 Descendants of the Edomites). Only 7,000 (approximately 3 percent) of the Israeli Bedouin are Arabs, the only ones whose ancestors were not part of the People of Israel in the past. These Arabs are scattered in a belt that runs from Beersheva to the Dead Sea, where their dialect[56] and their accent is different from the other Bedouin in the country. Together with the Bedouin who reside in the Gaza Strip, there are 247,000 Bedouin west of the Jordan River.

Of the 195,000 non-Jewish residents of East Jerusalem, 80,000 are Descendants of the People of Israel. Some 45,000 are Kurds who came during the reign of Saladin. Some 32,000 are Brethren of Israel (24,000 Descendants of the Moabites and 8,000 Descendants of the Edomites). Some 27,000 are of Arab origin, and constitute the main concentration of population of Arab origin among Israeli citizens today. This includes 9,000 members of the Judham Tribe, and 14,000 Descendants of the Arab Army living in the Mount of Olives neighborhood.

In East Jerusalem there are another 11,000 inhabitants who are recognized as non-Arabs: 5,000 Armenians and 6,000 non-Arab Christians from distance locations. Among the Descendants of Israel living in East Jerusalem there are 7,000 who are Christian. All told, today the number of Christians in East Jerusalem stands at 18,000, alongside 177,000 Muslims.

The number of Muslims living in East Jerusalem does not mesh with the number in the Israeli Population Registry, which puts the number of Muslims at 210,000 out of a total non-Jewish population of 228,000 in East Jerusalem. The gap is the product of 33,000 Palestinians who live in various places in Judea and

---

[56] The dialect of Arabic they speak.

Samaria but are registered as East Jerusalemites and enjoy Israeli residency rights.

The primary reason for this phenomenon is the lucrative government social welfare allowances (child welfare, national health insurance, social security, etc.) to which residents of the State of Israel are eligible. At the same time one cannot ignore the security risk of so many residents of Judea and Samaria with Israeli identity cards that allow them to travel with relative freedom, and aid and abet terrorists if they wish, which some, indeed, have done.

Approximately 510,000 non-Jews populate the **mountain country in the north** – that is, **the Galilee and the Carmel Range** (excluding Haifa). They are divided among four groupings: Surprisingly, 30 percent of all Bedouin in Israel – 78,000 persons – live in the Galilee. The Galilee Bedouin constitute 15 percent of the Palestinians in the Galilee, and their composure is similar to the general one among all the Bedouin in the country, as described above. Another 17 percent of the Palestinians in the northern mountain country, or 85,000 of the Galilee Palestinians, are Descendants of Israel who became *Musta'arbim* (i.e., were Jewish by faith, in the past).

Most of the Palestinian population in the northern mountain country, some 250,000 or 49 percent of the of this population, are Descendants of Israel who were Christian during the Byzantine Period who at the advent of the Arab period for the most part became Christian *Musta'arbim* (as well as some who remained Christian to this day). As described above, in the 19th Century, two-thirds of this population went to Syria and Lebanon, and returned to Eretz-Israel only in the 20th Century. Out of the 335,000 non-Bedouin Descendants of Israel in the Galilee, all told, 3,000 are Descendants of the Samaritans who for the most part were forced to convert to Christianity, then forced to covert from Christianity to Islam.

The remaining Palestinians in the Galilee – marginal in number – are 300 Descendants of Egyptian Immigrants and Descendants of the Moabites, all together some 1,000 persons. In addition to these, there are 87,000 Druze who live in the northern mountain regions, the largest concentration on the Carmel, near Haifa (28,000). The remainder are comprised of Foreigners from Distant Places: 6,000 Circassians, Bosnians and Turks and some 2,700 Christians in Nazareth. All the latter are neither Arabs nor Palestinians.

In **Haifa** there are some 20,000 Palestinians, most in the port area and some 5,000 Druze and 6,000 Foreigners from Distant Places. Within **the entire coastal plain and the valleys within the Green Line**, including Haifa,[57] but not the Negev, 182,000 persons, that is, approximately 29 percent of the 630,000 non-Jewish longtime residents living there are descendants of Israel, including 6,000 that originally were Samaritans. The rest are other permanent inhabitants of Eretz-Israel on both sides of the Jordan River – approximately 150,000 Descendants of the Roman Army, approximately 70,000 Descendants of the Edomites and 165,000 Descendants of the Moabites.

For instance, in the Triangle there are 70,000 Descendants of the Roman Army, while most of the residents of Wadi Ara are Brethren of Israel. A small minority of the remaining inhabitants of the low-lying regions are 8,000 Arabs, most of them the offspring of seven large families – the descendants of 19th Century immigrants from Egypt. Approximately 100 residents of Ramle are Arabs from the Judham Tribe.

The other inhabitants of the low-lying areas are some 30,000 Druze (primarily in Haifa and in the Zebulon Valley north of the city) and 4,000 Foreigners from Distant Places who reside in Jaffa (together with Haifa – 10,000 persons). The inhabitants of these

---

[57] Haifa has been included among the low-lying areas since most of the non-Jewish residents reside in neighborhoods in the shoreline, not the Hadar or the Carmel neighborhoods on the upper slopes of the city.

areas include 15,000 Bedouin (the detailed components cited above do but not include them in the tally). In the Negev (in addition to the Jews) there are only Bedouin (some 151,000).

The sum total within the Green Line demonstrates **that 621,000[58] out of 1,291,000 longtime non-Jews within the Green Line (not counting East Jerusalem), or <u>48 percent are Descendants of the People of Israel.</u>** The sum total of veteran inhabitants who are not Palestinian and are not Jewish is 136,000 and includes 117,000 Druze[59] and 19,000[60] Foreigners from Distant Places. If one subtracts this number from the 1,291,000 long-term non-Jewish veteran inhabitants living within the State of Israel, the number of Palestinians within the Green Line is 1,155,000. **Among the Palestinians within the Green Line (<u>not</u> including East Jerusalem) the percentage who are <u>Descendants of the People of Israel is close to 54 percent.</u>**

If one adds the residents of East Jerusalem, they constitute an additional 139,000 Palestinians – 80,000 of them Descendants of the People of Israel; in addition there are 56,000 Foreigners from Distant Places. **The tally of the Descendants of Israel in the State of Israel <u>including</u> East Jerusalem stands at 701,000, or 47% of all the 1,486,000 veteran non-Jews there, and 54% of all 1,294,000 Palestinians there.**

<u>There are 369,000 Brethren of Israel in the State of Israel</u>[61] (and another 32,000 in Jerusalem), or 32 percent of all the Palestinians there (401,000 or 31 percent, including Jerusalem).

---

[58] 104,000 Bedouin and 335,000 non-Bedouin in the Galilee and 182,000 non-Bedouin in the coastal plain and the valleys.

[59] 87,000 in the northern mountain country and another 30,000 in Haifa and in non-mountain areas.

[60] 6,000 Circassians, Bosnians and Albanians in the Galilee, 4,000 residents of Jaffa, and 6,000 residents of Haifa and 2,700 residents of Nazareth.

[61] 235,000 in the coastal plains and valleys without the Bedouin, and 133,000 Bedouin and approximately 1,000 in the Galilee.

362

A further breakdown of this figure shows that <u>Descendants of the Edomites</u> number 158,000,[62] and constitute 14 percent (of the Palestinians in the State of Israel, or 166,000 or 13 percent, with Jerusalem). The <u>Descendants of the Moabite</u>s number 211,000,[63] and constitute 18.5 percent (235,000 or 18 percent with Jerusalem). <u>The Descendants of the Roman Army number 150,000,</u> or 13 percent (approximately 11.6 percent with Jerusalem). The rest, some <u>15,000</u>[64]<u>, or 1.3 percent, are Arabs,</u> (42,000 or 3 percent with Jerusalem)

.

---

[62] 88,000 Bedouin and 70,000 in the low-lying areas.

[63] 45,000 Bedouin, 165,000 in the low-lying areas and less than 1,000 in the Galilee.

[64] 8,000 in the low-lying areas and another 7,000 among the Bedouin.

APPENDIX 5

Tables of the Various Groups of the Population of Eretz-Israel along the History

70 A. D. – After the Great Revolt		
Ethnic Group	No. of Inhabitants	Percentage of Population
Jews	1,850,000	75%
Samaritans	280,000	11%
Edomites & Moabites	150,000	6%
Arabs	40,000	2%
Phoenicians	30,000	1%
Philistines	28,000	1%
Canaanites	24,000	1%
Other Small Nations	67,000	3%
Romans	10,000	0%
Total	2,479,000	100%

Table 2: The Population After the the Great Revolt.

End of the 6th Century		
Ethnic Group	No. of Inhabitants	Percentage of Population
Jews	950,000	36%
Samaritans	254,000	10%
Edomites & Moabites	46,000	2%
Arabs	470,000	18%
Small Nations	300,000	11%
Foreign Christian Civilians	50,000	2%
Roman Army	600,000	22%
Total	2,670,000	100%

Table 4: Ethnic distribution at the climax of the Byzantine Era.

364

End of the 6th Century		
Religious Group	No. of Inhabitants	Percentage of Population
Christians	1,668,000	62%
Jews	726,000	27%
Samaritans	250,000	9%
Pagans	26,000	1%
Total	**2,670,000**	**38%**

Table 5: The Religious distribution at the climax of the Byzantine period.

640 – After The Arab Conquest		
Ethnic Group	No. of Inhabitants	Percentage of Population
Jews	472,000	28%
Samaritans	70,000	4%
Edomites & Moabites	30,000	2%
Small Nations	220,000	13%
Foreign Christians	4,000	0%
Arab Civilians	126,000	8%
Arab Army	40,000	2%
Roman Army	700,000	42%
Total	1,662,000	100%

Table 6: The Ethnic Distribution at the Time of the Arab Conquest.

640 – After The Arab Conquest		
Religious Group	No. of Inhabitants	Percentage of Population
Christians	1,115,000	67%
Jews	430,000	26%
Samaritans	70,000	4%
Muslims	46,000	3%
Pagans	1,200	0%
Total	1,662,200	100%

Table7: The Religious Composure after the Arab Conquest.

1044 – After the Repeal of the al-Khaken Edict		
Religious Group	No. of Inhabitants	Percentage of Population
Muslims	74,000	8%
Outwardly Muslims	517,000	56%
Jews	194,000	21%
Jews-Muslims	92,000	10%
Christians	17,000	2%
Christians-Muslims	11,000	1%
Allawis	3,800	0%
Samaritans	12,000	1%
Samaritans-Muslims	3,000	0%
Total	923,800	100%

Table 9: The Results of the Religious Coercion by al-Khakem and its partial correction.

1099 – Before the Crusader Conquest		
Ethnic Group	No. of Inhabitants	Percentage of Population
Jews	580,000	65%
Samaritans	70,000	8%
Edomites & Moabites	30,000	3%
Roman Army	129,000	14%
Arab Civilians	16,000	2%
Arab Army	68,000	8%
Total	**893,000**	**100%**

Table 10: The Ethnic Composure before the Crusader Conquest.

1099 – Before the Crusader Conquest		
Religious Group	No. of Inhabitants	Percentage of Population
Muslims	74,000	8%
Musta'arbim	681,000	76%
Jews	73,000	8%
Jew-Muslims	27,000	3%
Christians	17,000	2%
Allawis	11,000	1%
Samaritans	8,000	1%
Samaritans-Muslims	2,000	0%
Total	**893,000**	**100%**

Table 11: The Religious Composure before the Crusader Conquest.

1100 – After the Crusader Conquest		
Ethnic Group	**No. of Inhabitants**	**Percentage of Population**
Jews	575,000	65%
Samaritans	70,000	8%
Edomites & Moabites	30,000	3%
Roman Army	129,000	15%
Arab Civilians	16,000	2%
Crusaders	60,000	7%
Total	**880,000**	**100%**

Table 12: The Ethnic Composure after the Crusader Conquest

1100 – After the Crusader Conquest		
Religious Group	**No. of Inhabitants**	**Percentage of Population**
Muslims	6,000	1%
Musta'arbim	642,000	73%
Christians	127,000	14%
Jews	75,000	9%
Jews-Muslims	20,000	2%
Samaritans	10,000	1%
Total	**880,000**	**100%**

Table 13: The Religious Composure after the Crusader Conquest.

1291 – Under Full Mameluk Rule		
Religious Group	**No. of Inhabitants**	**Percentage of Population**
Muslims	25,000	3%
Musta'arbim	735,000	88%
Jews	34,000	4%
Jews-Muslims	21,000	3%
Christians	13,000	2%
Samaritans	7,000	1%
Total	**835,000**	**100%**

Table 14: The Religious Composure after the Crusader Defeat.

The Turkish Conquest - 1517		
Religious Group	**No. of Inhabitants**	**Percentage of Population**
Muslims	11,000	7%
Musta'arbim	131,000	87%
Jews	5,000	3%
Christians	4,000	3%
Samaritans	270	0%
Total	**151,270**	**100%**

Table 16: The Composure of Religions after the Ottoman Conquest.

The Turkish Conquest - 1517		
Ethnic Group	No. of Inhabitants	Percentage of Population
Descendant of Israel	106,000	70%
Brethren of Israel	5,000	3%
Jews	5,000	3%
Samaritans	270	0%
Roman Army	24,000	16%
Arabs	2,000	1%
Kurds	2,000	1%
Turkish Army	7,000	5%
Total	151,270	100%

Table 17: Ethnic Distribution at the Ottoman Rule beginning.

1550 – The Stabilzation of the Turkish Rule		
Ethnic Group	No. of Inhabitants	Percentage of Population
Descendant of Israel	220,000	72%
Jews	42,000	14%
Brethren of Israel	5,000	2%
Samaritans	700	0%
Roman Army	24,000	8%
Arabs	4,000	1%
Kurds	2,000	1%
Turkish Army	7,000	2%
Total	304,700	100%

Table 18: The Ethnic Distribution in Mid 16th Century.

370

1550 – The Stabilzation of the Turkish Rule		
Religious Group	No. of Inhabitants	Percentage of Population
Muslims	13,000	4%
Musta'arbim	243,000	80%
Jews	42,000	14%
Christians	6,000	2%
Samaritans	700	0%
Total	304,700	100%

Table 19: The Composition of Religions in the Country in 1550

1800 - The Sanjaks of the West						
Ethnic Group	Inhabitants in the West		Inhabitants in the East		Inhabitants in Both Sides	
	Number	Percentage	Number	Percentage	Number	Percentage
Descendants of Israel	35,000	50%	195,000	93%	230,000	82%
Roman Army	22,000	31%	2,000	1%	24,000	9%
Jews	8,000	11%			8,000	3%
Kurds	3,000	4%			3,000	1%
Arabs	2,000	3%	13,000	6%	15,000	5%
Total	70,000	100%	210,000	100%	280,000	100%

Table 20: The Population in 1800 of the Area Mistakenly
Considered as West of the Jordan Only

1800 - The Entire Country						
Ethnic Group	Inhabitants in the West		Inhabitants in the East		Inhabitants in the Entire Country	
	Number	Percentage	Number	Percentage	Number	Percentage
Descendants of Israel	35,000	50%	195,000	75%	230,000	70%
Roman Army	22,000	31%	2,000	1%	24,000	7%
Jews	8,000	11%			8,000	2%
Kurds	3,000	4%			3,000	1%
Arabs	2,000	3%	63,000	24%	65,000	20%
Total	70,000	100%	260,000	100%	330,000	100%

Table 21: The composition of the Population of the Entire Country, including both sides of the Jordan in 1800.

1840 - The Entire Country						
Ethnic Group	Inhabitants in the West		Inhabitants in the East		Inhabitants in the Entire Country	
	Number	Percentage	Number	Percentage	Number	Percentage
Descendants of Israel	131,000	75%	95,000	44%	226,000	58%
Roman Army	21,500	12%	2,500	1%	24,000	6%
Arabs	9,000	5%	59,000	27%	68,000	17%
Jews	10,000	6%			10,000	3%
Kurds	3,000	2%			3,000	1%
Brethren of Israel	700	0%	59,300	27%	60,000	15%
Total	175,200	100%	215,800	100%	391,000	100%

Table 23: The Composition of the Population of the Entire Country following the end of the Rule of Mohammad Ali.

372

APPENDIX 6

Glossary of Terms

The following terms and their definitions are not necessarily in general usage, rather they are primarily used in the context of the volume at hand.

Small Nations, The Small Nations of Eretz-Israel: The small nations that inhabited Eretz-Israel by the side of the People of Israel and others, such as the Philistines and the Canaanites.

Ethnic Jews: Members of the tribe of Judah and those who joined them during the First Commonwealth Period, such as some of the sons of the tribe of Simon and some of the tribe of Levi who were dispersed among the other tribes. This designation does *not* include converts, such as the Edomites and Moabites. This designation *does* include Jews who converted to Christianity, and later even Jews who accepted Islam in one form or another, provided that they resided in Eretz-Israel.

Jews: In addition to Ethnic Jews, the term Jews includes converts, and in the context of this volume, primarily the Edomites and the Moabites.

People of Israel: as distinguished from the **Jewish People**, includes Jews and Samaritans together.

People of Israel from an ethnic standpoint: does not include the Edomites and the Moabites.

Religion of Israel: includes the Jewish and Samaritan religion as one religion.

Descendants of the Roman Army, the Roman Army: Members of the Byzantine Army and their families who remained in Eretz-Israel after the Arab Conquest, and their descendants throughout the generations.

Brethren of Israel: Descendants of the Edomites and Moabites after they temporarily left Eretz-Israel beginning at the outset of the 16th Century.

Descendants of Israel, Descendants of the People of Israel, Descendants of (the People of) Israel in the Narrow Sense: Descendants of the *Musta'arabim* of Jewish origin from an ethnic standpoint and descendants of Samaritan *Musta'arabim*.

Descendants of Israel in the Broad Sense, Descendants of (the People of) Israel in the Broad Sense: Descendants of Israel together with the Brethren of Israel.

Distant Foreigners and **Foreigners of Distant Places**: Foreigners of various kinds, Christian and Muslim, who are not Arabs, who settled in Eretz-Israel, mainly after 1840. This concept does not include the Druze; it includes Armenians, Germans, Greeks, Circassians, Turks, Bosnians, Albanians, Gypsies and Kurds.

Lovers of Eretz-Israel: Christians and others from distant lands who settled in Eretz-Israel out of religious devotion and love of the Holy Land – due to their devotion to the Bible and the belief that their presence would help bring the Redemption of humankind – a Second Coming that would come out of Zion.

Internal immigrants are people whose forefathers originated in Eretz-Israel who migrated from place to place within Eretz-Israel beginning in the 18th Century – particularly between eastern Eretz-Israel to western Eretz-Israel, or immigrants whose forefathers originated in Eretz-Israel and they or their forefathers had gone to neighboring countries (primarily Syria and Lebanon) and ultimately returned to their native soil in Eretz-Israel (sometimes generations later).

External immigrants: Immigrants whose origins or whose forefathers did not originate in Eretz-Israel, and who came to Eretz-Israel from elsewhere, beginning in 1831.

374

Made in the USA
Columbia, SC
13 June 2024

37042637R10212